Confronting Environmental Change in East and Southeast Asia: Eco-politics, Foreign Policy and Sustainable Development

T0322895

Confronting Environmental Change in East and Southeast Asia: Eco-politics, Foreign Policy and Sustainable Development

Edited by Paul G Harris

London • Stirling, VA

First published in 2005 by the United Nations University Press and Earthscan
Publications Ltd

ISBN 92-808-1113-4 (UNUP paperback; not for sale in Europe and the
Commonwealth, excluding Canada)
1 85383 972 8 (Earthscan paperback; not for sale in the USA and Canada)
1 85383 971 X (Earthscan hardback)

The views expressed in this publication are those of the author and do not
necessarily reflect the views of the United Nations University.

United Nations University Press
The United Nations University, 53–70, Jingumae 5-chome,
Shibuya-ku, Tokyo, 150-8925, Japan
Tel: +81-3-3499-2811 Fax: +81-3-3406-7345
E-mail: mbox@hq.unu.edu
http://www.unu.edu

United Nations University Office at the United Nations, New York
2 United Nations Plaza, Room DC2-2062, New York, NY 10017, USA
Tel: +1-212-963-6387 Fax: +1-212-371-9454
E-mail: unuona@igc.apc.org

United Nations University Press is the publishing division of the United Nations
University.

Earthscan
8–12 Camden High Street, London, NW1 0JH, UK
Tel: +44 (0)20 7387 8558 Fax: +44 (0)20 7387 8998
Email: earthinfo@earthscan.co.uk

Cover design by Ruth Bateson
Printed and bound in the UK by Cromwell Press, Trowbridge, Wiltshire

Confronting environmental change in East and Southeast Asia : eco-politics, foreign policy
and sustainable development / edited by Paul G. Harris.
    p. cm.
Includes bibliographical references and index.
    ISBN 9280811134 (pbk)
        1. Environmental policy—East Asia. 2. Environmental management—East Asia. 3.
    Sustainable development—East Asia. 4. Environmental policy—Asia, Southeastern.
    5. Environmental management—Asia, Southeastern. 6. Sustainable development—
    Asia, Southeastern. I. Harris, Paul G.

  GE185.E18C66 2004
  333.72'095--dc22
                                                                    20040125444

Contents

Part 1 Environment, Foreign Policy and Diplomacy in East Asia: Actors, Institutions and Forces

List of Figures and Tables

Figures

Tables

List of Acronyms and Abbreviations

ADB	Asian Development Bank
AFTA	Asean Free Trade Area
AOSIS	Association of Small Island Sates
APEC	Asia-Pacific Economic Cooperation
ASEAN	Association of Southeast Asian Nations
BAP	Biodiversity Action Plan
BCN	Biodiversity Conservation Network
BD	biological diversity
BIOTHAI	Thai Network on Community Rights and Biodiversity
BOOT approach	build, own, operate and transfer
CBD	Convention on Biological Diversity
CBO	community-based organization
CCP	Chinese Communist Party
CDM	Clean Development Mechanism
Cdn$	Canadian dollars
CEN	Canadian Environmental Network
CEPD	Taiwanese Council for Economic Planning and Development
CFC	chlorofluorocarbon
CHAD	Conflict and Humanitarian Affairs Department
CIDA	Canadian International Development Agency
CITES	Convention on International Trade in Endangered Species
CM	conflict management
CMA	China Meteorological Administration
CO_2	carbon dioxide
COA	Taiwanese Council of Agriculture
COP1	first Conference of the Parties to the FCCC
COP3	third Conference of the Parties to the FCCC
COP4	fourth Conference of the Parties to the FCCC
COP6	sixth Conference of the Parties to the FCCC
COP7	seventh Conference of the Parties to the FCCC
COP8	eighth Conference of the Parties to the

	FCCC
COP9	ninth Conference of the Parties to the FCCC
CTE	WTO Committee on Trade and Environment
Danida	Danish Agency for International Development
DFID	UK Department for International Development
DPP	Taiwanese Democratic Progressive Party
DSB	dispute settlement body
DSP	Japanese Democratic Socialist Party
EA	Japanese Environment Agency
EANET	Acid Deposition Monitoring Network in East Asia
EC	European Commission
EIA	environmental impact assessment
ENGO	environmental non-governmental organization
EPA	Taiwanese Environmental Protection Administration
EPB	environmental protection bureau
EPC	Chinese Environmental Protection Commission
ET	emissions trading
EU	European Union
FCCC	Framework Convention on Climate Change
FOE	Friends of the Earth
FPCD	Foundation for People and Community Development
G-7	Group of Seven industrialized countries
G77	Group of 77 developing countries
GATT	General Agreement on Tariffs and Trade
GCM	general circulation model
GCWG	Global Change Working Group
GDP	gross domestic product
GEF	Global Environment Facility
GHG	greenhouse gas
GLOBE	Global Legislators Organization for a Balanced Environment
GRAIN	Genetic Resources Action International
GSI	Green Silicon Island
ICAD	Integrated Conservation and Development

ICJ	International Court of Justice
ICPB	International Capacity-Building Project
IDA	International Development Association
IFAD	International Fund for Agricultural Development
IGO	intergovernmental organization
IMF	International Monetary Fund
INC	Intergovernmental Negotiating Committee of the FCCC
IPCC	Intergovernmental Panel on Climate Change
ITTA	International Tropical Timber Agreement
IUCN	World Conservation Union (formerly International Union for the Conservation of Nature)
IWC	International Whaling Commission
JEC	Japan Environmental Council
JI	joint implementation
JICA	Japan International Cooperation Agency
KMT	Taiwanese Nationalist Party
LDC	less developed country
LDP	Japanese Liberal Democratic Party
MAC	Thai Ministry of Agriculture and Cooperatives
MARPOL	International Convention for the Prevention of Pollution from Ships
MC	Mekong Commission
MEA	multilateral environmental agreement
METI	Japanese Ministry of Economy, Trade and Industry
MFA	Thai Ministry of Foreign Affairs
MITI	Japanese Ministry of International Trade and Industry
MOEA	Taiwanese Ministry of Economic Affairs
MOF	Japanese Ministry of Finance
MOFA	Chinese Ministry of Foreign Affairs
MOFA	Japanese Ministry of Foreign Affairs
MOP	Meeting of the Parties to the FCCC
MOSTE	Taiwanese Ministry of Science, Technology and Environment
MOSTE	Thai Ministry of Science, Technology and Environment
MOSTE	Vietnamese Ministry of Science, Technology

	and Environment
MPH	Thai Ministry of Public Health
MRC	Mekong River Commission (formerly the MC)
MRCWG	APEC Marine Resource Conservation Working Group
MtC	metric tonnes of CO_2
MW	megawatt
NCPCC	National Coordination Panel on Climate Change
NCSD	Taiwanese National Council of Sustainable Development
NEA	Vietnamese National Environmental Agency
NEAP	National Environment Action Plan
NEPA	Chinese National Environmental Protection Agency
NGO	non-governmental organization
NPC	National People's Congress (China)
NPESD	National Plan for Environment and Sustainable Development
NR	natural resources
NRDC	Natural Resources Defence Council
NRTEE	National Round Table on the Environment and Economy
OCS	Thai Office of the Council of State
ODA	official development assistance
ODC	ozone-destroying chemical
OECD	Organisation for Economic Co-operation and Development
PA	participatory analysis
PKO	peacekeeping operations
PNG	Papua New Guinea
RFD	Thai Royal Forest Department
SCEP	Chinese State Commission on Environmental Protection
SCI	Sustainable City Initiative
SDF	Japanese Self-Defence Force
SDPC	Chinese State Development Planning Commission
SDPJ	Socialist Democratic Party of Japan
SEPA	Chinese State Environmental Protection

	Administration
Sida	Swedish International Development Cooperation Agency
SL	sustainable livelihoods
SMA	Chinese State Meteorological Administration
SPC	Chinese State Planning Commission
SPS Agreement	Agreement on Sanitary and Phytosanitary Measures
SSTC	Chinese State Science and Technology Commission
TBT Agreement	Agreement on Technical Barriers to Trade
TEAN	Taiwan Environmental Action Network
TERRA	Towards Ecological Recovery and Regional Alliances
TREM	trade-related environmental measure
TRIPs Agreement	Agreement on Trade-Related Aspects of Intellectual Property Rights
TVA	Tennessee Valley Authority
UK	United Kingdom
UN	United Nations
UNCED	UN Conference on Environment and Development (Earth Summit)
UNCHE	UN Conference on the Human Environment
UNCLOS	UN Convention on the Law of the Sea
UNDP	UN Development Programme
UNEP	UN Environment Programme
UNESCO	UN Educational, Scientific and Cultural Organization
UNFCCC	UN Framework Convention on Climate Change
US	United States
WCS	Wildlife Conservation Society
WCU	World Conservation Union
WFP	World Food Programme
WG	working group
WMA	wildlife management area
WMO	World Meteorological Organization
WSSD	World Summit on Sustainable Development
WTO	World Trade Organization
WWF	World Wide Fund for Nature

About the Contributors

Jonathan Harrington is an assistant professor of International Relations at Troy State University, Alabama, US.

Paul G Harris is an associate professor of politics at Lingnan University, Hong Kong. He directs the Project on Environmental Change and Foreign Policy.

Philip Scott Jones is a reader at the Centre for International Development and Training, University of Wolverhampton, UK.

Yuka Kobayashi is a Junior Research Fellow and doctoral candidate at the University of Oxford, UK.

Tran Dinh Lan is a senior researcher and deputy director of the Hai Phong Institute of Oceanology, Vietnam.

Ho-Ching Lee is an associate professor in the Centre of General Education and director of the Centre of International Programmes at Chung-Yuan Christian University, Chung-Li, Taiwan.

Tse-Kang Leng is a professor of political science, National Chengchi University, Taipei, Taiwan

Pham Van Luong is a senior researcher and deputy director of the Station for Marine Environment Monitoring, Hai Phong Institute of Oceanology, Vietnam.

Mika Merviö is a professor of political science at the University of Shimane, Hamada, Japan.

Hiroshi Ohta is a professor in the School of International Politics, Economics and Business at Aoyama Gakuin University, Tokyo.

Jak Sangchai is an officer in the Ministry of Foreign Affairs of Thailand. He received his doctorate in politics from the University of Leeds, UK.

Judith Shapiro is the director of the Global Environmental Politics Program at the School of International service, American University, Washington, DC, US.

Wen-chen Shih is an associate professor in the Department of International Trade, National Chengchi University, Taipei, Taiwan.

Peter Stoett is an assistant professor in the Department of Political Science at Concordia University, Montreal, Canada.

Tran Duc Thanh is a senior researcher and director of the Hai Phong Institute of Oceanology, Vietnam.

Preface

This is the sixth book from the Project on Environmental Change and Foreign Policy, which I began in 1998 at London Metropolitan University (then London Guildhall University). The project and I are now based at Lingnan University, Hong Kong.

The goals of the project are to better understand the role of foreign policy, broadly defined, in efforts to preserve the environment and natural resources. More specifically, the project seeks to understand foreign policy processes in international efforts to address adverse environmental changes at the local, regional and global levels; to analyse the actors and institutions – both domestic and international – that constrain and shape national actions on environmental issues; to show how environmental changes influence foreign policy processes; and to critically assess environmental foreign policies. Other objectives of the project are to 'test the waters' of research in this field; to showcase research that has not been forced into traditional empirical, epistemological or ontological boxes in the expectation that new areas and issues will be illuminated; to give insight to governmental and non-governmental practitioners and activists, which can help to improve their understanding of environmental issues in foreign policy; to disseminate these ideas so that they might have some positive effect on policy-making and scholarship; and to enlighten students and laypersons interested in environmental protection, sustainable development, international affairs and foreign policy.

Over 60 scholars have contributed to the project's first six books. The first phase of the project examined the environmental foreign policies of the United States. Three books resulted from that phase: *Climate Change and American Foreign Policy* (St Martin's Press, 2000), *The Environment, International Relations, and US Foreign Policy* (Georgetown University Press, 2001), and *International Equity and Global Environmental Politics: Power and Principles in US Foreign Policy* (Ashgate Press, 2001). The second phase of the project, of which this book is a part, has been dedicated to environmental change and foreign policy in East Asia. Two other books emanated from this phase: *International Environmental Cooperation: Politics and Diplomacy in Pacific Asia* (University Press of Colorado, 2002) and *Global Warming and East Asia: The Domestic and International Politics of Climate Change* (Routledge, 2003).

Many of the contributors to the project are internationally acclaimed and recognized. Others work in niches that deserve wider attention. I have made an effort to include the views of people of varied institutional and national backgrounds. Doing so helps to erode some of the intellectual and normative constraints that sometimes straightjacket work in international environmental politics and policy. Just as no single scholar will have the key to solving environmental problems, no single paradigm or theory is adequate to such a huge and important task. In this book, and in the larger project, we often apply similar theories in diverse ways, and we may interpret the same events differently. I welcome these disparate perspectives and I hope readers do too.

By thinking systematically about the issues and approaches contained in this book, I trust that we will better understand how politics and people interact with the environment. This will move us a bit closer to a more harmonious relationship with the natural world upon which we depend for so very much.

I wish to thank the contributing authors for their scholarship and hard work over a prolonged period. All of us are indebted to anonymous readers commissioned by Earthscan and the United Nations University Press (UNUP). Their comments, and the guidance of editors at Earthscan and UNUP, have helped us to convey our ideas more effectively. For this we are most grateful. Lingnan University and its Research and Postgraduate Studies Committee have provided important financial aid to the Project on Environmental Change and Foreign Policy, and Ivy Tsang has given consistently professional administrative assistance. I am especially grateful to Chan Kwok Kin for daily encouragement and support.

Paul G Harris
Hong Kong
August 2004

Chapter 1

Introduction: Confronting Environmental Change – Lessons from East and Southeast Asia

Paul G Harris

Introduction

In an essay entitled 'The Filthy Earth', Nicholas Kristof poignantly portrays what he describes as an ongoing 'war' in Asia:

> *It kills 3 million people each year, mostly children and the elderly, and yet it is scarcely noticed. It is the war between humans and the environment, and it is one that both sides are losing. The environment is one of the bleakest prisms through which to view Asia, for it is becoming a brake on development and a challenge to the rest of the world as well. This environmental catastrophe is one reason to temper one's optimism about Asia* (Kristof, 2000, p291).

Kristof's comments emphasize what environmental analysts have been saying for several years: as their economies and populations expand, almost all Asian countries are experiencing profound ecological deterioration and degradation of natural resources. It is therefore imperative that they confront environmental change.

The countries of *East* Asia, which are the focus of this volume, are no exception to this general trend in the wrong direction. Most countries in East Asia are experiencing terrible *national* environmental problems, such as horrendous air pollution in cities, water pollution and water shortages, soil erosion and deforestation, and major depletion of natural flora and fauna (JEC, 2000; UNEP, 1999, pp72–97). The poorest of these countries often need, and can always use, financial and technical help from more developed countries in order to address local and national problems. The countries of East Asia also experience the adverse effects of *regional* environmental problems. They use polluted water from shared rivers, they often suffer transboundary air and marine pollution, and they endure the effects of acid rain that can originate far away. Countries of the region are also subject to the effects of *global* environmental problems, most notably global warming and resulting climatic changes (see Watson et al, 1998).

While the countries of East Asia are the victims of environmental change, they are also complicit in causing it at home and abroad. Japan, for example, has been responsible for substantial deforestation in East and Southeast Asia, and China – already the second largest source of greenhouse gases – will eventually overtake the US as the primary source of anthropogenic pollutants causing global warming. To be sure, the poor people of this region are, on a per capita basis, much less responsible for environmental problems than are residents of richer countries, and they do not bear the same *moral* burden to act to prevent and cope with these problems (see Harris, 1996, 1997, 2001a). However, it is impossible to deny that how they live and develop will have increasingly profound consequences for the entire world. For these and other reasons, when confronting the problems of global environmental change, it is certainly worthwhile – and even essential – to look carefully at East Asia.

The responses of East Asian countries to environmental changes are always complicated and frequently disparate. Different historical experiences, cultures, levels of development, political systems and policy-making structures (among many other variables) cause these countries to view their environmental interests differently, to participate differently in international environmental negotiations and to operate environmental protection schemes differently. Among the issues central to international environmental cooperation in East Asia are foreign policy and sustainable development. That is, the relationships of these countries with one another and with other actors outside East Asia, the motivations and processes underlying those relationships, and the ways in which they are (or are not) translated into environmental protection, matter for efforts at all levels to protect the environment of this region and, to an increasingly significant degree, the world.

With these considerations in mind, this book surveys several East Asian countries to better understand – and, hopefully, to better answer – these types of questions: What are the different environmental experiences of East Asian countries? What indigenous factors and particular foreign policy processes influence whether some countries are more willing than others to join international environmental protection efforts? What are the different underlying stimuli for these countries' positions in international environmental negotiations, and what role do foreign policy institutions play in fostering or preventing international environmental cooperation in East Asia? What variables stimulate governments and other actors to develop in environmentally sustainable ways, and what are the keys to success in this regard? Once environmental foreign policies are formulated by individual states and groups of states, what are the impacts of those policies in affected countries – and how should these impacts be considered when polices are formulated? Our particular interest here is in areas where domestic politics and policy-making interact with international politics and institutions. As such, we are particularly interested in the making and implementation of *foreign policy*, and its effects on environmental protection in East Asia.

Environmental change and foreign policy

Foreign policy encompasses the objectives that officials of national governments seek to attain, the values and principles underlying those objectives, and the methods by which they are sought (see Chapter 2; Barkdull and Harris, 2002). It almost goes without saying that foreign policy objectives and processes can play an important, often vital, role in determining whether countries cooperate to address environmental problems, and often whether they have the capabilities to do so. What is particularly important about foreign policy is that it involves the *crossover* and *interaction* between domestic politics and processes, on the one hand, and international relations and institutions, on the other. Looking at purely local or international variables seldom explains environmental policy within and among countries. Many issues, actors and forces, which act domestically and internationally, affect and influence countries' national environmental regulations and their environmental foreign policies. As a result, they impact upon international environmental cooperation. Yet, despite the clear connections between local and international policy processes, many studies do not account for the foreign policy aspects of environmental protection efforts. This book seeks to do just that, in the process delineating and explicating many of the factors driving policy.

Thinking about foreign policy focuses our attention on interactions among domestic political preferences and the positions governments take in negotiations; the balancing of economic capacity and popular demands for development with foreign pressures to join regimes; and the rivalries and alliances between foreign policy agencies and the individuals working in them (among many other considerations). A good reason for looking at foreign policy processes more systematically is that they can reveal important national characteristics that shape state behaviour, both domestically and internationally. Many foreign policy officials are simultaneously pressured to follow international norms and promote national interests and ideals. That is, they are buffeted by both domestic and international forces.

Foreign policy is, to be sure, about pursuing and promoting national interests. Complexities arise, however. It is not always clear what a country's national interests are or ought to be, particularly with regard to complex ecological issues, and it is almost always debatable how best to promote them (Webber and Smith 2002, pp43–44). As Roy argues in a discussion of contemporary Chinese foreign policy, policy-making elites will disagree over national goals and how to achieve them:

> *Beyond its most basic formulation, the national interest is not a monolithic, objective concept, but rather a dynamic and unsettled one, subject to constant debate. [Moreover,] powerful groups and individuals are subject to self-interested behaviour, and may support the policy option [that] they calculate will enhance their power and prestige, even if it is not necessarily the best option for the nation as a whole* (Roy, 1998, pp137–138).

Thus, defining national interests and the ways of achieving them is a problematic and complex undertaking, involving actors and institutions seemingly unimportant to the casual observer.

It would be fatuous to suggest that it is possible to *completely* abstract out the forces of foreign policy, particularly if 'foreign policy' is broadly defined. Foreign policy cannot be separated from, for example, domestic politics and institutions, at one end of a spectrum, and global regimes and international power balances, at the other end. To suggest this would be just as absurd as suggesting that everything that is important can be explained by the international distribution of power (Waltz, 1979) (if so, why are 'weak' states so powerful in international environmental politics?) or domestic interests (Milner, 1997) (why, then, do some states adhere to international environmental norms, even when, by any reasonable measure, those interests would not be advantaged, or would even be harmed, by doing so?). Only rarely, if ever, are states 'unitary rational actors' (Green and Shapiro, 1994; Friedman, 1996), particularly in the environmental issue area. This is why looking specifically at foreign policy can be helpful. What is useful, perhaps, is to go beyond thinking in terms of domestic and international levels of analysis to a 'two-levels-plus' game (cf Putnam, 1988; Evans et al, 1993). In other words, we ought to consider international political dynamics and domestic politics; but we can also think *explicitly* about the additional 'level' of foreign policy processes, which almost always falls between and affects the international- and domestic-level factors.

With this in mind, this book seeks to bring these considerations into analyses of how states and other actors in East and Southeast Asia confront environmental change through international cooperation and environmentally sustainable development. Although foreign policy processes and factors receive some attention in many studies of international environmental cooperation in East Asia (see Harris, 2002), they are seldom the focus of those studies. And while environmental foreign policy has been the focus of quite a number of excellent journal articles and book chapters, very few books have been dedicated to it. Material is scattered in journals and in books on broader topics. This book, and the larger Project on Environmental Change and Foreign Policy of which it is a part, endeavours to remedy this by bringing together the work of scholars examining, in one way or another, the role of foreign policy in global environmental politics (see Harris, 2000a, 2001a, 2001b, 2002, 2003). By focusing more scholarly attention on foreign policy processes and international variables that shape sustainable development, we can improve our understanding of how, why and when international environmental cooperation happens, how to foster more of it, and how to implement it most effectively.

Eco-politics and foreign policy: Lessons from East and Southeast Asia

This book comprises two parts. The first examines many of the actors, institutions and forces shaping environmental diplomacy and foreign policy in East Asia, with particular emphasis on case studies of China and Japan. The second part of the book looks deeper within the countries of East and Southeast Asia to help us to better understand the relationships between ecological politics, international relations and environmentally sustainable development. Several chapters in the second part focus on how environmental foreign policies impact upon countries in the region as they endeavour to implement environmentally sustainable development. Together, the case studies illuminate how environmental change is confronted – or not – in East Asia. Very importantly, they also teach us general lessons about environmental politics and policy, as well as international environmental cooperation, which can be applied to other regions and other countries.

Environment, foreign policy and diplomacy in East Asia: Actors, institutions and forces

Our case studies begin with Paul G Harris's survey of actors and forces affecting the environmental foreign policies of China and Japan. Chapter 2 describes some of the domestic environmental problems and transnational environmental issues of concern to each country; domestic policy processes related to environmental regulation; variables more obviously associated with foreign policy; and each country's record of international environmental diplomacy. Harris also introduces some theoretical approaches that can focus our attention on key variables. What he finds is that interesting and sometimes overlooked variables can be profoundly important. For example, China's historical near obsession with sovereignty and Japan's sometime obsession with being viewed as a major power shape their *environmental* foreign policies every bit as much as other factors. Indeed, the bilateral environmental relationship between these two countries remains deeply influenced by forces seemingly unrelated to the environment, in particular their 20th-century wartime history.

Chapter 2 serves as a primer for the more detailed case studies in subsequent chapters, which begin with Mika Merviö's analysis of the ideological foundations of Japan's environmental foreign policy. He argues in Chapter 3 that Japan's environmental policies, both domestic and international, are based on 'anthropocentric ideologies' that often neglect the environment per se. He introduces notions such as 'chauvinist anthropocentrism', where environmental protection is presented as an obstacle to economic development and the narrow interests of the local political elites guide policy. While Japan's environmental foreign policy is based on anthropocentric thinking, it is also influenced by broader foreign policy goals. Japan uses environmental issues to expand its influence abroad through, for example, its large amount of development assistance to other countries – much of it tied to environmental objectives. As such, the environment has taken on a more prominent role in Japan's foreign policy and has increasingly permeated other aspects of it. Thus, while anthropocentric ideologies and Japan's more narrow interests remain central, they have had to be reconciled with concerns about the environment.

In Chapter 4, Hiroshi Ohta examines Japanese foreign policy on global climate change to illustrate the intersections between domestic politics and environmental diplomacy. Ohta argues that Japan's domestic political framework, as well as its quest to make a greater contribution to international affairs (using non-military means), has generated rationales for it to undertake new initiatives in environmental diplomacy. Ohta describes several important events in the recent history of Japan's diplomacy and politics on global climate change, particularly its adoption of the 1992 United Nations Framework

Convention on Climate Change (FCCC). He does this from the perspective of Robert Putnam's 'two-level game' analysis (Putnam, 1988). Putnam proposed a conceptual framework for the analysis of international negotiations, whereby diplomats try to negotiate agreements that satisfy the demands of their domestic interest groups while minimizing the adverse effects of their counterparts' domestic interests. After using the conceptual framework of the two-level game to reconstruct the stories of Japan's domestic politics related to international climate change negotiations, Ohta evaluates the implications of this approach. In the process he highlights the importance of political leadership, public opinion and the active participation of environmental non-governmental organizations (NGOs).

In Chapter 5 Judith Shapiro turns our attention to China. She is particularly interested in the lessons we can learn from the environmental history of 20th-century revolutionary China. During the Great Proletarian Cultural Revolution (1966–1976), the Chinese state displaced millions of people and relocated them to the hinterlands. Hundreds of factories and entire work forces were moved to regions inhospitable to human habitation. Coercive and semi-voluntary relocations of people to pristine wilderness areas damaged or destroyed ecosystems even as they created enormous human hardships, exemplifying the link between the suffering of people and the abuse of the land characteristic of the Mao years. Shapiro's case study provides a stark example of the environmental and human repercussions of policies based on narrow conceptions of national interests – in this case, international security concerns. She demonstrates how a preoccupation with perceived external threats can shift attention from other priorities and, specifically, have profoundly negative effects on the environment.

In Chapter 6, Yuka Kobayashi looks at China's environmental policies and diplomacy over the last three decades. While China has become more active in environmental protection regimes during recent years, some observers criticize it as a laggard and as an obstructive, uncooperative actor in these regimes. However, Kobayashi argues that we should consider the extensive domestic implementation efforts that China has been making in order to comply with international environmental agreements. Criticizing China as a recalcitrant actor in international environmental regimes risks being simplistic. China has many impediments that keep it from being more proactive in environmental protection. Kobayashi shows that constraints at both the international and domestic levels, and their interplay, explain Chinese behaviour on environmental issues. Domestic factors, such as geography, demography and history, constrain and shape China's environmental policies. Its role as a leader of the developing world also influences its policies. These constraints are made worse by top-level leaders who still focus on economic growth. Thus, Kobayashi argues, considering these and other constraints, China looks more like a 'troubled modernizer' than a recalcitrant participant in international environmental regimes.

China is one of the most important actors in international environmental affairs, and arguably the most important actor in Asia. In Chapter 7, Jonathan Harrington continues our examination of how it confronts environmental change. He is particularly interested in explaining the role of 'state environmentalism' and the use of environmental issues by senior Chinese leaders to bolster and legitimize their regime. Among other things, Harrington asserts that following the bloody 1989 Tiananmen incident the Chinese leadership sought new ways of boosting its image, both domestically and internationally. The leadership latched on to a 'safe' and symbolic issue that had both domestic and international appeal – namely, expanding participation in global eco-politics – one that it could use to claw its way out of diplomatic isolation. But attention to environmental issues took on a life of its own in China, showing how environmental diplomacy for other reasons can, nevertheless, lead to environmental protection efforts at the national level.

In Chapter 8, Wen-chen Shih analyses Taiwan's international environmental policies, particularly its efforts during the 1990s to balance trade with environmental protection. Taiwan is in a strange position by international standards. It is subject to international criticism for its environmental conduct, yet it is unable to participate in most international forums that deal with environmental issues (because mainland China will not permit this to happen). Shih argues that Taiwan now has a policy of voluntary compliance with multilateral environmental agreements (MEAs), although he shows that the underlying reason for this policy is the protection of Taiwan's economic and trade interests – not environmental protection per se. This policy followed threats of trade restrictions and sanctions during the early 1990s from some MEAs to which Taiwan is not a party. This puts Taiwan in a very difficult position in the international debate over the compatibility between free trade and MEAs. In undertaking his analysis of Taiwan, Shih highlights some of the principal forces and actors shaping the environmental foreign policy of an important actor in East Asia.

Eco-politics, international relations and strategies for sustainable development in East and Southeast Asia

In the second part of this book we look more specifically at the effects that environmental politics and diplomacy have upon the negotiation and practice of environmentally sustainable development, and vice versa. We are concerned with how environmental foreign policy emanating from individual states and from international institutions is implemented in East and Southeast Asia, and the lessons from these experiences for those who formulate environmental foreign policies. In Chapter 9, Ho-Ching Lee explores China's policies toward the climate change agreements, which require little of China. Lee's chapter exposes some of the issues that must be addressed if China is to take on a greater role in combating climate change. Lee argues that major factors influencing China's actions include, for example, access to financial assistance and technology transfer, and China's desire for greater international recognition. Lee suggests that reducing carbon dioxide emissions through domestic measures (such as improved energy efficiency and tree planting) would promote China's current and long-term interests. In promoting its broader interests, China may reduce its environmental footprint, even if it is not required to do so by international environmental treaties.

In Chapter 10, Jak Sangchai examines Thailand's policy toward the Convention on Biological Diversity (CBD). Thai politics are often described as being dominated by bureaucrats. The government wants to join the CBD because it contains provisions for financial aid and technology transfer, and could help conserve Thailand's biodiversity. However, since the late 1980s there have been an increasing number of Thai NGOs claiming to represent the people and trying to influence government policies. NGOs can use environmental issues to further their objectives, such as promoting the rights of the poor, farmers and local communities. Some Thai NGOs view the CBD as a trap set by developed countries and transnational companies wishing to take advantage of rural people and the poor. Sangchai describes the struggles among the government and other actors as Thailand debates whether to implement the CBD. He shows, in particular, how NGOs can be active in shaping national policies toward international environmental goals, and how they use environmental issues to promote their own particularistic interests.

Many countries face serious challenges related to the resources they share with neighbours. This is often the case with states who share rivers susceptible to upstream development initiatives that can result in serious ecological consequences. Power relations between countries, and the advantages of upstream states, often define the issue. The Mekong River in Southeast Asia provides such an example as downstream states deal with China's construction of dams on the river's upper reaches. In Chapter 11, Peter Stoett examines the national, human and environmental security aspects of international efforts to manage the Mekong River. Stoett describes the current situation within and among countries along the Mekong's course, highlighting the foreign policy dilemmas raised by disputes over the river and its resources. In the view of Stoett, human security must be considered alongside, or even above, national security. He argues that scholars should look more carefully at the impact of environmental alterations on the people who rely on rivers for their well-being and who are often marginalized in decision-making processes related to river management.

The role played by international assistance in Vietnam's efforts to protect its marine environment is examined by Tran Duc Thanh, Tran Dinh Lan and Pham Van Luong in Chapter 12. The Vietnam Sea, with its densely populated islands and coasts, has become an area of active economic development. Human activities have resulted in many new problems for Vietnam's marine environment, making its protection an urgent requirement. Chapter 12 shows how Vietnam has undertaken substantial domestic efforts toward this end. These efforts derive much of their strength from international relationships, which have often emanated from Vietnam's participation in international environmental agreements. Indeed, Vietnam's international relations in the area of environmental protection have been among its most open policies over the last decade. Importantly, Vietnam's marine protection efforts have been bolstered by international assistance for capacity-building and local development projects. NGOs have also been involved through implementing small-scale projects. The authors show that international assistance, when wisely allocated, can be instrumental in bringing about major advances in environmental protection at the national level.

Using Canadian experiences and practices as a comparative backdrop, Tse-Kang Leng, in Chapter 13, analyses sustainable development in Taiwan. Taiwan's rapid economic development has caused environmental pollution and deterioration of natural resources. The Taiwanese and Canadian experiences suggest that sustainable development requires the integration of different national goals, an open process for public participation, accountability through multi-stakeholder supervision and market-based incentives for international participation. Economic development and sustainable development are not necessarily in conflict. Marketable environmental technologies, such as high-efficiency clean technologies, are important in creating win–win relationships between the state and the business community. Participation in international environmental cooperation can boost technological innovation and increase business opportunities for environmental industries. International cooperation, combined with mechanisms for collaborative governance among government, business and civil society, can move countries toward successful sustainable development.

Effectively confronting environmental change in East Asia will require the involvement of the international community. But doing so cannot be divorced from the priorities of people on the ground, their group interests and their everyday conflicts. Bearing this in mind, we conclude our look at strategies for sustainable development in East Asia with a study of how community-based conflict management has assisted environmental protection in Papua New Guinea (PNG). In Chapter 14, Philip Scott Jones describes projects in 'sustainable livelihoods' related to the implementation of international environmental objectives. He is particularly interested in policy approaches that enable local people and vulnerable groups to participate in policy-making, thereby improving policy formulation and implementation. He argues that the tools and principles of conflict management, appropriately applied within a framework of sustainable livelihoods, provide flexible methods for managing environmental conflicts and for developing appropriate policy mechanisms. Well-designed, locally relevant conflict management and sustainable livelihood training can be powerful entry points for bringing stakeholders at all levels into the process of confronting and managing environmental change in East Asia.

Conclusion

The findings of the contributors to this volume enhance our understanding of how and why states and other actors work to protect the environment – or fail to do so. We are particularly interested in the important role played by foreign policy processes, broadly defined, in influencing international environmental cooperation and in the implementation of environmentally sustainable development. We have reached many interesting and important conclusions, including – but certainly not limited to – the following.

Domestic politics can be the determining variable in shaping environmental foreign policy, even in nominally less pluralistic countries. In many or even a majority of cases, the most important determinants of environmental foreign policy are found within countries. This will come as no surprise to students of international environmental politics. We know, for example, that domestic politics are very important in shaping the foreign policies of the US, including its policies related to the environment (Harris, 2000, 2001a, 2001b). However, while the US case shows the importance of pluralism – the degree of access that civil society actors have in the policy process – it is not always clear how this plays out. A case in point is Japan. Although Japan is a recognized and well-established democracy, there is relatively little pluralism, especially compared with the US. Non-governmental actors and the public have less influence than many casual observers would expect, whereas bureaucrats and business interests are very influential in shaping policy. In contrast, and perhaps paradoxically, in China – a country ruled by an authoritarian government and hardly classified as democratic – quite a large number of actors shape policy. These actors range from interested governmental officials and scientists – even foreign scientists – to local officials and industry leaders, among others. Even the semi-independent media and NGOs have played a more important role than one might expect – perhaps a more important role than in Japan and some other more democratic countries, at least with regard to *global* environmental issues (at times the Japanese public has vigorously pushed the domestic environmental agenda, especially at the local level).

In contrast to the power of domestic forces, international factors can, at least in some cases, shape environmental foreign policy; in short, international politics can shape foreign and domestic policy on the environment. To say that domestic politics can be paramount is, of course, not to say that international influences are not germane in many cases. Indeed, they can be central to policy formulation. Japan is again a case in point. Its environmental foreign policy is arguably not driven by domestic politics, or even by concern about threats posed by global environmental changes for the nation or its people. Instead, Japan's environmental foreign policy has been driven by its desire to be viewed as a legitimate major power in the eyes of other industrialized countries. Environmental diplomacy is a way for Japan to peacefully increase its power vis-à-vis other states. Similarly, China has substantial 'environmental power' because its growing contribution to global pollution gives it the ability to make or break many international environmental agreements. It wields this 'power' to enhance its international position and reputation, not simply to join others in addressing environmental problems or to respond to environmental concerns among influential actors in the policy process. Taiwan provides another example of how international forces can be important. Its environmental policies are arguably a function of its dependence upon international trade and its desire to avoid environmental sanctions. Environmentalism on the part of the government and the people of Taiwan has a relatively minor role in shaping its environmental foreign policies.

History matters, sometimes a great deal, even if it appears to be totally unrelated to the global environment. This is one of the more interesting conclusions that come from studies of environmental politics and policy in East Asia. History quite unrelated to the environment can shape environmental foreign policy. China, for example, has been (at least until recently) virtually obsessed with its treatment by foreign powers in past centuries. One of its primary goals when joining and implementing environmental accords – and, indeed, other international agreements – is to avoid the humiliation it experienced during the 19th and 20th centuries. This has practical consequences – for example, when China refuses to be bound by certain verification measures that are viewed as important to effectively implement international agreements for sustainable development. In the case of Japan, war history shapes much of its foreign policy, including its *environmental* foreign policy and the responses to that policy by other countries in East and Southeast Asia. Japan's environmental aid to other countries in the region is, to a significant degree, an effort to atone for (or appear to atone for) the way it treated neighbouring countries during the first half of the 20th century, and its neighbours expect it to be this way. In short, wars and colonialism of a century ago can be central determinants of current policies on, for example, financial assistance for sustainable development in East Asia. Thus, the degree to which history influences environmental foreign policy in East Asia should not be underestimated.

The number and type of actors shaping most environmental foreign policies is usually very large. There is an understandable tendency among some scholars to seek parsimonious explanations for environmental foreign policies and international environmental affairs more broadly. However, as in other issue areas, the process of environmental policy-making and implementation is complex, and seldom as easy to explain as many would have us believe. In addition, the usual actors we identify as being important may not be working in the way that we expect. An example might be the role played by NGOs in shaping US environmental foreign policy. The US has many prominent organizations with environmentally friendly names that, in fact, work hard to prevent their government from joining or implementing international environmental agreements. But it gets even more complicated. For example, the case of Thailand and the biodiversity convention shows that even pro-environmental organizations may oppose international environmental accords if, in so doing, they can achieve other important (and usually laudable) goals or (more cynically) if they or their officials can garner additional power in or with government. Which actors, institutions or forces are the most important? It depends upon the country being studied, the particular environmental issues at stake, the country's level of economic development and (among many other variables) the combination of domestic and international forces at play – including the ecological problems themselves.

Environmental foreign policy is often not about the environment. As indicated by several case studies in this volume, countries may act on environmental issues for reasons partly or totally unrelated to the environment. As suggested previously, Japan's environmental foreign policy is, in part, about establishing itself as a credible global power and an influential actor in this issue area, to some degree because it cannot easily do so in others (for example, security affairs). China's substantial efforts to join international environmental negotiations and regimes during the early 1990s were much less motivated by environmental concerns than by the desire to garner international financial assistance and technology for its economic development, its interest in being viewed as a leader of the developing world in this issue area, and (most interestingly, perhaps) its efforts to escape the diplomatic isolation imposed on it by much of the Western world following the Tiananmen crackdown in 1989.

We can conclude that foreign policy processes are crucial in shaping the domestic and international environmental policies and behaviours of states. Foreign policy processes are conduits of communication and influence among individuals, bureaucracies, states, international institutions and forces, and foreign policy-makers. They are the venues for forming *environmental* foreign policy, determine the degree to which it enters international dialogue, and influence its implementation. In short, whether (and the degree to which) the natural environment is protected is in large part a function of foreign policy and all of the actors, institutions and forces of which it is comprised.

Part 1

Environment, Foreign Policy and Diplomacy in East Asia: Actors, Institutions and Forces

Chapter 2

Environmental Politics and Foreign Policy in East Asia: A Survey of China and Japan

Paul G Harris

Introduction

For those concerned about the global environment, arguably the most important countries in East Asia are China and Japan. China is the most populous country in the world and its fast-growing economy is amongst the largest. Consequently, it is one of the world's largest polluters. Furthermore, China's population is adversely affected by many environmental changes and resource scarcities. Japan has the second largest economy in the world. It contributes to global environmental changes and has financial and technological resources that can help to address environmental changes and implement environmentally sustainable development in East Asia. In short, these two countries are crucial to regional and global environmental protection efforts. Understanding their domestic and foreign environmental policies is therefore important for scholars, practitioners and citizens interested in international environmental affairs. Looking at their policies can also help to illuminate variables influencing the domestic and international environmental policies of other countries in East Asia.

This chapter surveys China and Japan to help us better understand their environmental policies and to frame the debates and detailed analyses of environmental politics, diplomacy and foreign policy of East Asian countries in subsequent chapters. The main concern is to shed light on the crossover and interaction between domestic and international variables – what we can refer to as the domain of *foreign policy*. Foreign policy can be defined as the objectives that officials of national governments seek to attain, the values and principles underlying those objectives and the methods by which the objectives are sought (see Barkdull and Harris, 2002). Foreign policy is characterized by the processes through which these objectives, values, principles and methods are developed and implemented, as well as the actors and forces involved.

Foreign policy analysis is well suited to studying responses to environmental changes because it considers the 'continuing erosion of the distinction between domestic and foreign issues, between the socio-political and economic processes that unfold at home and those that transpire abroad' (Rosenau, 1987, p3). Foreign policy is the interplay between domestic forces, institutions and actors (such as democratic principles – or lack thereof – civil society, executive and legislative power structures, government agencies and diplomatic personnel) and international forces, institutions and actors (such as globalization – economic, environmental, cultural – international organizations and regimes, and powerful countries, corporations and non-governmental organizations, or NGOs). As Gerner (1995, p17) has observed:

> *Although no subfield in political science is completely self-contained, the study of foreign policy is somewhat unusual in that it deals with both domestic and international arenas, jumping from individual to state to systemic levels of analysis, and attempts to integrate all of these aspects into a coherent whole.*

While foreign policy analysis and explanation can be complicated, they get us closer to understanding the reality of how domestic and international forces – and those in between – coalesce into environmental cooperation and sustainable development within and among countries.

Many variables that are not purely *foreign* or obviously *international* in nature can affect national and international environmental policy by shaping national interests, preferences and values. These can, in turn, shape foreign policy attitudes and behaviours. Some of the most obvious variables are introduced in this chapter. Among these are local ecological problems and transnational environmental concerns, domestic environmental policies and regulations, foreign policy actors and processes, and each country's history of environmental diplomacy. Subsequent chapters look at these and other variables in more detail (see especially Chapters 4, 6, 7 and 9).

The following sections (1) introduce a number of theoretical approaches to environmental foreign policy; (2) summarize domestic environmental policy-making, foreign policy processes and environmental diplomacy of China and Japan; (3) highlight underlying characteristics and purposes of these countries' environmental foreign policies; and (4) reference major theories of foreign policy to illustrate how we can focus on key variables in, and explanations for, international environmental policies. Taken together, this and subsequent chapters give a detailed picture of environmental politics, foreign policy and international relations in East and Southeast Asia.

Theoretical approaches to environmental foreign policy

We can use theory to help us think systematically about the relationship between foreign policy and environmental change. Barkdull and Harris (2002) have undertaken a comprehensive survey of environmental foreign policy. They propose a framework (see Figure 2.1) that focuses on a variety of potentially important variables in the shaping of foreign polices in particular circumstances. No single theory is necessarily best for explaining and understanding the environmental foreign policies of all countries in all circumstances; indeed, approaches might suitably be combined to arrive at the richest explanations for policy.

Barkdull and Harris (2002, p66–67) draw on Ikenberry et al (1988) to suggest that theoretical approaches to foreign policy can be characterized as systemic, societal or state-centric. Systemic theories argue that foreign policy stems from the role, identity or interests given to the state by systemic factors (for example, regional or global configurations of power and hegemonic ideas). Societal theories point to the preferences of domestic actors, which are translated into policies adopted and implemented by the government. From this perspective, explanations for foreign policy 'are found in the ongoing struggle for influence among domestic social forces or political groups' (Ikenberry et al, 1988, p7). In contrast, state-centric approaches argue that foreign policy is shaped by the structure of government and the individuals and institutions that promulgate and implement foreign policies on its behalf, with the emphasis 'on the goal-oriented behaviour of politicians and civil servants as they respond to internal and external constraints in an effort to manipulate policy outcomes in accordance with their preferences' (Ikenberry et al, 1988, p10).

These three broad approaches to understanding foreign policy – system, society and state – can be further refined by also focusing on the roles of power, interests and ideas (Barkdull and Harris, 2002, pp67–68; cf Hasenclever et al, 1997). According to some power-based approaches, often characterized as 'realism', countries join international regimes due to hegemonic or oligopoly distributions of power. Hegemons (or small groups of leading powers) create regimes that serve their interests, and then force them upon other countries. Alternatively, interest-based theories, often associated with 'liberal institutionalism', posit that international cooperation stems from the desires of states to promote their interests in a given issue area. According to this perspective, hegemonic power is not essential because rational state actors will cooperate to achieve joint gains. Yet another set of theories focus on ideas. Ideas can direct international actors toward new ways of pursuing their interests, whether unilaterally or multilaterally. From this 'constructivist' perspective, material interests and power may have limited influence compared to even more influential identities that the international system generates for global actors.

These theoretical approaches can be portrayed in a matrix of environmental foreign policy (see Figure 2.1). They serve as reference points in the final section of this chapter, which focuses on the actors and forces shaping the environmental foreign policies of China and Japan.

Figure 2.1 *A Typology of (Environmental) Foreign Policy*

	Systemic	Systemic	Systemic
Power	Structural realism, hegemonic model	Elite theory, class analysis	Executive — legislature relations
Interests	National interest model	Interest group politics pluralist models	Bureaucratic politics model
Ideas	Sociological approach to international regimes	Media studies; social movements; public opinion	Media studies; social movements; public opinion

Source: Barkdull and Harris (2002, p69).
Note: Cells in the matrix show examples of illustrative foreign policy studies. See Barkdull and Harris (2002, pp66–84) for a detailed exposition of this typology and references to the examples shown.

People's Republic of China

China's population has reached about 1.3 billion people, and its economy is one of the largest (by most measures in the top ten), growing about 8 per cent per year since the mid 1980s (UNEP, 1999, p73). Consequently, China is experiencing tremendous environmental problems with severe local, national and regional consequences (see Smil, 1993). China has highly developed urban areas that experience modern forms of pollution (for example, automobile exhaust fumes) and vast rural areas that have long suffered from destruction or overuse of environmental resources (for example, deforestation and soil erosion). Other environmental problems include pollution from heavy industry; air pollution and acid rain, particularly from coal burning; water shortages and pollution; degradation of farmland and desertification; huge volumes of solid and toxic waste; and other environmental effects of urbanization and burgeoning consumerism (JEC, 2000, pp98–100; see Johnson et al, 1997). Regulations and improved efficiency have reduced some pollution, but economic growth still outpaces efforts to limit environmental damage.

The Chinese government recognized some environmental problems and began addressing them as early as the 1950s; but into the 1970s it argued that as a socialist state it did not have environmental problems. However, the increasingly obvious damage to China's natural environment and, importantly, resulting adverse impacts on economic development caused the government to be more concerned during the 1980s. In 1982 the Chinese constitution was rewritten, with the government pledging to 'protect the environment and natural resources by controlling pollution and its societal impact, ensure the sensible use of natural resources, and safeguard rare animals and plants' (cited in Tseng, 1999, p383). The following year environmental preservation was declared one of China's basic national policies, and by the end of the decade China started its first major campaign to combat pollution (Tseng, 1999, p383). During the 1980s the government also instituted new environmental protection laws in the areas of solid waste, noise, air and water pollution, and in 1989 the government strengthened the Environmental Protection Law (UNEP, 1999, pp241–42).

By the mid 1990s the government was becoming more serious about environmental issues, even closing some polluting factories. In 1994 the Chinese State Council adopted *China's Agenda for the 21st Century: White Paper on China's Population, Environment and Development in the 21st Century*. The main themes were economic development (first) and environmental protection (second). A new environmental awareness at the national level was evidenced in the pronouncements of national leaders. For example, in 1995 Premier Li Peng told the National People's Congress (NPC) to follow the national policy of environmental protection, and in 1997 President Jiang Zemin reported to the Chinese Communist Party's (CCP) National Congress that pressures on the environment caused by overpopulation and economic development were harming the country (Tseng, 1999, p383). The agency tasked with promoting environmental protection was elevated to ministerial status, becoming the State Environmental Protection Administration (SEPA).

By the late 1990s, the central government was allocating substantial (if grossly inadequate) funds to environmental and resource protection, and it reportedly shut down tens of thousands of polluting enterprises and implemented emissions fees and clean technologies (UNEP, 1999, p246).

However, the environmental benefits of these actions have often been limited. Implementation of environmental laws is hindered by lack of money, corruption, the refusal of local authorities to take the laws seriously and the inability or unwillingness of higher officials to force them to do so. Beijing often has limited control over the vast bureaucracy, particularly outside Beijing, and the institutional structure of China's environmental management system is extraordinarily complex. Underlying the inability to implement environmental protections is a strong nationwide fixation on economic growth. According to Tseng (1999, p390), even 'the government often ignores some of its environmental policies and regulations and does what it thinks is necessary for economic advancement'. Wealth creation in the short term usually trumps environmental protection.

Chinese foreign policy

China's political system remains predominantly authoritarian. The two main domestic forces in its foreign policy are the CCP and government ministries. Citizens have seldom had great impact on foreign policy. The paramount civilian leadership – usually the president, premier and/or chief of the CCP – is the ultimate arbiter of foreign policy decisions. The 'top leader' can have decisive influence, but this is not always the case; bargaining usually occurs even at the highest level (Bachman, 1998, p42). Other actors can be influential in shaping foreign policy, notably the military and the Ministry of Foreign Affairs (MOFA). Roy (1998, p138) argues that 'Chinese foreign policy may be seen to be the result of an ongoing debate between self-interested groups or factions arbitrated by a paramount leader who may be swayed toward one viewpoint or another on a given issue'. According to Whiting (1992, p241):

> ... *only under unique circumstances is policy the dictate of a single official acting wholly on his own initiative. Instead, specific interests and responsibilities shape the perceptions, information intake and policy output of organized groups inside and outside the government. It is their complex interaction that defines policy in specific situations.*

This is truer now than in the past because charismatic and powerful leaders (for example, Mao and Deng) have been replaced by weaker leaders who need support to make policy, and because international affairs create new constraints not faced when China was more closed to the world.

Chinese foreign policy is increasingly bureaucratic, with experts and specialists taking on greater importance. In practice, this bureaucratization can lead to 'irrational' outcomes as officials promote the interests of their bureaucracy or higher-level officials promote competing objectives, rather than the country's best interests. In routine matters, bureaucratic management takes on great importance, whereas when fundamental national interests are at stake individual leaders are more important (Breslin, 1990). In most cases, competing bureaucracies must reach consensus and use collective decision-making, and a process of investigation, argumentation and negotiation must be completed before complex foreign policy issues are decided. Foreign policy decisions are formulated incrementally and implemented in an organizational fashion. Often, the result is inefficiency (Whiting, 1992, pp243–245). While we can point to the most visible agencies in foreign policy, it can be difficult to determine which is most important in a given policy area.

Underlying Chinese foreign policy is the desire for power and prosperity, which are deemed essential for national security and economic vitality. Security interests will, of course, affect foreign policy, including policies on the environment. For example, China's scepticism regarding the Law of the Sea might be attributed to its claims to vast swathes of the South China Sea – including the sea lines of communication and natural resources found there. Pervading China's foreign policy is an obsession with the prerogatives of sovereignty that is 'particularly extensive and absolutist', often preventing Chinese policy-makers from agreeing to international environmental commitments that might require it to allow intrusive inspections or might limit its 'sovereign right to develop its resources as it sees fit' (Johnston, 1998b, p73). In recent decades, economic development has become a preoccupation of China's foreign policy. The CCP derives its legitimacy from its ability to raise living standards, and it is mesmerized by the prospect of catching up to more economically developed countries (Roy, 1998, p139). A closely related characteristic of China's foreign policy is its support for the right of developing countries to grow free of outside hindrances. An important feature of Chinese foreign policy is the lingering assumption that outsiders seek to exploit China. China's perceptions of other countries and of international institutions can be clouded by this assumption.

China's environmental diplomacy

China has a central role to play in international environmental diplomacy. It is a huge developing country that is having profound adverse impacts upon the natural environment. It already produces vast amounts of greenhouse gases (GHGs), which will increase in coming decades, and pollution from its factories and cities contaminates regional seas and air – even spreading to other continents. The Chinese have a massive and unrelenting demand for living and non-living natural resources, causing great harm to wildlife and ecosystems both inside China and beyond its borders. These and other environmental effects of its development mean that China cannot be ignored in international environmental protection efforts. More broadly, China is a powerful member of the developing world, and its political and diplomatic powers mean that it can influence international environmental negotiations.

China's environmental diplomacy seeks to further three goals: protect its sovereignty, acquire foreign aid and technical assistance, and promote its economic development (Economy, 1998, p264). China has used its dual status as a developing country (with rights to, and needs for, development) and its growing role as a major contributor to global environmental problems (such as GHG emissions) to acquire substantial influence in international environmental negotiations (Economy, 1998, p265). It has consistently sought 'new and additional' funds from developed countries in international environmental deliberations of all kinds in return for its support for, or acquiescence to, environmental agreements. These efforts have paid off; China is the largest recipient of environmental aid from the World Bank and receives large amounts of aid from other international funding agencies. Indeed, 80 per cent of its environmental budget comes from abroad (Economy, 1998, p278). In addition, China benefits from environmental technologies, such as those offered in the context of the Framework Convention on Climate Change's (FCCC's) Clean Development Mechanism (JEC, 2000, p106).

The most important actors in China's environmental diplomacy are MOFA, SEPA, the State Development Planning Commission (SDPC, formerly the State Planning Commission, or SPC) and the State Science and Technology Commission (SSTC). MOFA has generally viewed environmental issues from the perspective of fairness, seeing industrialized countries as responsible for solving problems and helping China and other developing countries to implement sustainable development. Other agencies view environmental problems in terms of their harm to the Chinese people and China's developmental prospects (Economy, 1998, pp270–271). The increasing salience of environmental issues in international relations has strengthened environmentally proactive bureaucrats and technocrats (Economy, 1998, p265), as well as government-approved think tanks, such as the Council for International Cooperation on Environment and Development.

The cases of stratospheric ozone depletion and climate change help to illustrate some general themes in China's environmental diplomacy. By the mid 1980s, China's consumption of ozone-destroying chemicals (ODCs) was only about 3 per cent of the world total. However, a decade or so later it had jumped to 18 per cent (Economy, 1998, p270). China initially opposed the

Montreal Protocol on Substances that Deplete the Ozone Layer, fearing that limitations on ODCs would hinder its development. Increased use of chlorofluorocarbons (CFCs) would aid dissemination of affordable refrigeration, thereby raising living standards and improving health. There was also the concern (shared by Japan) that CFCs were needed for the electronics industry. China agreed to the protocol only after it was clear that developing countries would be allowed a long grace period to use ODCs and, perhaps more importantly, after the Montreal Protocol Multilateral Fund was established to assist developing countries in making the transition to alternative chemicals. A year after the 1990 London amendments to the protocol to set up such a fund, China announced its full accession to the agreement. This demonstrates how important national developmental concerns have been in shaping China's environmental foreign policies.

China has been intimately involved in international deliberations on global warming and resulting climate change (see Chapter 9). China produces about 15 per cent of the world's carbon dioxide emissions – the chief 'greenhouse' gas contributing to global warming – in large part a consequence of its heavy reliance on coal to power its economic development, making it second only to the US in carbon emissions (Marland et al, 1999). Although China's per capita GHG emissions remain low relative to those of the industrialized countries, its overall emissions will inevitably increase, and it will surpass the US in coming decades. This prospect becomes clear when one considers the burgeoning middle class in China, whose lifestyle choices will lead to dramatic increases in per capita energy use.

During early negotiations on climate change, China sought to protect its sovereignty. Asserting its leadership among developing countries (see Chayes and Kim, 1998, p528) and protecting its freedom to pursue economic growth, it opposed every effort to require GHG limits for developing countries – even those calling for *voluntary* commitments to restrict future emissions *increases* (Harris, 2000b, p15). China has consistently demanded that developed countries provide assistance to developing countries to help them cope with climate change and to implement sustainable development. It has usually resisted any links between financial and technical assistance from developed countries in the context of the climate change regime and emissions limitations by developing countries. Instead, it has demanded transfers of funds on non-commercial and preferential terms, and has rejected most of the market-based international mechanisms for emissions reductions advocated by developed countries and their industries (Linnerooth-Bayer, 1999, p59). According to one observer, 'Only when outsiders (for example, the GEF [Global Environment Facility]) have paid the incremental costs has China been willing to implement global warming projects' (Victor, 1999, p203). However, once it was established that developing countries would not be required to take on any obligatory commitments under the climate convention, China joined the Kyoto Protocol on implementing it.

China's varying positions in the climate change negotiations show that domestic politics, a complex foreign policy-making apparatus and international affairs can combine to shape its environmental foreign policies. According to Chayes and Kim (1998, p528), China's diplomacy was affected by internal politics and bureaucratic manoeuvring among at least 18 government agencies. In early climate change negotiations, MOFA and the SDPC eventually took control of policy, although not without other agencies getting involved at times (notably SSTC, SEPA and the China Meteorological Administration, which influenced scientific understanding on the issue). China's position has been 'susceptible to domination by foreign policy and state planning officials' (Chayes and Kim, 1998, p529). However, it eventually became clear to senior policy-makers that joining the Kyoto Protocol could be in China's economic, environmental and diplomatic interests. The Clean Development Mechanism would provide new funds to aid economic development, domestic pollution would be mitigated by the resulting new technologies, and announcing accession to the treaty at the 2002 World Summit on Sustainable Development would show the world that China was leading developing countries in addressing an important global issue.

Japan

Japan's environmental experience has been characterized by a concerted focus on economic development leading to domestic environmental damage, followed by measures to clean up pollution and limit future environmental harm (see Chapter 4). The 'Big Four' pollution incidents of the 1950s – 'Minamata disease' mercury poisoning in Kumamoto and Niigata Prefectures, air pollution in Mie Prefecture and *Itai-Itai* disease in Toyama Prefecture – sparked environmental concern in Japan (Akaha, 1999, pp531–532). These and other incidents led to the 1967 Basic Law for Pollution Control (strengthened in 1970) and the creation of the Environment Agency in 1971 (Akaha, 1999). However, these and other environmental initiatives of the late 1960s were unable to keep pace with rapid industrialization (UNEP, 1999, p241). By the early 1970s public and official opinion were concluding that 'the nation's mindless pursuit of economic growth had caused serious environmental problems and a paradigmatic shift was necessary to improve the environmental situation' (Akaha, 1999, p533). Combined with measures to conserve energy following the 1970s oil shocks, new measures by the Environment Agency led to reduced air and water pollution. Japan now has some of the world's strictest environmental standards (UNEP, 1999, pp245–246).

Much of the impetus for environmental legislation in Japan came from local government initiatives (JEC, 2000, p56), which were the consequences of pressure from localized citizens' movements. By the late 1980s these were supplemented by growing international attention to environmental problems, which 'forced a re-evaluation of environmental and development goals' (UNEP, 1999, p241). Partly due to public pressure, the Basic Environment Plan was introduced in 1993, although by the 1990s public concern about Japan's environment had lowered substantially – despite many remaining national environmental problems. Instead, *global* environmental changes became important for the Japanese public, far exceeding concerns about domestic pollution. Overall, however, environmental concern among the Japanese public has been quite low, and the Japanese generally expect their government, scientists and international institutions to find solutions to environmental problems (Akaha, 1999, pp534–538).

Japan's Environment Ministry was, until early 2001, only an agency; as a result, it has not had the bureaucratic importance of a ministry. Indeed, when it became a ministry the number of ministers was reduced. It is supposed to coordinate national environmental policy, set environmental standards and monitor their implementation (Akaha, 1999, p539). However, many other agencies and ministries, such as the Ministry of Construction, Ministry of Economy, Trade and Industry (METI, formerly Ministry of International Trade and Industry, or MITI), Ministry of Transportation and the Economic Planning Agency, are involved in environmental policy-making. These bureaucracies must reach a consensus before proposals are presented to the cabinet and environmental legislation is prepared for the Diet. Hence, environmental policy is made slowly and is rarely innovative (Akaha, 1999, p539). Much as American politics are sometimes characterized by 'iron triangles', Japanese politics are heavily influenced by collaboration among bureaucrats, powerful industries and politicians. This can prevent clear leadership, with differing goals and consensus-seeking among powerful groups stifling innovation. Policy-making therefore tends to be reactive and incremental. According to Calder (1997, p1), 'Institutions are, to be sure, crucial in shaping policy options everywhere in the world. But nowhere is this truer than in Japan.' Consequently, individual innovation is discouraged and political leaders – including even the prime minister – can be extraordinarily weak relative to the bureaucracy.

The Japanese electoral system has been characterized by medium-sized electoral districts that contribute to a reactive and indecisive policy-making process (in both domestic and foreign policy) by increasing the influence of large factions within parties and by encouraging politicians to cater to small, sometimes localized, special interest groups. These liabilities were reduced somewhat when electoral changes were passed in 1994, the expectation being that politicians would seek to broaden their bases of support (Calder, 1997, p20). However, the effect of the changes has been limited, and the influence of factions and specialized interest groups remains. Chief among the powerful interests is Japanese industry, which uses its connections with politicians, parties and the bureaucracy to limit the reach of environmental legislation. However, this may be changing as more industries view being clean and energy efficient as potential business opportunities – both within Japan and overseas.

Civil society's role in policy-making is usually constrained in Japan. Most public pressure for environmental action still occurs at the local or prefecture level, although when the public, media and scientists become concerned simultaneously they can have broader influence (Akaha, 1999, pp540–541). Compared to other industrialized democracies, independent environmental NGOs have much less influence on national policy-making (Maull, 1991, p254). NGOs have relatively little influence, in part, because they have limited funds, few members and few legal options to push policy change (Akaha, 1999, p542). The Japanese political system favours groups and individuals with political connections, often through the ruling party or via retired bureaucrats who routinely go to work for the industries they once regulated (or related think tanks). This, combined with the Japanese tendency to avoid public conflict and to resolve issues through negotiation and dialogue, contributes to an atmosphere where NGOs have limited power. This equation can change when catastrophe strikes, as it did when mercury poisoning killed and sickened people at Minamata, or when international issues take on major salience, as happened in the run-up to the 1992 United Nations Conference on Environment and Development (UNCED, or Earth Summit) in Rio (see Chapter 4).

Japanese foreign policy

As with China (and other countries), the foreign policy process acts as a conduit between Japan's domestic politics and policies and the outside world. Like the domestic policy process, the foreign policy process is characterized by strong bureaucratic agencies, powerful industrial groups and political factions seeking to defend their turf. Largely as a consequence, foreign policy is fragmented and often lacks clear leadership. The ministries most central to shaping Japanese foreign policy are the Ministry of Foreign Affairs (MOFA), METI, and the Ministry of Finance (MOF). Importantly, the latter agencies can be more powerful than MOFA, particularly in foreign economic policy. They are often more powerful in other areas simply because substantial funding is needed or the issues affect the Japanese economy. The economic agencies are heavily inclined toward promoting Japan's economic interests and, in the case of MOF, mostly domestic economic issues. They are also larger and have more influence in the cabinet. The dedicated foreign policy bureaucracy in Japan is small – METI is three times the size of MOFA – even smaller than that of the UK and dwarfed by similar agencies in the US (Calder, 1997).

The prime minister and party policy-makers, notably in the ruling Liberal Democratic Party (LDP), have sometimes actively shaped foreign policy (Scalapino, 1992, p201). Nevertheless, in comparison with other industrialized democracies, the prime minister frequently has limited authority over the foreign policy bureaucracy. His staff is small and generally unable to force policies upon agencies. Indeed, it is often the other direction in which influence flows. But even the bureaucrats find their power constrained by the influence of industrial interests, particularly in areas where the economy is affected (in other words, most areas). The close relationship between bureaucrats and industry ensures that the latter's interests will be considered very seriously, even more so than in most other developed countries. Thus, private-sector organizations such as Keidanren (Federation of Economic Organizations) can have profound influence on foreign policy. Many 'para-public' organizations supported by the state and working in loose alliance with it also have a significant role in Japanese foreign policy. Among these types of groups are the so-called 'external organizations', which are maintained by government ministries – for example, the MOFA-supported Japan Institute of International Affairs. These groups are often staffed by former bureaucrats (Calder, 1997, pp15–17). Interest groups and public opinion are becoming more important forces in Japanese foreign policy, although the latter is often inward looking (Scalapino, 1992, pp201–202). The media also has increasing influence on foreign policy; but its impact is seldom decisive.

As in China and other countries, Japanese foreign policy-makers use economic instruments to promote Japan's national interests (Scalapino, 1992, p207). By the 1980s, official development assistance became a core feature of Japan's national economic strategy. In 1989 Japan became the largest provider of international development assistance by most measures, overtaking the US, and it is the largest donor to the Asian Development Bank. Almost two-thirds of its foreign aid has been directed at Asian countries, being 'carefully coordinated to develop structural complementarities with the Japanese economy' (Pyle, 1998, p128). Recently, however, Japan's foreign-aid spending has declined amid stagnation in its economy.

Overall, Japan's foreign policy has several longstanding and distinctive traits (Pyle, 1998, pp122–124; see Chapter 3). First, with some exceptions, Japan's foreign policy has tended to be a reaction to outside influences. Japan is inclined to join the prevailing international order and adjust to that order as it changes. Second, Japan has been pragmatic in its foreign policies. In pursuit of its national interests, it adopts 'an opportunistic adaptation to international conditions in order to enhance the power of the Japanese nation' (Pyle, 1998, p122). Third, Japan has been very concerned about its international status and place in the international hierarchy. Fourth, Japan has seldom played a *leading* role in international organizations, despite the size of its economy and its large financial contributions to the United Nations (UN) and other organizations.

Japan's international environmental policy

Until fairly recently, Japan was physically isolated from many of the world's environmental problems. Combined with an historical aloofness, this delayed realization that it cannot ignore regional and global environmental issues. However, many transboundary environmental problems now affect Japan. These include pollution from China in the form of acid rain; management of environmental commons, such as regional seas; the stratospheric ozone layer and atmosphere; environmental restrictions on trade (for example, the Convention on International Trade in Endangered Species, or CITES); the use of aid to promote Japan's environmental and economic objectives in other countries, and the environmental consequence of Japanese-funded development projects; and the internationalization of the Japanese economy, including the environmental impacts of the activities of Japanese multinational corporations (JEC, 2000, p48). According to some prominent observers, Japan has done very little to address these issues, at least insofar as environmental protection is concerned (JEC, 2000, p48).

Mirroring the surprisingly limited role of MOFA in overall foreign policy, Japan's environment ministry has not been heavily involved in shaping Japan's international environmental policies. The environment ministry is generally classified as a 'domestic' agency, partly explaining why Japan has not been more active in some international environmental regimes (such as biodiversity) (Pharr and Wan, 1998, p622). Japan's positions on international environmental issues are seldom the result of pressure from the public or interest groups. Hence, the Japanese government felt little domestic pressure to, for example, to join international efforts to limit trade in ivory or to end whaling and driftnet fishing (Porter et al, 2000, p40). These factors, combined with new emphasis on global environmental issues surrounding UNCED, meant that 'foreign pressures' had a greater impact on Japan's environmental policies than did domestic actors (JEC, 2000, p42). One important 'domestic' influence, however, has been Japan's desire to develop a good reputation on international environmental issues – with the ongoing exception of whaling.

Keidanren has persuaded the government to fund environmentally harmful overseas resource extraction. Occasionally business interests have very direct influence on Japanese international environmental policy, as when the president of the Japanese Whaling Association – which represents Japanese whalers

– served as Japan's representative to the International Whaling Commission (IWC) (Day, 1987). More broadly, Japan is most active in international environmental negotiations when its economic interests are at stake. It usually resists international agreements that would add to domestic regulation, and supports those agreements that benefit its industries. Hence, Japan has pushed for broad regulation of some fisheries outside of national jurisdictions so that other countries' fishers would be subject to standards such as those in Japan. Japan's eventual agreement to stop producing ODCs came only after domestic industry indicated willingness to adopt international regulation. Japan will support international regulations that enhance demand for environmental technologies where it has a development lead. When Japanese auto-makers decided to improve the fuel efficiency of their products during the early 1990s, the government committed the country to stabilize its GHG emissions in accordance with the climate change regime.

During the late 1980s Japan began to focus much of its foreign aid on environmental issues, in large measure to promote Japanese businesses (Maull, 1991, p258). Japan has also used foreign economic assistance to promote its environment-related objectives (JEC, 2000, p105). For example, it has funded clean-energy programmes to limit China's emissions of pollutants that cause acid rain in Japan. In contrast, it has also given money to other countries in return for their support in Japan's efforts to lift the international ban on commercial whale hunting (Gibbs, 2002). Through its Green Aid Plan, Japan is funding new environmental industries and the transfer of environmental technologies throughout Asia (half goes to China) (JEC, 2000, p105). Indicative of this has been Japan Environment Cooperation and the related Japan Fund for Global Environment, which started in 1993 (UNEP, 1999, p247). However, this aid is often tied, with much of it spent inside Japan. Recently, Japan has indicated that it will reduce its environmental aid (although as a percentage of reduced overall foreign aid it may actually increase). In addition to the effects of economic stagnation on Japanese foreign-aid spending, the Japanese believe that they are not getting much in return by way of environmental protection and gratitude from neighbours (China, for example, continues to criticize Japan for atrocities committed during the first half of the last century).

In summary, Japan's position with regard to several environmental issues show that it has not readily supported international environmental regulation. It was one of the holdouts during negotiations in the 1970s on limiting maritime pollution from ships (Mitchell, 1995, p211). Throughout the 1980s, Japan was one of several developed countries seeking to limit restrictions on mining in Antarctica and surrounding waters, although by 1991 it joined other countries in banning these activities. In international deliberations to limit the export of pesticides to developing countries, Japan was among countries opposing more stringent rules (Paarlberg, 1995, p320). It was among the developed countries that were sceptical of efforts to control access to biodiversity, fearing that this might limit the ability of Japanese firms to gain access to genetic resources. Japan was also one of the countries that tried, during the 1990s, to prevent a complete ban on trade in hazardous wastes. Japan opposed creating a global forest convention and its companies have been very active in financing logging in Southeast Asia, Brazil and Siberia. The Japanese government has subsidized these activities.

The government has worked to help Japanese distant-water fishing fleets retain or expand their fishing opportunities (Peterson, 1995, pp259–260). It was a reluctant participant in international negotiations on straddling fish stocks, particularly insofar as any agreement might be enforceable by convention. While Japan signed the straddling fish stocks agreement, it resisted ratifying it under pressure from its fishing industry. Japan agreed to restrict its fishers from using drift nets, although enforcement has been lax. On the issue of trade in endangered species, Japan was the largest importer of ivory products. However, demand dropped a decade ago after an international campaign by European and North American NGOs persuaded the Japanese government, in effect, to implement a ban on the trade of elephant ivory negotiated under the auspices of CITES (Harland, 1990). Japan eventually joined the ban because it wanted to protect its international image, and because it was concerned about its economic and diplomatic relations with other trading states (Porter et al, 2000, p142).

One of the most visible environmental issues related to Japan, particularly for outsiders, is whale hunting (see Porter et al, 2000, pp93–98). As the world's leading whaling nation, Japan has consistently sought to thwart efforts by other countries and by environmentalists to permanently end commercial whaling. Since the late 1980s, it has circumvented hunting bans by taking whales for 'scientific' purposes, which is permitted under the International Whaling Convention. Japan is also by far the main market for whale products from other countries, thus fuelling demand internationally and inciting others to hunt whales. Japanese companies have been known to purchase whale meat caught by pirate whaling ships, and NGOs have found the meat of endangered species on sale in Japan. Japan continues to push aggressively for an end to the IWC's ban on commercial whaling (Gibbs, 2002). It may very well succeed in this, given the pull of its demand for whale products, its ability to withdraw from international controls altogether, and its power to use financial assistance to persuade many other IWC members to support a compromise more in line with the demands of the Japanese whaling industry (Fletcher, 2001). One primary reason for Japan's continued support for commercial whaling is the great influence of rural fishing communities and the whaling industry on the LDP and government (Day, 1987; Brooke, 2002).

As with China, the cases of ozone depletion and climate change illustrate important features of Japan's environmental foreign policies (see Chapter 4). During the early 1980s, Japan joined the Europeans in opposing international controls of ODCs. Relations between the Japanese government and its national producers of ODCs were very close, to the point where, during negotiations leading to the Montreal Protocol, industry representatives were official members of the Japanese negotiating team (Parson, 1995, p37). Japan also joined the US and other developed countries in initially opposing the creation of the Montreal Protocol's ozone fund, which would help developing countries to limit their emissions of ODCs. Japan joined the ozone protection regime once its industries were ready, passing the Ozone Layer Protection Law in 1988 (JEC, 2000, p49), and it has provided aid to Asian countries in order to help them phase out ODCs (UNEP, 1999, p238).

Japan produces about 5 per cent of the world's carbon dioxide emissions, making it more efficient than most other countries. This resulted from conscious policies to limit the economic impacts of the country's reliance on imported fossil fuels. During the early phases of the climate change negotiations, MITI opposed freezing Japan's GHG emissions. However, MOFA wanted the freeze and, after these agencies' differences became news abroad, MOPA's position prevailed (Maull, 1991, p261). By 1990, Japan agreed that a treaty calling for the stabilization of GHG emissions was needed. This would force other developed country industries to compete on a level playing field with Japanese firms, which were already required to be more efficient (in the transitional stages Japanese firms would be at an advantage). In 1991 Japan adopted the Action Programme to Arrest Global Warming, and it became a full party to the climate change convention in 1993. However, Japan opposed emissions *reductions* into the late 1990s. At a major 1997 conference of the parties to the convention in Kyoto, it agreed in a protocol to a 6 per cent cut in its emissions by about 2010 (the developed country average was about 5 per cent) – double what it had proposed but far less than what scientists and environmentalists said would be necessary. Japan implemented measures to reduce GHG emissions, although they have had very limited effect because the industry and transport sectors, not to mention the Japanese public, have relatively few real incentives to lower their emissions (JEC, 2000, p49). In ongoing negotiations Japan has sided with other developed countries, seeking to use emissions trading and joint implementation to limit the impact of emissions reductions on its national economy. In 2002 it began to break away from the US and join European countries in ratifying the Kyoto Protocol; but concessions in implementing measures meant that its required reductions were less than the 6 per cent agreed. In sum, like many other developed countries, Japan's policies on climate change have been compromises between international demands for action and preferences for incremental action from Japanese industry – with emphasis on the latter.

Characteristics and purposes of Chinese and Japanese policies

Briefly comparing China and Japan can highlight some important actors and themes in their (and other countries') environmental foreign policies. However, it may first be useful to summarize some of the major characteristics and purposes that underly each country's environmental foreign policies, as suggested by the preceding survey. Importantly, many of these characteristics and purposes are evident in other countries.

Some characteristics of environmental foreign policy in China and Japan

China's environmental foreign policies are characterized by increasing cooperation and engagement on regional and global issues, often in line with the policies of other developing countries. China supports the notion of 'common but differentiated responsibility' – all countries should protect the environment, but developed countries have more responsibility to do so – and, more particularly, it generally supports regimes that benefit developing countries through transfers of aid. Along these lines, Chinese policy has been characterized by support for multilateral environmental funding mechanisms, 'new and additional resources' for environmentally sustainable development (aid above and beyond non-environment-related aid) and technology transfer. China has often resisted mandatory implementation of agreements by developing countries and it usually rejects projects for sustainable development that include intrusive inspections (especially in multilateral agreements; less so in bilateral ones).

Among the prominent features of Japan's environmental foreign policy are its increasing cooperation and engagement on regional and (less so) global issues. It has generally followed the US on global issues; but more recently it has shown greater independence from the US and more willingness to join other major industrialized countries in specific regimes. It has even shown some leadership on the Kyoto Protocol – for which if felt a degree of 'ownership', given where it was signed – and limited willingness to join Europe in opposition to the US, as demonstrated by its move to ratify the protocol and thereby bring it into force, even without the US. Having said this, its policies have also been characterized by strong resistance to some regimes that threaten domestic interests, with whaling being perhaps the most visible example. During the 1990s, a key characteristic of Japanese policy was providing substantial environmental aid, particularly to China and within East/Southeast Asia – aid that often (but not always) helped to limit transboundary pollution from entering Japan (for example, acid rain). Japan has shifted away from state support of policies and Japanese industries that cause environmental harm in other countries. Like China, it has resisted international environmental agreements with implementation measures requiring domestic economic changes not already adopted by industry, although it has sought to 'export' Japanese environmental and energy standards abroad to create a level playing field for its industries.

Some purposes of environmental foreign policy in China and Japan

What are the underlying purposes of the environmental foreign policies of China and Japan? We might summarize these under the rubrics of environment, economics and politics. Note that *environmental* foreign policies of these countries (like almost all others, in my view) are *not just about environmental issues*.

In the case of China, there is now a genuine desire among policy-makers to protect the country's dwindling natural resources and to reduce 'natural' disasters, particularly floods (which are often a consequence of past and present overuse of resources), as well as to preserve dwindling biodiversity and, increasingly, to limit environmental threats to human health and the economy. This leads us, more specifically, to economic purposes for China's environmental foreign policies: recognition of the connections between environmental changes and economic development; protection of natural resources essential to development; and realization that foreign investment is related to environmental conditions and regulations (investors might avoid investing due to pollution or the high cost of complying with environmental regulations; investors might be more likely to invest knowing that facilities meet international standards for environmental quality). China also seeks through its environmental foreign policies to secure foreign aid and environmental technology for economic development. Turning to the political purposes of China's policies, the additional resources that come to China via environmental agreements enhance the legitimacy of the state and the CCP and provide the government with resources to assuage new domestic demands for action on severe local environmental problems. China also uses environmental diplomacy to assert, affirm and protect its sovereignty and to show leadership among developing countries. During the 1990s international environmental negotiations were likely also used as an inroad to engagement with other states on largely unrelated issues (for example, to escape from the diplomatic isolation following the 1989 Tiananmen incident; see Chapter 7).

Similarly, there are environmental, economic and political purposes behind Japan's environmental foreign policies. In the case of the former, the Japanese government seeks to limit threats to the health of the Japanese people and to its domestic natural environment resulting from regional pollution. But, like China, economic priorities can overshadow environmental concerns. For example, increasingly important purposes of Japan's environmental foreign policies are promotion of foreign demand for its environmental technologies, to protect domestic industries from international environmental agreements until they are prepared for additional regulation, and to create a level international economic playing field for Japanese industry. Politically, Japan seeks to use environmental diplomacy to assuage the entire region, which is still critical of Japan's war history. It also seeks to justify its 'great power' status and membership in the club of leading industrialized states, and to demonstrate international leadership in lieu of assertive security policies (see Chapter 4). Domestically, the government may also seek to use international environmental cooperation to satisfy occasional public demand for action to protect the global environment, as happened in the run-up to UNCED and the Kyoto climate change conference.

Chinese and Japanese environmental foreign policy: selected variables and possible explanations

Which variables shape the international environmental policies of these (and other) countries? The typology of theories described in Barkdull and Harris's (2002) survey can point us to important and interesting actors, institutions and forces (see Figure 2.1). Importantly, there are many potential crossovers between and among these approaches and the variables to which they point. What follows is intended to highlight some variables and possible explanations, most of which will be prominent in the environmental policies of other countries in East Asia.

Systemic variables and explanations

A system- and power-based focus suggests that China was able to prevent the imposition of GHG emissions limitations on developing countries during the climate change negotiations due to its increased 'environmental power'. Industrialized countries were inclined to take China seriously because its growing GHG emissions have the ability to greatly alter the climate system and prevent future efforts to effectively address this problem. With a similar focus on Japan, one might conclude that Japan followed the US on climate change because of American power in this (and most other) issue areas; but when the US effectively withdrew from serious climate change negotiations, and as the Europeans took the issue more seriously, Japan was persuaded by an issue-specific redistribution of power to join the Europeans. From the same perspective, we might argue that environmental foreign aid garners regional and global power for Japan, increasing its influence in other issue areas. Alternatively, systemic and interest-based approaches might show that China joined international environmental regimes because the costs were very low and benefits were high (environmental aid and technology). In Japan's case, national interests were promoted by supporting environmental regimes that require more regulation abroad (especially when it pertained domestically) in order to limit pollution that reaches Japan. However, its interests were promoted by opposition to regimes that threaten industrial interests (perceived as coinciding with national interests).

In terms of systemic and ideational influences, we might say that the notion of protecting the global environment has permeated international politics, at least to the point where all able states are now expected to have an environmental ministry (which will attempt to influence policy) and to support, at least nominally, multilateral environmental protection efforts. Hence, both China and Japan created environmental agencies and wanted to be seen taking environmental issues more seriously. In the specific case of China, its foreign policy has been enabled by the increasing international acceptance of the idea that developing countries have a 'right to development', rich countries are mainly responsible for global pollution, and the latter ought to help the former to achieve sustainable development. For Japan, international norms and ideas regarding climate change have started to influence policy, and the country wants to be among new 'global stewards', even while hegemonic economic ideas (that is, open trade) create conflicts and compete with newer ideas about environmental preservation.

Societal variables and explanations

Focusing instead on societal variables, approaches that point to the role of power suggest that Chinese elites have dominated environmental foreign policy. While powerful elites in society still prioritize economic development, their views on domestic environmental policy are gradually changing, increasing opportunities for more pro-environment foreign policies. In Japan, industrial interests can sometimes virtually dictate foreign policy, with the limited pluralism in politics preventing more influence by NGOs and interested public opinion (when it is interested). From the perspective of society and interest-based explanations, societal interests in China have sought to use environmental foreign policy to garner economic advantages for themselves, and civil society groups and independent media are still too weak to greatly influence environmental policies. In Japan, circumstances occasionally increase the importance for policy-makers of listening to sometimes environmentally oriented civil society actors (the public, NGOs and think tanks), such as around the time of UNCED and the Kyoto Protocol. Even industry actors are sometimes interested in environmental protection, perhaps reflecting public opinion, and they, in turn, push government toward policies that are more favourable to a pro-environment foreign policy. Societal approaches focusing on ideas can highlight the spread of capitalist economics and consumerism in China, as well as the growing preoccupation with wealth generation in society, which in turn permeate foreign policy – that is, push the government to support international environmental agreements that aid these sentiments through whatever means, and to oppose those that do not. In Japan, belief in market mechanisms is generally strong in society and national ennui over economic stagnation makes movement toward pro-environmental foreign policy difficult and a collective belief in technological progress hinders development of environmental consciousness, although it is there and perhaps growing.

State variables and explanations

A state- and power-based approach to Chinese policy points to powerful central state actors who have resisted more environmentally friendly foreign policy until recently, but with a new shift in favour of the environment as leading officials begin to recognize the importance of environmentally sustainable development and the external resources that can help to actualize it. From the same perspective, we can point to bureaucratic turf battles, where economic growth usually wins out over environmental protection – at least until recently – and there is ongoing bureaucratic resistance to implementing policies in many provinces. Using the state and power approach when looking at Japan points to the weakness of the prime minister and politicians vis-à-vis bureaucrats, and struggles within government in which economic and finance ministries usually win out over foreign and environmental ministries. The state-centric approach reveals that the Chinese government's interests are often not conducive to a pro-environment foreign policy, favouring, instead, pro-economic growth policies. However, as environmental regimes are increasingly seen as tied to the interests of the state (that is, the CCP), they are correspondingly being supported. The state-and-interests perspective focuses our attention on the manner in which bureaucratic agencies in Japan push their own agendas (for example, MOFA in support of environmental aid; METI in favour of industrial interests) and sometimes try to use concern about global environmental issues and environmental security to increase or protect their resources.

If we think in terms of the state and ideas, we notice that ideas which favour environmental protection and sustainable development are slowly spreading throughout the Chinese government, especially given the new recognition of the increasingly tight connections between environmental harm and economic development. We also notice that this change is largely because 'knowledge brokers' and scientists are gradually affecting policy, including foreign policy supporting membership in international environmental regimes. In contrast, while the notion of sustainable development is firmly part of Japanese development assistance policies, the ideology of consensus limits the impact of policy innovators and critics of foreign policies who are more pro-environment. Having said this, foreign NGOs have had some success in influencing public and governmental actors' perceptions of the global environment.

These are but some of the ways of 'approaching' Chinese and Japanese environmental policies – notably, those that are international. In reality (although theoretical purists may not agree), the most complete and accurate depiction of environmental foreign policy in these and other countries will come from combinations of the aforementioned approaches (and possibly others), with some being more useful than others, depending upon the country case and the issue being explored.

Conclusion

What does all of this tell us about how and why East Asian countries – namely, China and Japan – confront environmental changes? This survey suggests that different environmental experiences are important variables in shaping the international environmental policies of East Asian countries. For example, while China's chief goal may have been to use environmental regimes as a means of extracting financial and technological resources from the developed countries (including Japan), Chinese policy-makers now see pollution and destruction of environmental resources as important policy issues, if for no other reason than the fact that they are now adversely affecting economic development. In the case of Japan, local demands for a cleaner environment and its national requirements for energy and environmental efficiency are being translated into its environmental foreign policies. In short, Japan is more willing to join international environmental regimes because, in many ways, they codify domestic practice on a global scale.

We can also conclude that indigenous factors – notably, national foreign policy processes – influence whether and how countries are willing to join international environmental protection efforts. For example, whether powerful officials and agencies take an interest in international environmental regulation will shape much of their country's policies. When the foreign affairs ministries are influential (which, surprisingly, they frequently are not), China will tend to view environmental regimes as potential violations of principles of international fairness, resisting demands from developed countries to join them, and as a means of bolstering its credentials as a 'leader' of the developing world; whereas Japan will view the regimes as a means of demonstrating Japanese leadership in the region and the world, and as a way of affirming its status as a member of the club of leading industrialized countries. If economic ministries have more influence (as they often do), international environmental regimes will be treated by China as potential hindrances on economic development and/or as a means of extracting resources for development from the wealthy countries, while in Japan they may be seen as a way of promoting the interests of Japanese multinational corporations and as potential instruments for exporting Japan's environmental technologies.

These are only some examples of the ways in which foreign policy processes, broadly defined, can shape these countries' positions in international environmental negotiations. This is also true of other countries. We can conclude that foreign policy actors and processes – that is, actors and processes at the domestic *and* international levels and the crossover between them – have important roles to play in fostering or preventing international environmental cooperation among East Asian countries, and between each of them and the broader international community. Theories of (environmental) foreign policy can direct our attention at key variables shaping policies and behaviours. China and Japan are not unique in the means by which they confront environmental changes within their borders and within the region. Understanding their policies can help us to comprehend similar policies of other countries in East Asia and beyond. Subsequent chapters will go into greater detail in exploring these and other countries' responses to environmental change. They will posit specific explanations and appropriate theories, expanding understanding of how East Asian countries manage environmental changes that are likely to become more severe in the coming decades.

Chapter 3

The Environment and Japanese Foreign Policy: Anthropocentric Ideologies and Changing Power Relationships

Mika Merviö

Introduction

Japanese politics is strongly based on anthropocentric ideologies. The Japanese political culture has been shaped by decades of conservative political rule, where a political elite, often former bureaucrats or sons of politicians (or both), have dominated the ruling party and have thwarted all attempts to widen political participation. At the same time, the political alternatives of opposition parties have appeared too vague and unconvincing to the majority of voters. The majority of Japanese citizens apparently feel quite uneasy with existing political alternatives, but they are reluctant to do much about it. After all, most Japanese people seem to be relatively satisfied with their current socio-economic conditions and have suspicions and reservations about the social and political models of other countries, and especially about their applicability to Japanese conditions.

As for environmental awareness in Japan, knowledge about global problems does not necessarily translate into local action and real concern. The Japanese political system and culture do not encourage people to stand out and question practices that they know to be harmful to the environment or contrary to their expressed purposes. It is also clear that a clean, healthy and comfortable environment has its costs, and that in the future ever-increasing amounts of money will be spent on fighting against environmental degradation in its various forms, whether people like it or not. Japan already has its share of environmental problems because high population density, together with consumerism and waste, put a heavy strain on the environment. Japan also has its share of environmental activism and activists, and environment-related information and research results are readily available. However, for various reasons ecological arguments and Green political philosophy seem to have difficulties entering the political agendas of the country. When Japanese individuals actually do something about the environment, they are much more concerned about, for example, the extremely high levels of dioxin that can be found in Japan or in their immediate neighborhood than they are about environmental problems that do not constitute a direct and clear health risk.

Chauvinist anthropocentrism

The impact of social and environmental movements has its limits in Japan, and the postwar history of Japanese society has been shaped by conservative political forces that have usually ignored environmental issues as long as possible. Quite a few Japanese conservatives openly advocate what can be called *chauvinist anthropocentrism*, where environmental protection is presented as an obstacle for economic development, and it is argued that the narrow interests of local political elites (such as the local construction sector and cooperatives) represent the wishes of local people and therefore should guide all political action. At worst, the chauvinist anthropocentrism among politicians leads to such bizarre behavior as eating whale meat in public or strongly defending such environmentally destructive and economically and socially unsound projects as most of the current dam projects or reclamation projects for creating new farming land, usually in regions where there already are large areas of unused farm land. Quite a few of those politicians, who do not listen to the opinions of the environmentalists or political opposition in Japan, are happy to defy the so-called international pressure or international public opinion.

Such chauvinist anthropocentrism is by no means restricted to Japan. In fact, it is closely related to a group of ideologies, which often are sanitized by calling them versions of political realism or conservative nationalism, and these ideologies have remarkably wide support in many affluent industrialized countries. It could be argued that chauvinist anthropocentrism provides an ideology that justifies selfishness in all human relations and in relations between humans and nature, and when raised to the international level fits well with foreign policy doctrines that emphasize traditional nation-state sovereignty and disrespect for international cooperation and international treaties. It is no wonder that most Japanese politicians were delighted to see the Republicans returning to the helm of American politics in 2001. The Japanese chauvinist anthropocentrism perfectly complements an isolationist and unilateralist US foreign policy that emphasizes national interest and military power and attaches little importance to environmental issues. The so-called international pressure (*gaiatsu*) in the Japanese context has usually meant only pressure coming from the US, and a Republican administration is always expected to be more predictable and easier to cope with. At its best, a Republican administration could be satisfied with Japan as a loyal and indispensable military ally. The conservative wing of the Republican party is known for having chauvinist anthropocentrists, with the best example being President George W Bush.

Technocratic anthropocentrism

A widespread and more moderate version of anthropocentric environmental policy can be called *technocratic anthropocentrism*. In Western Europe, the European Commission (EC) and its agenda of economic rationality have created an atmosphere where anthropocentric politics rule, and where even its critics usually have to be satisfied with moderate reformist policies. In spite of all the criticism against the elitism and lack of transparency, the work of the EC and the European Union (EU) bureaucracy remains technocratic at its best, and full of red tape at its worst. For a long time environmental legislation was largely smuggled into directives by referring to various human-prudential causes in an almost total lack of common agreement on environmental policy, and still this is often the most effective way of reaching objectives. The result is that the EU and its directives have set an example for the rest of the world of how to build an international environmental policy on legal principles and an ideology of technocratic anthropocentrism.

In Japan, the Ministry of the Environment (which was upgraded from the Environment Agency in January 2001) with its more than 1000 regular staff members often represents technocratic anthropocentrism. Even the basic organizational structure of the ministry suggests a strong anthropocentric ideological basis. The founding of the agency in 1971 was itself largely a result of awakening to the dangers of industrial pollution and responding to growing public concern and political pressures. The opposition won several local elections during the early 1970s by using the environment as one of its main themes, and the government has since tried to avoid being seen as totally ignorant about environmental issues and risks. Japan has also had clear success with its fight against industrial pollution, and the government may use this as an example of its environmental concern. The focus in environmental policy has been in safeguarding public health, and the history and activities of the Environment Agency reflect this pursuit. Environment Agency publications, including the most informative Annual White Paper (*Kankyô Hakusho*), tend to focus on technical details. Technocratic anthropocentrism may also provide civil servants with a survival strategy in a political environment that is largely hostile to more bio-centric or global approaches. In the end, the Environment Agency has for almost all of its existence served ruling Liberal Democratic Party governments that have supported political agendas in which the environment is in a subordinate position.

Japanese environmental foreign policy and the power of foreign aid

The *omnipresence* of power and the *chain-like nature* of power relations make it difficult to define what kind of power relations exist between Japanese society and other societies. In spite of the 'lost decade' of Japanese economic recession, Japanese economic power is perceived with certain uneasiness among its Asian neighbors. Japan is still an economic superpower, with its 15 per cent share of the world gross domestic product (GDP) (the other economic power is China; but its economy is seven times smaller than Japan in terms of GDP). The other countries in the region have been influenced by Japan and applied the Japanese experience in their own modernization policies. This has given Japan a very special position in East Asia. There are still fresh memories of Japanese colonialism in East Asia. In spite of all the assistance that Japan has provided its neighbors, one of the most obvious traits of regional foreign policy is a lack of trust for Japanese motives. Japanese diplomacy has obviously not been the most effective in conveying its message. It is, indeed, difficult to explain the finer details of foreign policy doctrines because politicians themselves show little interest in foreign policy formulation and debate.

An important characteristic of Japanese domestic and foreign policies is the tendency to rely on long and thorough negotiations in the policy-making process, which itself is characterized by compromises that are supposed to produce consensus, but all too often leave participants unsatisfied. When policies are finally announced it is difficult to make adjustments. Japanese public administration (and sometimes even large private corporations) provides a wealth of examples of huge projects that are kept alive even after no one seems to have a clear idea of the original or current aims of the project. With so many foreign counterparts, this 'normal' Japanese practice may easily result in something very different. *The Diplomatic Yearbook* describes a typically Japanese approach to solving the global environmental problems: 'Views on the content and extent of environment-related efforts also frequently differ even among the developed countries. In resolving global environmental issues, it will therefore be indispensable to coordinate the different positions and persist with negotiations until agreement can be reached' (MOFA, 2000, p107). This 'traditional Japanese' approach hardly demonstrates any leadership role, although it may be effective with the United Nations (UN) type of multilateralism. If the formula of endless consensus-seeking with all legitimate actors is used in dealing with all global environmental problems, the result is that there may never be significant agreements.

The Japanese negotiating style on the issue of global warming and in the series of conferences related to the UN Framework Convention on Climate Change (UNFCCC) has in many ways been reminiscent of *The Diplomatic Yearbook* description: Japan tried to coordinate views and served as the host for the third Conference of the Parties (COP3) to the climate change convention held in Kyoto in 1997 even while the negotiating position of the Japanese government remained quite hostile to the environment. The process that led to the Kyoto Protocol demonstrated the unwillingness of the Japanese government to make significant unilateral cuts to slow down climate change, reflecting the positions of various Japanese politicians and ministries who were primarily concerned with narrow interests of specific industries. The Kyoto Protocol, in its attempt to produce consensus, was made so hollow that often the whole process came close to a collapse over key concepts, such as the role of forests as sinks and the idea of trading greenhouse gas reductions.

The subsequent decision of the Bush administration to turn against the protocol was a heavy blow to Japanese diplomacy and left the Koizumi government in a difficult situation, even as the active support of the EU kept the protocol alive. Japan needed to save this key international treaty, which is associated with Japan's new diplomatic role. However, Koizumi also needed to take care of maintaining good relations with the US government. However, the whole issue of US policy on the Kyoto Protocol has not significantly changed the perceptions of US foreign policy among Japanese people in the way that it has damaged relations with other countries, such as Germany (as seen during the German parliamentary elections in 2002).

The economic might of Japan, with all its consequences, is a fact that the Japanese and the rest of the world have to live with. It may cause fear among some, but it is also a sign of hope for many, and it can be (and has been) used as a tool of Japanese foreign policy. In all concerns, Japan's international aid programme, including environmental aid, is closely reflecting changing political considerations: new Japanese activities are already changing the regional system and all of its power relations. The question asked in most other East Asian countries has been whether Japan remains committed to help its neighbors even when the wealth and development gap between them narrows. Moves in Japan to cut its official development assistance (ODA) have caused worries that it may radically reassess its aid diplomacy. After all, ODA has never enjoyed wholehearted support among the Japanese population, and much of the domestic discussion has been related to the abuse and waste that have accompanied ODA. In fact, popular support for ODA has been in decline. Only 23 per cent of poll respondents seem to support it (*Daily Yomiuri*, 2001, p2). Many cite the nation's own economic problems as the reason for their lack of support. Furthermore, new contacts between Japan and North Korea in the summer of 2002 opened a way to eventual normalization of relations and significant aid to North Korea. Such aid is unpopular in Japan and may contribute to further waning of enthusiasm in Japan for all ODA.

Another long-term issue is the position of China in Japanese ODA. Since the normalization of relations with China, Japanese foreign policy has tried to promote stability, economic development and modernization in China. Japanese assistance and technology have been indispensable in China's modernization; but it is unclear whether China is now an easier neighbor for Japan. Japanese perceptions of China are gradually changing. While China's economy has been able to narrow some of the wide gap with Japan's, the Chinese political sector has remained closed. China grows more affluent and, at the same time, more nationalistic. That kind of China would be a difficult partner for Japanese foreign policy. Already, many people in Japan are asking why China has remained among the largest recipients of Japanese aid even as it has become a serious rival to the Japanese economy, maintains huge military forces, possesses nuclear weapons, has obvious problems with human rights, shows little gratitude for past assistance, and is a donor itself. In the end, aid to China has turned many Japanese people against ODA, in general.

Japanese foreign policy and emancipatory ideals

Japanese foreign policy liturgy has discredited the use of (openly) *repressive power* in international relations. It creates a picture of a world and an Asia where power relations have a more *emancipatory* nature. However, it remains unclear what kind of regional system is actually emerging in East Asia, and specifically what kind of region we are really talking about and which actors are going to be most significant. It is much easier to preach the emancipation of potential in others if they are much weaker and pose no real danger. In a contradiction to the emancipatory ideals and orientations behind Japanese policies, there are signs of the emergence of the old type of militarism, and some researchers predict that Japan is already on its way to playing a much greater military role, probably in the shadow of the UN. The Republican administration in the US has asked Japan to play a more visible military role in the region and to play a decisive part in the global war against terror. Politically, the easiest way to achieve that goal would be to widen Japanese participation in UN peacekeeping operations. Naturally, a rise of Japanese militarism would threaten the emancipatory power relations that have been formed in the region. However, judging from social discourses in Japan, the basic policy orientation of a more or less omni-directional and constructive foreign policy will continue, and Japanese foreign policy and diplomacy will become more multilateral and diversified. This means that most people in Japan reject the more hawkish policy alternatives; for instance, in September 2002 only 5 per cent of respondents in a *Mainichi Shimbun* poll supported what looked to be a looming American attack on Iraq (*Mainichi Shimbun*, 2002).

Although most Japanese would like to emphasize cooperation over conflict in international relations, there are also significant threats. The most widely perceived threat scenarios are:

- major regional military crises (most notably on the Korean Peninsula);
- Chinese foreign policy becoming more aggressive and turning against Japan; and
- continued inability of the Japanese government to take more decisive measures to fix structural problems in the economy, with a possibility of serious economic crisis.

Any of these scenarios would rapidly change the regional status quo, and with it Japanese foreign policy. However, the risks are clear to everyone and therefore we should treat these scenarios as highly unlikely. Since policy-makers are so concerned with the traditional type of risks, they seem to have little time for something like global environmental problems. Everything global, and especially everything related to large multinational organizations, is often regarded by the foreign policy decision-makers as 'idealistic', less urgent and too far from reality.

Omni-directional foreign policy (*zenhôi gaikô*) was often used by Japan during the late 1970s and the early 1980s as the official characterization of its equidistant foreign policy. The idea was that Japan would try to maintain good relations with all countries, even if the world was plagued with divisions. The term 'multilateral foreign policy' (*takakuteki gaikô*) also became widely used in Japan during the 1970s when China and South Korea became partners in Japanese foreign policy, relations with the Southeast Asian countries were strengthening, Japan's ODA was increasing, and North–South relations and UN policy became major issues in Japanese foreign policy. The emergence of the EU as a major player in foreign policy contributed to a sense of *trilateralism* among Europe, Japan and North America. But the link between Japan and Europe is the weakest of all the three, and trilateralism is often hollow. Nevertheless, European integration and, in particular, the launch of the Euro currency have contributed to a sense in Japan that foreign policy must turn more global and multilateral.

Multilateral foreign policy was contrasted with an earlier situation in which the US did not leave much room for multilateral relations. Thus, *takakuteki gaikô* came to be strongly associated in Japan with a new historical period in which Japanese relations with the rest of the world would be diversified and Japan would have a more active role in international politics. This new multilateralism in Japanese foreign policy was directly related to increased foreign aid. Multilateralism helped to change the nature of Japanese ODA from being tied to the economic objectives of Japan (and wider political and strategic objectives of the US), to a policy with a great diversity of objectives, including the environment (cf Yasutomo, 1995). During recent years, Japanese diplomacy has increasingly used the term 'human security' to emphasize the comprehensiveness of its security concerns (see Merviö, 2002). The direct participation in ODA projects in most parts of the world has brought better knowledge about contemporary global problems to a fair number of Japanese specialists. The hidden objectives of Japanese politicians may be narrower than the officially stated ones; but years of Japanese ODA have created a new class of specialists and bureaucrats who are far better accustomed to dealing with a great diversity of societies and political conditions.

It was only with changes in the relationships between the US, Russia and the Western European countries that the foreign policy paradigm of Japan started to change to give Asia and the Asia–Pacific region a much more important role in Japanese foreign policy and diplomacy (Watanabe, 1997, pp18–23). The original motive for change was simply a feeling of being left out. Japanese diplomacy is characterized by being rather reactionary in its nature, cautious of making too many commitments. While gradually shifting the focus of Japanese diplomacy toward the rest of Asia, given the global reach of Japanese economic and other interests, it is most unlikely that Japan will push for any kind of exclusive economic or political zone in Asia (Unger, 1993, pp163–166). However, regional multilateral and bilateral cooperation and ODA activities have provided ample tools to stress new priorities and contribute to a better future in most Asian societies. The volume of Japanese ODA is so large that it will continue to have visible effects in the recipient societies. Even if Japanese ODA has not been able to win wide gratitude in the developing world, at least it has brought a new type of acceptability for Japan within the Asian community.

The sheer magnitude of Japanese economic and political presence in Asia and other parts of the world has changed world power relations, no matter how 'soft' these forms of power may be. Some researchers point out that it is often difficult to even recognize Japanese manifestations of power because they do not fit traditional notions of power, especially military power (Drifte, 1996, pp85–92). However, the lack of great-power 'bully' behavior may only improve the general image of the Japanese diplomacy. Furthermore, there seem to be situations in international relations where economic power and influence is the only kind of power that has some use, and even it may prove to be insufficient. As for the definition of the positive role that Japan played, in general, in world affairs during the 1990s, another alternative has been as a 'facilitator' (Shibusawa et al, 1992, pp123–142). By serving its role as facilitator of peaceful change and development, Japan can help to create more cooperative kinds of power relationships and encourage the emergence of emancipatory forms of power.

When it comes to a more constructive global and regional role for Japan in the future, much of the discussion in Japan has often been overshadowed by rather narrow domestic concerns. Ronald Dore points out that during the early 1990s, it was the nationalists, preoccupied with power and prestige, who were the most vocal supporters of high-profile Japanese participation in building a UN-based security system, and many of the people most prone to having internationalist ideas were so fixated on defending Japan's 'Peace Constitution' that they saw embarking on peacekeeping as yet one more concession to American attempts to subvert it (Dore, 1997, pxv). Without a perception of a common threat, there is more scope for Japan and the US to pursue security policies independently of each other (see, for example, McDougall, 1997, p72). As for the UN, it seems that virtually no one in Japan is in favor of a so-called super-Scandinavian option (Dore, 1997) – making Japan the champion of the UN. It seems likely that future regional policies of Japan will continue to be rather conservative and cautious, and largely confined to bilateral relations between countries. In addition, there is the sub-regional level where the collapse of the Cold War system has created more room for new ways of linking countries and their regions across boundaries. However, even at the sub-regional level the legacy of Japanese imperialism tends to cast a shadow over most attempts to deepen relationships with its neighbors (which, of course, would make the best candidates for sub-regional partnerships) (Hook, 1996, pp21–24). Furthermore, the great disparities in wealth between Japan and the other East Asian countries easily make all sub-regional links appear rather asymmetrical in their nature.

To sum up the development of the emancipatory elements in Japanese foreign policy, we can distinguish between the periods of omni-directional foreign policy and multilateral foreign policy. During the period of omni-directional foreign policy, Japan tried to be friendly with almost everyone while still hiding behind the US. It regarded its political passivity as often the best that it could do to help other countries, especially other Asian countries, develop their own societies. Under a multilateral foreign policy, Japan has adopted a more active role and has been giving significant assistance to those countries that have made efforts to show their friendliness to Japan and responsiveness to the new priorities of Japanese aid diplomacy. The diversity of the Japanese foreign policy objectives should have made it reasonably easy for most countries to deal with Japan. For many developing countries, Japan has been one of the least selfish of the wealthy industrialized countries and there is, indeed, a slow shift toward more environment-friendly and human development-concerned aid diplomacy.

At the special environmental session of the UN General Assembly in 1997, then Prime Minister Hashimoto summed up the new, more environment-conscious priorities of Japanese ODA. He said that Japanese 'initiatives for sustainable development' were based on the principles of promoting human security, ownership (self-help efforts of developing countries) and environmental cooperation for sustainable development (Matsushita, 2000, p18). This mixed bag of principles apparently was intended to win wider support of recipient governments and other partners. These principles showed a clear respect for the recipient governments and their own policies and priorities. The 'sustainability' in these principles seems to be subject to other anthropocentric objectives. 'Human security' is a convenient term, which clearly includes meeting the basic needs of people but may also be interpreted as a reference to human rights and to social and political rights in other societies. The underlying assumption seems to be that sustainable development should be achieved together with human security and ownership, and that usually there is no conflict between these principles or priorities.

No matter what is the real content of Japanese responses to global environmental problems, it seems to be the most popular of Japan's international contributions among Japanese survey respondents. Some authors have pointed out that the strong support for international environmental efforts reflects the thinking that Japan should contribute only to 'low' politics and avoid getting involved in 'high' politics (military and security issues), and that the support for foreign aid is a sign of ambivalence or a reluctant attitude toward internationalization (Itoh, 2000, pp38–42). There can be some truth in that interpretation; but I would consider it a positive sign that the Japanese people identify environmental cooperation as the field where Japan could most easily contribute to global governance. Some scholars acknowledge that environmentalism as a new and rising international norm fits particularly well with long-held, domestically embedded Japanese norms (Hook et al, 2001, p388).

It may, indeed, be a good idea to think about the change in Japanese foreign policy in terms of gradually adopting or rejecting global norms, and adjusting those with domestic norms.

Japanese global environmental cooperation: Domestic discourses on environmental protection and conservation

Japan was not among the first countries to raise issues of global environmental problems. However, the growing activity of other governments was keenly observed in Japan. For instance, the 1972 UN Stockholm Conference on the environment awakened the Japanese bureaucracy and scientific community to the changing role of the environment in international relations. Japanese cabinets dealt with the issue by establishing advisory bodies and discussion groups during the early 1980s. However, it took a long time before environmental diplomacy really hit the whole of Japan. Interestingly, some observers give credit for bringing global environmental issues to the mainstream of Japanese foreign policy to Prime Minister Takeshita Noboru, whose political support organizations were ideologically quite removed from environmentalism. Takeshita was said to have realized the importance of global environmental issues at the Toronto Group of Seven (G-7) meeting in 1988. Thereafter, he repeatedly raised environmental issues and even said that 'Politicians who do not know and act for environmental issues are those who lack intelligence, education and courage' (Ohta, 2000, pp96–101). In 1989, Japan hosted Global Environment and Human Response, a major international conference on global environmental issues. At that time it was Prime Minister Kaifu who could take credit for Japanese initiatives. However, the Rio de Janeiro UN Earth Summit in 1992 was the place where Japan – and Prime Minister Miyazawa – made it clear that Japanese priorities had changed. Japan was now serious about Green aid, with money being no problem.

Japanese governments have used ODA to take an active role in environmental protection. They realized that ODA often provides the only tool with which Japan can mitigate environmental damage caused by economic activity. Japanese companies have often been involved in practices that destroy nature, especially in Southeast Asia. The Japanese government wanted to improve the country's reputation by being active in environmental ODA, even when the recipient governments were sometimes less than enthusiastic. Most other East Asian countries have a stronger belief in the benefits of rapid economic growth than does Japan. It is quite telling that after the financial crisis hit East Asia in 1997, the government of Thailand was quick to slash its environment-related budget (Matsushita, 2000, p16).

Internationally, Japan is perhaps most widely criticized for 'scientific whaling', driftnet fishing and import of timber from Southeast Asian tropical forests. Whaling has become a kind of diplomatic prestige issue as successive Japanese governments (like Norwegian governments) have raised the issue of protecting local cultures and traditions. The International Whaling Commission (IWC) meeting in Shimonoseki in May 2002 served as a reminder of how serious the Japanese government is about its whaling policy and how little support there is for the Japanese position in the rest of the world, despite its vote-buying to win other IWC members over to its position. Whale eating is not a particularly important part of Japanese culture, and modern whaling has very little to do with traditional coastal whaling. The argument about 'traditions' is just one more excuse to withdraw from global whale-protection efforts. Interpreting cultural meanings and differences in Japan (and Norway) is done in ways that simply serve nationalistic purposes, and have, indeed, become issues of national prestige. Economically, whaling is less important, and ordinary Japanese people do not have very strong opinions on the issue itself in spite of newspapers supporting the government line by steadily carrying pro-whaling articles. The foreign pressure attached to this issue has developed into an issue itself. Some foreign environmental organizations have even campaigned against giving a permanent UN Security Council seat to Japan on the basis of its whaling.

Drifte (1998, pp123–124) identifies foreign criticism of the ecological consequences of Japanese economic activities, and the realization of transboundary pollution from China and South Korea entering Japan, as the reasons for Japan's new activity in the field of global environmental cooperation. Foreign pressure may be important in Japanese foreign policy decision-making, but there are quite a few individuals in the Japanese decision-making elite who are aware of the magnitude of global environmental problems. For these people, spending on environmental aid is less wasteful than many other forms of spending, and foreign pressure can be convenient support for their arguments. In addition, most people who are familiar with the rapidly worsening environmental situation in East Asia know well that in the future vast amounts of money need to be spent on the environment, and that in most cases it would be much cheaper to start as soon as possible. The real motivations behind the sudden awakening of Japanese decision-makers to global environmental problems are as varied as their ideological convictions. Especially in foreign policy, otherwise conservative politicians may suddenly display very 'progressive' views. Sometimes there is a marked difference between the domestic track record of Japanese politicians on environmental issues and their enlightened views on global environmental cooperation. Apparently, the number of chauvinist anthropocentrists may be, after all, fairly small among the Japanese political elite – at least in foreign policy.

In accordance with new priorities, Japanese ODA has, after some delays, institutionalized environmental impact assessment, and advanced environmental technology has been applied in many development projects. Some Japanese researchers are concerned that there are problems when the most advanced environmental technology is being applied in ODA projects even when the general infrastructure is not commensurate with that technology, and that the real purpose of the assistance is to support Japanese industry. Some of the money designated for environmental ODA is spent on training foreign environmental researchers, officials and administrators in Japan, and the idea is very much to spread the latest Japanese know-how to other countries. At least some of the more advanced Japanese practices and technologies have a positive impact upon the environment. For instance, Thailand has engaged with Japan in a long-term environmental training programme (including dispatch of Japanese experts, acceptance of Thai trainees and the provision of equipment and materials) and Japanese grant aid was used already in 1983 to establish the Environmental Training and Research Centre in Thailand.

Japanese aid has also greatly contributed to environmental information-gathering systems in developing countries. Soon after the Japanese government started to emphasize environment in its aid diplomacy, it conducted environmental surveys and drew up environmental profiles of most key countries receiving Japanese aid. In addition, there have been quite a few large-scale environmental studies, often in cooperation with foreign counterparts, aimed at generating data for formulating comprehensive plans to control environmental problems in specific locations, such as in Bangkok, Thailand, and Liuzhou, China. In short, Japanese aid has added to the knowledge of environmental problems. Japanese researchers and administrators often generate this information, and it is therefore readily usable for Japanese ODA decision-making. Japanese aid projects aimed at contributing to the preservation and improvement of the environment include improvement of 'community environment' (such as improvement of water supply, sewer systems and waste management systems), preservation of forests and reforestation, prevention of disasters, pollution control and ecological conservation. The share of aid for community environment has been more than the others combined, with the second most costly being the fight against pollution. The share of natural conservation and biodiversity-related projects has remained negligible. The actual content of Japan's environmental policies points once again to anthropocentric priorities, which should be no surprise since ODA tends to reflect the domestic policies and values of donor countries. However, Japan has added to its bilateral environmental aid by contributing to multilateral environmental efforts, such as those of the UN Environment Programme (UNEP) (MOFA, 1994, pp173–191; 1996, pp183–197).

The emphasis on community environment can help to steer ODA away from large-scale infrastructure projects, which are prone to cause environmental destruction and embarrassing questions about political and business connections. The community environment-related projects are, in most cases, based on the similar type of technocratic knowledge, skills and management that have always served Japanese ODA programmes, and therefore the biggest change may occur in methodology rather than actual work. The emphasis on preserving forests is interesting against the sorry state of Japanese forests and since Japanese economic activities (especially the pulp and paper industry, construction and building) continue to consume tropical timber from Southeast Asia in great quantities. Japanese ODA has for many years included several forestation projects, although their scale is still small compared with the damage created to foreign forests by Japanese economic activities (see Dauvergne, 1997; Yamada, 1997).

For some international environmental issues there is a direct link to the environment in Japan. For instance, global warming has a major impact on Japan, and much of the world's carbon dioxide emissions will originate in the East Asian region where rapid economic growth continues and governments are often reluctant to cut industrial emissions. Marine pollution and depletion of fish stocks in the region have hit the Japanese hard because they are among the heaviest consumers of fish and seafood. China's environmental problems already constitute a global problem that is getting worse. China's pollution is also a regional problem, and Japan probably is the only foreign government in the region that can have a major impact on China's environmental policy. China's economy annually emits an estimated 20 million tonnes of sulphur oxides into the air, or about 20 times the amount generated by Japan. Japanese authorities feel quite powerless to fight against acid rain in Japan when so much of the region's emissions originate in China (and other East Asian countries). China depends heavily upon the use of low-grade coal as its energy source, and much of that coal is burned inefficiently and without the use of adequate desulphurization equipment. Of course, the consequences of acid rain and air pollution hit the Chinese people hardest, and air pollution of most big cities in China clearly poses a major health risk there.

Emissions of sulphur oxides have increased rapidly in East Asia. Together with other emissions, they have made East Asian countries' air the most polluted anywhere. Due to Chinese emissions, the concentrations of sulphate aerosol are now often as high above the remote islands of Okinawa as they are above Japan's largest urban centres. The Japanese government has, through research organizations and the Ministry of Economy, Trade and Industry (METI), supported cooperative research with the Chinese and other East Asian partners on acid rain. The most ambitious initiative is the Acid

Deposition Monitoring Network in East Asia (EANET) launched by Japan's Environment Agency in 1998, and which now has cooperation in ten different countries. EANET provides technical assistance in monitoring and collecting data, and it tries to establish uniform monitoring data (see Matsushita, 2000 pp17–18; Tanaka, 2000, pp32–33).

In spite of all the good intentions of Japanese environmental ODA, it has not met the highest criteria for ecologically sound behavior. Japan's ODA in the Pacific Asia region has been, as described in the ODA charter of 1992, more of 'a support for self-help efforts of developing countries toward economic take-off' than a force to move towards sustainable development (MOFA, 1996, p253). It still remains to be seen whether it will ever be possible to combine both of these goals. For most successful industrial states of Pacific Asia, including Japan, it will be very difficult to substantially modify their cultures to enable them to better conform to the principles of environmentally sustainable growth.

However, there is some cause for optimism. Various Japanese private corporations have voluntarily adopted the cause of environmentalism and are trying to benefit from their new environment-friendly image at home and abroad. For instance, Canon bases many of its highly visible advertisement campaigns on environmental themes. Some companies, such as Ricoh, have very ambitious environmental plans and have provided resources for a wide range of environmental activities. Ricoh has consequently won several domestic and international environment-related awards (Ricoh Corporation, 2001). These and other global Japanese corporations seem to be fully aware of the need to build up their environmentalist credentials in order to appeal to the tastes of a significant segment of their customers. In this case the laws of the market are contributing to more environmentally conscious business practices.

For their part, Japanese environmental non-governmental organizations (NGOs) tend to be focused on local environmental issues. At the local level, environmental issues can occasionally become the focus of politics, as has taken place in the Yoshinogawa River basin area or in Nagano Prefecture (where Governor Tanaka has successfully tied his political future to a 'no dams' policy). But the membership figures for most Japanese national environmental organizations tend to be modest and most are too weak to have a significant independent role outside Japan, and sometimes even within Japan. This reflects the difficulties that many Japanese NGOs have in securing their financial and organizational maturity. Frequently, Japanese authorities have been reluctant and unprepared to cooperate with environmental NGOs. That lack of cooperation has certainly hindered more balanced development of Japanese global environmental activities. Many of the people who are responsible for official Japanese environmental cooperation are displaying the traditional attitudes and behavior of Japanese civil servants, rather than the enthusiasm and environmental consciousness that would be needed to convince their foreign partners of their sincerity and good intentions.

Conclusion

In domestic environmental controversies, citizens and community members (*shimin*) have organized themselves with great efficiency, and environmental movements themselves have given new meaning to the whole concept of *shimin* (cf Kitô, 1999, pp10–26). Since the current decision-making system of Japan is based on the close interaction of conservative politicians, top bureaucrats and narrow business interests, any kind of change in the direction of democratization would serve the cause of environment, although it remains likely that anthropocentric ideologies in their different forms will continue to be strong in Japan. In its foreign policy, Japan has demonstrated that it is possible to integrate elements of emancipatory foreign policy in an international environment that has not always appreciated Japanese attempts to bear its global responsibilities. Japan became a major donor of development assistance by the 1980s, and in the early 1990s it rapidly changed the priorities of its assistance, making environmentally sustainable development and human security key principles of its aid and foreign policy. Together with Japanese pacifist traditions, new 'softer' principles have had a significant and constructive role in East Asia and beyond. But the question remains as to whether anthropocentric ideologies and centralized, technocratic decision-making will characterize Japan's environmental foreign policy and its influence in international environmental cooperation in the future.

Chapter 4

Japan and Global Climate Change: The Intersection of Domestic Politics and Diplomacy[1]

Hiroshi Ohta

Introduction

This chapter examines Japanese foreign policy on global climate change, focusing particularly on the role of domestic politics. It argues that Japan's basic domestic political framework, as well as its quest to make a non-military contribution to international affairs, generated the rationale for taking initiatives in environmental diplomacy. The chapter recounts stories about Japan's diplomacy and politics on global climate change from the aspect of two-level games. The bulk of the chapter analyses domestic politics associated with the adoption of the 1992 United Nations Framework Convention on Climate Change (hereafter, FCCC) in Rio de Janeiro, the third Conference of the Parties (COP3) to the FCCC in Kyoto in 1997, and the sixth Conference of the Parties (COP6) in The Hague in 2000.

Putnam (1988, pp427–460) has proposed a conceptual framework for analysing international negotiations, what he calls 'level 1', and domestic politics, or 'level 2'. At level 1, diplomats negotiate a tentative agreement, and at level 2 each country's domestic political process decides whether such a negotiated international agreement should be ratified or not. In this context, domestic politics includes '[political] parties, social classes, interest groups (both economic and non-economic), legislators, and even public opinion and elections, not simply executive officials and institutional arrangements'

(Putnam, 1988, p432). The intersection of domestic politics and diplomacy is the 'win-set', which is defined 'for a given level 2 constituency as the set of all possible level 1 agreements that would "win" – that is, gain the necessary majority among the constituents – when simply voted up or down' (Putnam, 1988, p437).

Drawing upon this theoretical framework, this chapter focuses analytically on the domestic politics of Japan's diplomacy on climate change. However, it does not deal with the ratification phase of the international convention, nor does it examine the Kyoto Protocol on global climate change. Rather, it takes a close look at the domestic political dimension of the international negotiation phases of the convention and its protocol. The conclusion briefly evaluates the implications of one assumption presented by Putnam – namely, that 'the size of the win-set depends on the distribution of power, preferences and possible coalitions among level 2 constituents' (Putnam, 1988, p442).

Analysing Japan's diplomacy and the politics of climate change

The overall argument of this chapter rests upon one constant and one semi-constant factor, three main variables and two parameters, all of which explicate the level 2 game of Japan's diplomacy and politics of climate change. The constant factor is the Japanese constitution – above all, Article 9. The semi-constant factor is public opinion. Three variables include political leadership, bureaucratic politics and two non-governmental organization (NGO) sectors, including the business (or private) sector and non-profit (environmental) organizations. Overshadowing all of these are the domestic and international political economic contexts, which act as parameters that promote or discourage action or inaction in Japan's diplomacy and politics of climate change.

The rule of the game in Japan's level 2 is the quest for ways of making a contribution to international affairs by non-military means. This rule of the game has not changed throughout the period covered by this chapter. There are two reasons for this continuity. One is straightforward and involves Article 9 of the constitution and its governmental interpretation prohibiting the use of the armed forces except for self-defence. The other reason for continuity is the semi-constant factor shown in the results of public opinion polls. With relatively small ups and downs, the Japanese public has opted for non-military means with regard to the questions about how their country should contribute to international society. Making an international contribution has also been the measure for evaluating the importance of actions in the field of the environment, in general, and global warming/climate change, in particular.

Political leadership, bureaucratic politics and NGOs are the main variables, which together constituted win-sets at level 2 of Japan's politics during negotiations at the FCCC, COP3 and COP6. The relative strength of each variable determines the size of win-sets. Political leadership or its relative strength, including the presence or the absence of policy entrepreneurs (or policy brokers), is the prime source for determining the size of a win-set. It is presumed that the more influential the politician who plays a role of policy broker, the more likely it is that the win-set will grow (Kingdom, 1984; Walker, 1974, pp112–116; 1981, pp75–96). Bureaucratic politics, in turn, hinge on the relative strength or presence/absence of political leadership. For instance, strong political leadership may make it possible to overcome bureaucratic turf wars among economic and environmental bureaucrats for the sake of the environment. NGOs, which include for-profit organizations and non-profit environmental organizations, are another integral part of determining the size of the win-set. Neither environmental and economic bureaucrats nor politicians can ignore the pressure from NGOs. While pressure from the business sector largely leads to the smaller size of the win-set, pressure from environmental NGOs supports widening a win-set for international negotiation insofar as the government is active in promoting international agreements on climate change.

Major domestic and international political and economic events, which constitute a domestic and international context, act as catalysts, either activating or inactivating each variable. International relations surrounding Japan during the Cold War were relatively steady and constant, revolving around the Japan–US security arrangement. At the same time, major domestic political alignments, known as the 1955 system, became more or less fixed. However, once that international system collapsed and alternative political party alignments became possible, the Japanese domestic political context became fluid and more susceptible to external changes. Likewise, Japan's bubble economy or the Asian financial crisis of 1997 activated or inactivated environmental policy-making processes. Therefore, the international and domestic political and economic contexts during the negotiations of the FCCC, COP3 and COP6 were important parameters that encouraged or discouraged the activities of the political leadership, bureaucratic politics and NGOs.

The main trend since the signing of the FCCC to COP6 was shrinking win-sets, together with the decline of political leadership and the abating of bureaucratic turf wars, while pressures from NGOs, both those of the business sector and environmental NGOs, mounted. Since the first phase of domestic politics relating to international negotiation on the FCCC provides us with common features that are also applicable to the phases of COP3 and COP6, the first story requires the most detailed account.

Japan's diplomacy and politics: FCCC and UNCED

The period of negotiating the FCCC was an active one for diplomacy and domestic politics, with strong Japanese political leadership and political fluidity stimulated by an inflated economic upturn and extraordinary international events. The late politician Noboru Takeshita, shrewd, experienced and influential, played a significant role as a policy entrepreneur. In addition, plenty of political opportunists, who became extempore environmentalists, had emerged by the time of the run-up to the UN Conference on Environment and Development (UNCED, or the Earth Summit) held in Rio de Janeiro in June 1992. Nonetheless, bureaucratic turf wars, especially between the Ministry of International Trade and Industry (MITI) and the Environment Agency (EA),[2] were in evidence. During the same period, business and environmental NGOs gained momentum.

Japanese public opinion and inflated economic performance during the bubble economy formed a tail wind toward Rio, despite the fact that the asset-inflated economic bubble burst in October 1990, reaching near rock bottom nine months after marking a record high in December 1989 (Asahi Shimbun, 2000, pp12–13). The quest to contribute internationally, particularly to the betterment of the global environment as reflected in public opinion polls, strongly supported Japan's active role in negotiations for the FCCC. This public opinion, in turn, was heavily influenced by a sense of 'responsibility' as a 'great' economic power – that is, an inflated self-image fostered during the Japanese bubble economy after 1985. This quest for 'global leadership' for Japan was further intensified by international criticism of Japan's inability to take part in the multinational forces that expelled Iraqi forces from Kuwait in the Gulf War of January 1991. Therefore, contribution to the betterment of the global environment, in general, and the successful negotiations concluding the FCCC, in particular, were tailor-made issues into which Japan could throw itself wholeheartedly, without going against public opinion by overstepping the limits of the constitutional framework. Everyone climbed on the bandwagon and raised the entire stake of the win-set to the highest level during the negotiations of FCCC and at COP3 and COP6. Internal momentum generated within Japan itself might have been strong enough to carry out further environmental policy changes. Yet, the speed and scope of changes would have been much slower and narrower without the ever-growing international diplomatic concerns over the advancing destruction of the global environment.

The year of 1989 was a year of international environmental diplomacy. In March then UK Prime Minister Margaret Thatcher hosted an international conference on depletion of the stratospheric ozone layer. Soon after, the governments of France, the Netherlands and Norway jointly held an international conference in The Hague on depletion of the ozone layer and climate change.

On top of these events, the Group of Seven (G-7) annual meeting, held in Paris in July, symbolically highlighted environmental diplomacy. In September, these major waves of environmental diplomacy reached Japan. The Tokyo Conference on the Global Environment and Human Response toward 'sustainable development' was jointly held with the UN Environment Programme (UNEP) and the World Meteorological Organization (WMO). The main themes discussed were the issues of the changing atmosphere and development and the environment in developing countries.

The quest for 'internationalization' and 'international contributions'

Public opinion polls revealed the strength of Japanese desires for *kokusaika*, or the internationalization of Japan, during the latter half of the 1980s. For instance, the prime minister's office's monthly public opinion poll of 1987 began to include an item on the 'internationalization of Japan' as a regular feature. This increased self-awareness about Japan's role in the world coincided with the rapid valuation of the yen after 1985, when the exchange rate of the yen to the US dollar skyrocketed from 240 yen to 120 yen to US$1. This sharp increase in the Japanese exchange rate dealt a crushing blow to export-oriented industries in Japan. In order to salvage them, the Bank of Japan adopted an easy-money policy, lowering the official discount rate. For over a year, from January 1986 the Bank of Japan lowered the rate five times until it stood at 2.5 per cent. This easy-money policy, however, resulted in the so-called 'bubble' economy, which began to inflate in 1986 and burst in 1990.

The high value of the yen and the bubble economy at home served to increase aspirations for Japan's international role. These aspirations can be seen in the general trend of responses to the public opinion poll on foreign policy from 1987 to 1992. One question asked about public views on the 'internationalization of Japan'. Except for the poll of 1987, the largest number of people chose Japan's 'international obligation as a great power' as the reason Japan needed to promote internationalization. The next most popular reason given was to 'maintain Japan's mid- and long-term prosperity'. Actually, support for these two answers during the period between 1987 and 1992 was very close – on average, 44.8 and 42.0 per cent, respectively (Sorifu, 1988–1993). As for the role that Japan should play in the world, the option that received the greatest support was to 'contribute to solving global environmental problems'. During the period between 1990 and 1992, the rate of selecting 'contribution to the global environment' averaged 47.5 per cent, while 'contribution to mediating local conflicts' was 34.5 per cent on average. In addition, 'contribution to sound growth of world economy' was 33.8 per cent.

Thus, in the run-up to UNCED, the global environmental movement became the beneficiary of the general public's aspiration that Japan play a greater international role. Countless writers saw Japan as a 'great surplus power', one 'inflated' by a high-value yen and the 'bubble' economy, and overdue for making its contribution to the world. One business leader aptly captured the mood of the times – the heightened anxiety to make an international contribution – as *kokusai koken byo* (the 'international contribution disease'). But what kind of contribution should Japan make? In his view, the general public and most politicians were not comfortable with the idea of sending Japanese Self-Defence Force (SDF) personnel abroad. He felt they would be happy, however, to contribute to solving global environmental problems.[3]

On the diplomatic front of UNCED, especially in the process of negotiating the final terms of the FCCC, Nobutoshi Akao, an experienced career diplomat in the Ministry of Foreign Affairs (MOFA), was in charge. Before assuming his new position in January 1991, Akao had served as director-general of the UN bureau of MOFA, and he had experienced the political difficulties that surfaced during the autumn of 1990, prior to shelving a bill on Japanese participation in peacekeeping operations (PKO). (After the Gulf War, the Japanese government had made strenuous efforts to pass a PKO law aimed at enabling Japan to send SDF personnel for UN peacekeeping operations within the framework of the Japanese constitution. It was forced to withdraw the bill in the face of overwhelming opposition. A modified bill was passed in the Diet (parliament) in June 1992.)

Akao said that dealing with global environmental affairs was much easier than dealing with the PKO bill. He said that there was no political opposition to Japan's contribution to the betterment of the global environment.[4] This is not to say that the government was united in its policy on climate change. There was tension between principle beliefs in commitments to 'economic growth' and 'development' versus 'environmental protection' – that is, tension at the bureaucratic level between MITI and the Environment Agency. Nevertheless, both camps reached an agreement, however reluctantly, on the importance of a new global idea of 'sustainable development', and on the causal belief of the effect of greenhouse gases on the global climate system. This fundamental agreement kept their differences from growing into a serious domestic political issue. The fact is that politicians of both the ruling and opposition parties showed strong supportive interest in the global environment question. In terms of the 'international contribution' so much desired by all, Japan was able to make both financial and technological contributions to protecting the global climate. While engaged in the final round of negotiations in New York for the FCCC, Akao put it this way:

> *We tend to see Rio and the environment as offering Japan a key leadership role. It is tied directly to what we call* kokusaika *– the internationalization of policy, which is essential.* Kokusaika *is almost an obsession with our political and business leadership and with our*

people, in general. Our media bombard the public with articles about how we must internationalize. Rio is happening against that background. It was tailor-made for us (Newhous, 1992, p68).

This view was shared widely in Japan. In addition, Akao underscored the importance of Japan's contribution in view of the fact that other leading countries, such as the US, were not doing more.

Politicians climb on the bandwagon

Prime Minister Takeshita certainly played a significant role in domestic environmental politics and diplomacy during the late 1980s and early 1990s, particularly regarding financial matters. Despite his negative popular image as a typical 'pork-barrel' politician, Takeshita was considered an expert on financial issues and taxation. He was able to enact a consumption tax law after several attempts by his predecessors, including Masayoshi Ohira and Yasuhiro Nakasone, had failed. By passing the law he boosted his political credentials among bureaucrats, especially those in the Ministry of Finance.

Takeshita projected an image of an ardent advocate of the new 'creed' of global environmentalism. Particularly before the Earth Summit, speculation about his transformation was ripe among the analysts of Japanese politics. One theory went that he wanted to revive his reputation, which was tarnished by the Recruit 'Stock for Favours' scandal. Yet another speculated that he was seeking a comeback to the centre of power. However, it seems plausible that he wanted to protect his political stronghold and expand his influence in the realm of the environment, in addition to rehabilitating his own image. Above all, the global environment was a growing issue area with a rapidly expanding popular concern and national budget.

In addition, financial assistance to developing countries for preserving the environment became one of the most contentious issues between developed and developing countries in the months preceding UNCED. The world community hoped that Japan would resolve this issue, especially by making a financial contribution. By becoming the mediator for this matter, Takeshita (and his party) was able to exploit for his political gain Japan's national quest for 'internationalization' and 'international contribution'. Furthermore, to assume leadership in global environmental issues was politically safe. Takeshita was quoted as saying: 'Whereas Japan's participation in the UN Peacekeeping Operations stirs a political controversy, protection of the global environment is an issue area to which Japan can contribute without any hesitation' (*Asahi Shimbun*, 1992).

In February 1992, an informal group chaired by Ryutaro Hashimoto, the *Kankyo kihonmondai kondanhai* (Discussion Group for Fundamental Environmental Issues, hereafter the Hashimoto discussion group), was established by the LDP to support Takeshita's political endeavours. The core members consisted of Hashimoto, Kazuo Aichi, Masayoshi Takemura and Masahisa Aoki. Other influential senior politicians belonging to the Hashimoto discussion group included former Prime Minister Toshiki Kaifu and Keizo Obuchi, former LDP secretary-general (and subsequently prime minister from 1999 to 2000; Sato, 1992, p7). However, during its preparation period, the Hashimoto discussion group did not consult with the veteran LDP environmentalist Takashi Kosugi. In 1992 he succeeded US Senator Al Gore as president of the Global Legislators Organization for a Balanced Environment (GLOBE), which was established in 1989 by parliamentarians from the European Community (now the European Union) and the US (Japanese legislators joined GLOBE soon thereafter).

This highlights the real objective of the new 'greenish' political leaders who gathered under the banner of the Hashimoto discussion group. The importance of environmental issues had qualitatively changed and expanded. The vague and elusive concept of sustainable development is a case in point. Environmental problems in Japan had long been seen as synonymous with local pollution (*kogai*), a characteristic of industrial pollution since the late 1950s. By the late 1980s and early 1990s, a new emphasis had come with the recognition of emerging urban and global environmental problems. Moreover, by manipulating the internationally accepted concept of sustainable development, even long-time advocates of 'development', or the old-style politics of material prosperity, could project a 'greenish' image, even though their actual interest was not the environment but, instead, economic development. In any case, the 'brownish' politicians of the old school had begun to 'invade' and 'colonize' the environmental policy area.

Many politicians wanted to go to the 1992 Earth Summit, even though deliberations for two important bills were to reach their final stages in the Diet during the summit and elections for the House of Councillors were to be held during the summer. By late June, the Japanese Diet was to complete deliberations on a political reform bill and a bill regarding UN peacekeeping operations (hereafter the PKO bill). As pointed out earlier, there was strong disagreement over the PKO bill, in particular between a coalition of the LDP, Komeito and Democratic Socialist Party (DSP), on the one hand, and the Socialist Democratic Party of Japan (SDPJ) and Japan Communist Party, on the other hand. The crux of debate was whether or not Japan should and could send the SDF abroad for UN peacekeeping. UNCED was to convene from 1 to 12 June when the Diet deliberations over the PKO bill would reach their final phase. Nonetheless, a contingent of 13 politicians from different parties departed for Rio. Takeshita lead the main contingent of ten politicians. This was a stark difference from the Stockholm Conference of 1972, when no politician had accompanied the official delegation led by Buichi Oishi, then director-general of the Environment Agency (Yoshida, 1992).

NGOs become active

Following the Stockholm Conference, the UN came to consider NGOs as crucial for solving international environmental problems. Consequently, an international NGO conference, Global Forum 92, was set up for the Earth Summit. Responding to the forum, various grassroots groups organized the 92 NGO Forum–Japan during May 1991. Thereafter, Japanese environmental NGOs organized themselves and helped to raise popular awareness of international environmental issues. This visibility and collective voice began to exert social pressure, although still insufficient to directly influence national policy (Ohta, 1995, pp219–238). Among various activities, NGOs wrote their own report – *People's Voice of Japan: I Have the Earth in Mind, the Earth Has Me in Hand* – identifying global environmental problems, explaining how humankind came to face these problems and how to ameliorate them. The report was submitted to the Earth Summit. Even though some policy proposals required more scrutiny in order to become viable policy alternatives, the report was a comprehensive expression of grassroots views on the issue of environment and development.

The business sector also joined in. On 23 April 1991, Keidanren (Japan Federation of Economic Organizations, now Nihon Keidanren) adopted its Global Environment Charter. The charter is based on three premises. The first is that a new approach to the environmental problem is indispensable. In the past, Japanese industry was successful in containing industrial pollution and in developing energy conservation technology. However, a new set of urban environmental problems, resulting from household refuse, waste water and air pollution caused by the ever-increasing number of automobiles, could not be solved solely by anti-pollution measures and technology, nor could global environmental problems be dealt with effectively by technology fixes or by Japan alone. The second premise is that the current social and economic system must be fundamentally re-examined, while at the same time seeking technological breakthroughs. Third, cooperative efforts among the private sector, public sector, individuals as consumers and academia were seen as essential for success in overcoming environmental problems. Unlike past issues of industrial pollution, which were characterized by a confrontational relationship between producers and consumers, today's urban and global environmental problems require cooperation between them (Keidanren, 1991, p3). Thus, the charter's basic theoretical framework indicates a notable change in the attitudes of major Japanese corporations.

In 1992, 150 Japanese governmental officials were sent from Tokyo to the Rio Earth Summit. In addition to these governmental representatives, the above-mentioned 13 politicians took part in UNCED. About 50 Japanese NGOs were at Global Forum 92. Ten industrial organizations were also listed as NGOs and participants in the forum. They included Keidanren and the

Petroleum Federation (*Asahi Shimbun*, 1992). The upshot is that Japanese contingents were highly visible in both the official Earth Summit and the NGO Global Forum.

Japan's diplomacy and politics for COP3

The period from the FCCC's first Conference of the Parties (COP1) in 1995 to COP3 in 1997 was also characterized by relatively strong political leadership and enthusiasm for the successful conclusion of the Kyoto Protocol. Hashimoto, an influential policy broker, was then prime minister. He took charge at the final stages of the negotiations at the Kyoto conference in December 1997. Although the division between the EA, MITI and MOFA remained, they all wanted a successful conclusion of the protocol. The NGOs – above all, the environmental NGOs – were eager to support such governmental efforts, although they were dissatisfied with policy targets declared by the Japanese government and by the lack of dynamic leadership.

The core element of a 'categorical imperative' of the successful conclusion of the protocol at COP3 was closely related to Japan's quest for a role contributing to international society. Its contribution should be a substantive one; but the 'nominal' aspect of the protocol has become increasingly important. Toshiaki Tanabe, former ambassador in charge of global environmental issues, has pointed out the significance of giving the name of an old Japanese capital, Kyoto, to this significant protocol, along with Japan's actual contribution to the betterment of the global environment. In addition, Japan's hosting of COP3 gave it the opportunity to show the rest of the world the tremendous efforts it had already made to conserve energy in industrial activities (Tanabe, 1999, pp48–49).

Although the conclusion of the Kyoto Protocol was the categorical imperative for Japanese negotiators, voices from the policy alliance between MITI and the private sector were to stress the difficulty for Japan of accepting substantial reductions in its greenhouse gases (GHGs). Their main argument was that Japan had already made tremendous efforts to conserve energy, particularly after the two oil crises of 1973–1974 and 1979–1980. A further substantial reduction of GHGs essentially meant that even more energy conservation measures would have to be adopted. If Japan were compelled to accept a large reduction of GHGs, its industries would face impaired economic competitiveness due to increased production costs, which, in turn, could push Japan further down the recessionary slope. The Environment Agency, however, refuted this argument by insisting that past experiences had shown that surmounting energy crises had actually resulted in economic growth and the development of eco-industries and energy conservation technology that added 'comparative advantage' to Japanese products.[5]

While keeping an eye on the US, the chief negotiator representing MOFA and the Japanese negotiating corps stressed the importance of equity. The main point of the argument was that the starting lines for reducing GHGs were different among major developed countries. Japan had already achieved substantial energy efficiency and resulting reductions in carbon dioxide (CO_2) emissions. Japanese energy efficiency in 1990 was much better than, for example, that of Germany or the UK. Therefore, the Japanese negotiators argued, it would be unfair if Japan were forced to reduce GHG emissions at the same rate as other major developed countries (Tanabe, 1999, pp129–130). The business sector – MITI's policy ally – supported this argument wholeheartedly.

By contrast, environmental NGOs were very critical of the Japanese government's insistence on equity and its declared target for Japanese GHG emission reductions. They were sympathetic to countries belonging to the Association of Small Island Sates (AOSIS) and the less developed countries, and they therefore kept pressuring the Japanese government to adopt a more ambitious emissions-reduction target. Nevertheless, environmental NGOs worked hard to ensure that the protocol would be adopted at COP3, and they supported the Japanese government's efforts toward this end.

The international and domestic contexts were not favourable to promoting the Kyoto agreement. Japan was in the midst of the prolonged economic recession after the burst of the bubble economy and the Asian financial crisis of 1997. While Japan's economic recession continued, domestic politics became increasingly unstable. Amid political turmoil, the LDP stepped down from ruling party status, but later returned as the dominant party in a coalition government with SDPJ and the Sakigake party. The instability of Japanese party politics revealed itself at the most crucial moment of COP3. Hiroshi Oki, the co-chairperson for COP3 and the director of the EA, abruptly resigned the chair on the last day of the conference (11 December 1997). The main reason for his resignation was that he was forced to return to Tokyo to deal with a no-confidence vote against the Hashimoto Cabinet, which was presented that day by the Shinshin-to party. Associates caught up with Oki at the Kyoto station and brought him back to the conference room. It was reported that Japanese environmental NGOs asked some other Diet members to make arrangements on Oki's behalf so that he would be able to co-chair the conference until the end (*Japan Times*, 1997). What these events and situations suggest is that both international and domestic contexts discouraged the Japanese negotiators and domestic pressure groups (except for environmental NGOs) from taking a stronger leadership role in bringing the Kyoto Protocol to a successful conclusion.

Despite the odds, however, public opinion polls consistently supported Japan's international contribution in the field of the environment. One year before COP3, the Japanese public strongly supported the necessity of 'internationalization' and Japan's contribution, by peaceful means, to international society and to the betterment of the global environment, in general, and specifically to address global warming. The Japanese public favoured the internationalization of Japan because of its obligation as a great power and for the sake of maintaining Japan's mid- and long-term prosperity.[6] Regarding the question about Japan's role in world society, the largest support was for Japan to contribute to solving global environmental problems (44.2 per cent) and to help maintain international peace through human aid and efforts to facilitate the peaceful settlement of local conflicts (37.5 per cent). The public opinion survey that was carried out during the year that COP3 was convened indicated public concerns about global warming, with 25.3 per cent 'very concerned' and 54.1 per cent 'concerned to a certain extent'. Almost half of the respondents (49.7 per cent) regarded the problem of global warming as one of the most important issues that the government and international organizations had to address (Sorifu, 1999, pp77–78). In sum, the Japanese public still felt that Japan should be 'internationalized', and that it should contribute to world society through peaceful means, including in the field of the global environment, in general, and global warming, in particular.

Japan's diplomacy and politics for COP6

The distinguishing Japanese features of the periods before and during COP6 at The Hague were an absence of political leadership and further diminishing of political enthusiasm, although there was bureaucratic unity at the conference. Some of the most prominent Japanese political leaders had died or left office, notably Takeshita, Obuchi and Hashimoto. Their departure from the central political scene made it impossible to maintain dynamic political leadership on climate change. What is more, the erosion of the popular support for the LDP, which failed to give the public decisive political solutions or remedies for the long-term economic recession, uprooted the parliamentary seats of 'greenish' politicians. The fallout from electoral setbacks in the general election of the House of the Representatives (lower house) on 25 June 2000 hit hard for environmentally conscious and active politicians in both the ruling and opposition parties. Kosugi, who was a long-time promoter of environmental policies and even held the office of the minister of education, lost his Diet seat after serving six terms. Another 'greenish' LDP politician, Aichi, who once had been the EA director and chairperson of the Parliamentarian Federation for the Promotion of Natural Energy, also lost his seat in the lower house. So, too, did Masayoshi Takemura, one of the founders of the Sakigake party, which once played a pivotal role in forming the coalition government. Takemura was earlier a leading environmental parliamentarian – particularly by taking advantage of his experience in tackling the problem of effluents in Lake Biwa while governor of Shiga Prefecture. The defeats of these influential 'greenish' politicians and others substantially reduced enthusiasm for environmental policy initiatives.

The lack of political leadership, together with political indifference, partly led to unity among the main bureaucratic branches that formed the Japanese negotiating team at COP6. Japan belonged to the 'umbrella group' of the US, Canada, Australia and other countries, and it took a position distinct from the European Union (EU) and others who were advocating severe operational rules and tight restrictions on the utilization of Kyoto Protocol emissions reduction mechanisms.

In 1998, two years prior to COP6, the Japanese negotiating position was declared in *The Guideline for Measures to Prevent Global Warming: Measures Towards 2010 to Prevent Global Warming*, a document by the Global Warming Prevention Headquarters of the Japanese government.[7] This policy programme relies heavily on using forests to absorb CO_2, particularly through activities such as forest management, as suggested in Article 3.4 of the Kyoto Protocol. With regard to forest activities, Japan proposed 'essential measures' aimed at preventing global warming by meeting 3.7 per cent of the 6 per cent that was Japan's target under the Kyoto Protocol. There is another policy of reducing domestic GHG emissions by 2.5 per cent through energy conservation, introduction of new energy sources, and more construction of nuclear power plants 'with rigid nuclear safety measures'. However, the guideline estimated a 2 per cent increase of GHGs due to emissions of gases used as alternatives to ozone-depleting gases regulated under the Montreal Protocol. Therefore, Japan has to rely on the Kyoto mechanisms to find credits equivalent to 1.8 per cent of its emission reductions (this policy guideline can be utilized for an indication of the negotiating win-set).

Meanwhile, the Japanese business sector attempted to dissuade the Japanese negotiating team from agreeing upon any hasty regulatory restrictions on utilizing the flexible Kyoto mechanisms.[8] Environmental NGOs, on the other hand, insisted that Japan honour the rule of supplementarity, make further efforts to reduce GHGs at home, and not rely on forest sinks (Mizutani, 2000). The business sector's position of protesting the severity of the 6 per cent reduction target and insisting on no restrictions for the Kyoto mechanisms, and calling for the largest possible utilization of sinks, constituted straightforward pressure on the Japanese negotiators not to compromise with, for example, the EU position. On the other hand, the almost complete opposite demands of environmental NGOs, however desirable they might be environmentally, were not acceptable, particularly to the pro-industry negotiators, since the environmental NGOs claims were outside a negotiable range, notwithstanding the presence of pro-environment NGO sympathizers (EA bureaucrats) on the negotiating team. In addition, the conceptual bond among MITI, MOFA and EA was the strange combination of the concepts of national and global interests. To put into operation (or to save) the Kyoto Protocol was a 'categorical imperative' for the Japanese government because doing so would clearly demonstrate the Japanese contribution to the world community on an important global environmental issue – much as having the protocol named for Kyoto had done.

One year prior to COP6, the Japanese public still strongly backed Japan's contribution to international society in the field of the global environment, including the issue of global warming. In a 1999 public opinion survey, respondents continued to stress the need for Japan to 'internationalize' itself in order to maintain mid- and long-term prosperity and to fulfil its obligation as a great power (Sorifu, 1999, p102).[9] Regarding the question of Japan's role in world society, contribution to solving global environmental problems and maintaining international peace through human aid and efforts for a peaceful settlement of local conflicts shared the largest and almost equal degree of concern (40.2 per cent and 40.0 per cent, respectively).

Although public opinion polls still supported Japan's contribution in the field of the global environment, including climate change, the domestic and international contexts were not particularly favourable to helping regain political and diplomatic enthusiasm. In addition to diminishing political leadership and support from 'greenish' parliamentarians, the Japanese economy still lagged behind public hopes for slow but steady growth. In spite of the government's announcement of an economic stimulus package, the stock market did not respond favourably. The unemployment rate remained high (for Japan) at 4.7 per cent in 1999 (*Asahi Shimbun*, 2000, p13). Globalization continues to affect Japan's economy, and Japan itself is unable to regain a leading position in the 'flying geese' formation of the Asian economy (Hatch and Yamamura, 1996). This continued economic stagnation will have important implications for Japan's environmental foreign policy.

Conclusion

Towards the conclusion of the FCCC, Japan's win-set was enlarged through strong political leadership, political enthusiasm and the active participation of environmental NGOs. With favourable domestic political circumstances, the Japanese negotiating team promoted the conclusion of the FCCC. The quest for Japan's contribution to international society was the strongest of the three periods examined here, partly because of the inflated image of Japan as an ascending 'great' economic power, and partly because of the cold reception that accompanied Japan's monetary contribution to the Gulf War in early 1991. Japanese public opinion also wholeheartedly supported making an international contribution to arresting global warming.

When COP3 was held in 1997, international and domestic conditions had become unfavourable to an active promotion of Japanese policy on global climate change, although Prime Minister Hashimoto acted as an environmental policy entrepreneur (albeit much less influential than Takeshita before him). Economic recession within and surrounding Japan diminished political enthusiasm for the cause of the global environment, even as it strengthened the policy alliance between economic ministries and the business sector. Yet, as the host country of COP3, the Japanese government wanted to succeed in concluding the Kyoto Protocol. Japanese public opinion and environmental NGOs supported the government's efforts, in spite of their dissatisfaction with its GHG-reduction policy. However, reduction in the size of the win-set, due to the relative weakness of political leadership, declining political support and the increased relative strength of the economic policy alliance, was partially responsible for acceptance of the major preconditions for US participation in the regime – namely, the flexible (and arguably pro-business) Kyoto mechanisms and sinks.

Regarding level 2 of Japan's diplomacy and politics surrounding COP6, the persistent economic recession and resulting negative pressure from the private sector, the lack of dynamic political leadership, and diminishing political enthusiasm together reduced the size of the win-set. In other words, all of these negative factors discouraged the Japanese negotiating team from taking a bold step towards finalizing the detailed rules for the protocol. However, Japanese negotiators did not want to see the total failure of the protocol, either. The name of this protocol is indispensable for the Japanese government to show its contribution to tackling perhaps the most pressing global problem that human civilization has ever faced. The Japanese negotiating team was united at The Hague to save the protocol for the sake of the national interest, and for the interests of MOFA and the EA (now the Ministry of the Environment). Having said this, MITI held a tight rein over those ministries.

Although developments following COP6 are not included in the scope of this chapter, Japan's ratification of the protocol in June 2002 begs some explanation, particularly since the US has withdrawn from the protocol. Japan's initial hesitation at joining the EU in Kyoto Protocol negotiations during 2001 is explained by concerns about the perceived negative impact on its economy and the Japan–US relationship, which is, after all, Japan's most important foreign concern. Nonetheless, a compromise proposal, which allowed Japan to count the sequestration of CO_2 by forests, was actually more than Japan had demanded. Thus, the US defection indirectly boosted Japan's (and Russia's) negotiating position sufficiently to obtain substantial gains. It seems fair to say that the Kyoto Protocol is so important for Japanese foreign policy that Japan finally decided to step forward with the EU and the rest of the world, leaving the US behind, although the step forward was a small one.

Environmental Degradation and Security in Maoist China: Lessons from the War Preparation Movement

Judith Shapiro[1]

Introduction

During the Great Proletarian Cultural Revolution (1966–1976), the Chinese state displaced millions of people and relocated them to the hinterlands. The most well known of these displacements is the relocation of intellectuals and educated urban young people to the countryside in order to 'learn from' the peasants and bolster China's borders against enemy attack. Less well known is the 'Third Front' movement, during which heavy industry was transplanted to the interior in an effort to prepare China for expected war with the Soviet Union. Hundreds of factories and entire work forces were picked up and placed in regions inhospitable for human habitation. These relocations not only disrupted the lives of hundreds of thousands of urban workers but also brought intense extractive and manufacturing activity into remote areas. Among Third Front projects, one of the most heralded, and most environmentally destructive, was the steel manufacturing city of Panzhihua, carved out of a virtually uninhabited mountain area in southwest Sichuan Province.

This chapter, based on first-person interviews, Chinese-language archival records and books, and secondary material by Chinese and Western scholars, explores the relationship between China's war-preparation atmosphere and decisions that had severely negative environmental impacts. The story of Panzhihua and the larger militarization effort of which it was a part is representative of a pattern of poor decision-making motivated by security concerns, at a time when Maoist efforts to wage 'war' against the natural world were at their rhetorical extreme. During this period, coercive and semi-voluntary relocations of people to inhospitable regions and pristine wilderness areas damaged or destroyed ecosystems even as they created enormous human hardships, clearly exemplifying the link between the suffering of people and the abuse of the land that was so characteristic of the Mao years.

A broad 'war preparation campaign' during the late 1960s and early 1970s sent millions to China's hinterlands and frontiers in response to China's heightened international security concerns. One aspect of this movement was the 'educated youth movement' (*zhiqing yundong*), in which 20 million urban young people were sent to the countryside and frontiers. This movement intensified in late 1968 after the worst of the Red Guard violence. Among millions of youth 'sent down' to the countryside, more than 2 million were deployed to border areas to join the Production-Construction Army Corps under the People's Liberation Army (PLA) leadership. Another aspect of the war preparation movement, and the focus of this chapter, was the effort to create a 'Third Front' (*sanxian*), or inland industrial and military base (the First and Second Fronts were the vulnerable coastal regions and the mid-country regions that would be at risk during a long conflict[2]). Third Front construction began in 1964, with the Third Five-Year Plan, which called for building a base for rear-guard defence in the event of war. Both the Third Front and educated youth movements peaked in 1969, following border skirmishes with the Soviet Union, when the war preparation campaign reached its height.

From an environmental perspective, the Third Front primarily affected mountainous interior areas of west and southwest China. The new strategic base required roads and railroads to open up the hinterlands. Relocated industries engaged in mining for minerals with defence applications and logging for fuel and timber. They sent air pollution into narrow mountain valleys and chemical wastes into river headwaters. The 'war preparation' campaign epitomizes Mao Zedong's war against nature in its most explicit incarnation, for the Chinese people were called on to make war against the country's external and internal enemies and to conquer nature at one and the same time.

The Maoist war preparation movement demonstrates how a preoccupation with perceived external threats can draw attention away from other priorities and have profoundly negative effects on the domestic environmental situation. This dynamic can apply in other countries and other situations. The perceived urgency of the security situation led Mao and his followers to implement policies that shifted scarce resources from the provision of basic human needs, had long-term negative economic and environmental repercussions, and caused great human suffering. Similar choices, with similar consequences, have been made, to list just a few obvious examples, in the former Soviet Union, in today's North Korea, in Utah and Nevada at the heyday of nuclear testing, and on Vieques, the Puerto Rican island that the US has been using as a bombing range. In most cases, these choices have been made with little public discussion, and the environmental repercussions of security-based decisions have been given little or no weight.

The security environment and the Third Front

China's international isolation became profound after the 1960 Sino–Soviet split. War waged in Vietnam by American 'imperialists' and border skirmishes with Soviet 'revisionists' soon led Mao to see war as imminent in a world hostile to China. China lacked allies and feared attack from either or both superpowers. Mao's view that an apocalyptic struggle between the forces of revolution and reaction was imminent helps to explain why he intervened to put the country on a war footing just as consumption-oriented policies were bringing China's economy greater stability after the Great Famine.[3]

After the US bombed North Vietnam on 4 August 1964, Mao called for accelerated inland development in preparation for war, sounding his favoured themes of urgency, decentralization and self-reliance (Naughton, 1991, p157). Relations with the Soviet Union worsened as Khruschev's reforms and territorial disputes exacerbated differences with the former 'elder brother'. From 15 October 1964 to 5 March 1969 there were 4189 border incidents on the Soviet border, half again as many as during the period from 1960 to 1964. After Soviet troops marched into Czechoslovakia in August 1968, a large-scale invasion of China seemed increasingly plausible. In February 1969, Chinese troops were put on alert on the Far East border, and on 2 and 15 March there were armed clashes with the Soviets on Zhenbao Island in Heilongjiang Province. Mutual displays of aggression continued throughout the year. In the summer, clashes erupted in Xinjiang and Heilongjiang; a 30 July 1969 *People's Daily* editorial called on the Chinese people to expect war through surprise attack at any time. Soviet Premier Alexei Kosygin visited China on 11 September 1969, meeting Zhou Enlai at the airport in a failed attempt to defuse tensions, and in the latter half of 1969 the Soviets used even stronger anti-Chinese language. By mid October 1969, China was at a fever pitch of war preparation. Tensions decreased somewhat only when talks resumed on 20 October (Zhang and Li, 1998, pp349–354; Barouin and Yu, 1998, pp85–97). These talks failed, and on 31 January 1970, Mao called on the people to 'use the war preparation viewpoint to see everything, examine everything, implement everything'.[4] In his famous 20 May speech 'People of the World Unite, Defeat American Invaders and their Running Dogs', he declared: 'The danger of a new world war still exists, the people of each country should prepare.'

The army's participation in the Revolutionary Committees formed in 1967–1968, as mentioned, brought military governance to civilian institutions.

The country's increasingly militarized stance now coloured the domestic struggle against internal counter-revolutionary 'enemies' that was launched with the Cultural Revolution. As war preparation increased, the whole country came to resemble an army on alert. Mao maintained that 'all people are soldiers' (*quan min jie bing*). Green military clothing and red-starred PLA caps became the fashion. Party directives propounded such war-preparation slogans as 'Raise vigilance, protect the motherland' (*Tigao Jingti, Baowei Zuguo*) and 'Deeply dig tunnels, broadly gather grain, never seek hegemony' (*Shen Wadong, Guang Jiliang, Bu Chengba*). Military expenditures rose. In 1969, defence military preparations were 34 per cent greater than the previous year, and in 1970 and 1971 they continued to increase by 15 and 16 per cent, respectively (Zhang and Li, 1998, p351; Barouin and Yu, 1998, p90). Strategic considerations dominated, to the exclusion of other values.

'Prepare for war, prepare for famine, for the sake of the people' (*Bei Zhan, Bei Huang, Wei Renmin*) became the defining slogan for the war preparation phase of Mao-era environmental degradation. The formulation emerged during preparatory discussions for the Third Five-Year Plan (1966–1970), which specified that China's economic circumstances should be confronted through austerity and arduous struggle (Naughton, 1991, p157). Commenting on a draft document, Mao remarked on 16 June 1965 that the focus of the next period should be on the people, war preparation and the possibility of famine. An August version of the plan stated that China should prepare for a big, early war, place national defence first, speed up Third Front construction and slowly improve people's lives. Zhou Enlai is credited with creating the slogan and Mao with repeating it in March 1966. It was propagated nationwide with the April 1967 edition of Mao's *Little Red Book* (Zhang and Li, 1998, p343).

The Third Front strategy originated during the same period. In a 6 June 1964 'Talk on the Third Five-Year Plan', Mao commented, in his earthy fashion:

As long as imperialism exists, there is always the danger of war. We must build up the strategic rear... This does not mean that we no longer care about the seacoast, which must also be well guarded so that it can play the role of supporting the construction of new bases. Two fists and one rear-end. Agriculture is one fist, and national defence is another fist. To make the fists strong, the rear-end must be seated securely. The rear-end is basic industry (Mao, 1974, p354).

The Third Front would be built in the mountainous interior, where rugged terrain would provide protection in the event of a military attack. Urban factories, particularly strategic industries, would be relocated to remote areas for shelter and concealment.

The Third Front comprised two sections, corresponding approximately to interior mountainous regions above 500 metres in altitude (Naughton, 1988, p354). The southerly part included most of Yunnan, Guizhou and Sichuan and the southwest parts of West Hunan and West Hubei; the northerly one included all or parts of Shaanxi, Gansu and Ningxia, and Qinghai and the northwest parts of West Henan and West Shanxi. Each province was ordered to develop its own military industries and to manufacture rifles, bayonets, light and heavy machine guns, mortar, grenades and dynamite (Zhang and Li, 1988, pp340–341; Barouin and Yu, 1988, pp92–93). In September 1964, hundreds of inland sites were surveyed as possible Third Front locations. The ideal site was said to be 'in the mountains, dispersed and hidden' (*kaoshan, fensan, yinbi*). A report on Guizhou Province, home of the minority Zhuang people and one of China's most barren and sparsely populated regions, identified 48 suitable sites (Zhang and Li, 1988, pp344–345). The slogan 'In mountains, dispersed, in caves' (*Shan, San, Dong*), which at least one source attributes to Lin Biao (Panzhihua, 1997, p51), came to describe the ideal location.

Naughton, who has studied the Third Front's huge economic losses, describes the Third Front as the largest investment in military development ever pursued by any country:

> *The intention was to create an entire industrial base – not just an armaments industry – that could survive a prolonged war. The programme was so huge that it can fairly be said that, with the exception of petroleum development, the central government's industrialization policy from 1965 through 1971 was the Third Front* (Naughton, 1991, p158).

Some industries were rebuilt from scratch; but, especially in the machinery and chemical industries, relocations were common. Whole plants were moved, or split up and partially relocated. From 1964 to mid 1971, 380 factories were moved inland, representing one fifth of all large Third Front plants. Machine-building and arms factories in northern Guizhou, the Number Two Automobile Factory in Hubei, and nuclear and aerospace industries in the northwest were all part of Third Front policy, along with the Gezhou Dam on the upper Yangzi River (Naughton, 1991, pp159–160). In 1970, construction investment in the interior totalled 197.98 billion yuan, of which Third Front expenditures comprised 163.13 billion yuan – or most of the investment (Shi and He, 1996, p161).

The high costs were due not only to difficult terrain but also to the urgency with which Mao's directives were implemented. Site selection, design and construction were to be implemented simultaneously, with revisions conducted as needed; construction had the ad hoc character of a guerrilla war. Naughton (1991, p168) writes:

> *The great haste with which Third Front projects were initiated meant that in most cases design and preparatory work were inadequate or non-existent. Nearly every project about which we have information ran into substantial additional costs and delays because of inadequate preparatory work.*

Thus, with the Third Front, Mao again sounded the same theme of urgency that had devastated the environment during the Great Leap Forward. Apparently, Mao had not learned that political will alone could not force time to collapse.

The Panzhihua steel mill in southwest Sichuan, which ultimately cost the state 3.74 billion yuan, was the centrepiece of the Third Front and the primary reason for the construction of the Chengdu–Kunming railroad, which was to bring Guizhou coal to the mill and carry Panzhihua steel to Chongqing. Today, Panzhihua is trumpeted as a Third Front success story that validates Mao's strategic genius. An English-language investment brochure boasts, for example: 'Looking back into the past and forward into the future, we cannot help marvelling at the profound foresight of our great leader.' The brochure continues: 'Standing on the very spot where the construction of Panzhihua started, we can see a picture unfolding before us, a picture of man conquering nature' (Information Office of Sichuan Provincial People's Government, undated, pp32–33). The story of Panzhihua, as detailed in books and annals about the city and as reflected in interviews with ordinary people and officials, is a microcosm of Third Front relocations in many parts of the interior, a tale of arduous struggle by thousands of resettled individuals who had little say in their activities.[5] There were extraordinary engineering achievements in carving a complex mining and manufacturing operation out of an inhospitable landscape and building a railroad with so many tunnels. There were also enormous environmental and economic costs to placing strategic considerations above all else.

Panzhihua: A steel mill like a 'miniature carving in ivory'

Because of the extraordinary difficulty involved in building an enormous steel mill on only 2.5 square kilometres of land, official mythology compares the Panzhihua Iron and Steel Mill (*Pangang*) to a carved ivory miniature. Panzhihua city is named for the flower that is the region's botanical marvel, a rare and ancient fern-like plant called a cycad. The cycad is often described as a 'living fossil' and is listed together with pandas and dinosaurs as one of the three jewels of Sichuan. Until the late 1980s, the city was also known by its original name, Dukou, which means ford.[6] Created out of a tiny village in

1965, Panzhihua is located at the confluence of the Jinsha and Yalong rivers, 749 kilometres south of Chengdu and 351 kilometres north of Kunming. It shares a rift valley with Xichang, today's satellite-launching city. During the 1930s, beneath a seemingly barren landscape, geologists discovered tremendous mineral resources, which were confirmed through additional surveys in the early 1950s (Sichuansheng, 1994, pp8–9). Mao dreamed of tapping these resources, and by the mid 1960s, when war looked increasingly likely, he became determined to do so. The rich deposits include plentiful iron and coal – 47 minerals in all, including rare metals. Coal deposits include coking coal and anthracite, and iron ores included hematite and titanium-bearing titano-magnetite, all of which are highly suitable for the manufacture of steel. Panzhihua has 69 per cent of China's vanadium and 93 per cent of its titanium, both metals with defence applications. Its proven titanium reserves are first in the world (Foreign Investment Office of Panzhihua Municipal Government, undated, pp14–16).

Mao Zedong raised the question of exploiting Panzhihua's rich mineral resources for steel manufacture as early as a March 1958 meeting in Chengdu, but he put aside his ambition in the aftermath of the Leap. He revived the plan at the earliest opportunity. The official Panzhihua myth thus begins with 'a wise decision' of 4 March 1965, when Mao scrawled 'good proposal' on a Ministry of Mining and Industry report recommending construction of Panzhihua. In May, Mao criticized overly cautious leaders for abandoning plans for Panzhihua and the Kunming–Chengdu railroad, declaring: 'The decision to build Panzhihua City is not an issue concerning only one particular steel plant, but a strategic consideration.' He then made a dramatic offer: 'I cannot sleep until we build the Panzhihua iron and steel mill … If capital is lacking, I will donate the royalties from my own writing' (Sichuansheng, 1994, p3). From this meeting until 1967, Mao is estimated to have mentioned the Third Front 21 times in writings and speeches and to have explicitly linked it to Panzhihua more than 6 times. He is said to have been obsessed with Panzhihua (Panzhihua, 1997, p102). In a conversation about this history, a Panzhihua resident sighed and shrugged: 'What could we have done? Chairman Mao couldn't sleep, so we had no choice.' During the initial drafting of the Third Five-Year Plan, when other leaders sought to emphasize living standards, agricultural development and production of consumer goods, Mao intervened, rejected their plan and prevailed in his war preparation strategy.[7] Responsibility for implementing the plan was retained at the highest level, with Premier Zhou Enlai placed in charge of opening Panzhihua. In 1965, then Communist Party General Secretary Deng Xiaoping also reviewed the plans, as evidenced by a photo reproduced in many public settings in the city.

When the first 50,000 workers arrived from 10 Sichuan and Kunming work units in 1965, only 7 Han Chinese households consisting of about 70 individuals were living in the area (Sichuansheng, 1994, p3). The surrounding mountains were Yi minority territory, an ethnic group famous for its aggressive resistance to the Han. Today, the newcomers' early hardships are presented in museum dioramas illustrating Panzhihua's glorious origins. Pioneers built huts of thatch and rammed earth in the barren and dusty land. 'The pot on three stones is our kitchen, the tent in the open is our bedroom', boasts the legend (Information Office of Sichuan Provincial People's Government, undated, p34). Young men in mining hats stand below a slogan: 'Don't think of father, don't think of mother, until you produce iron, don't go home' (*Bu Xiang Die, Bu Xiang Ma, Bu Chu Tie, Bu Hui Jia*). In an odd item of memorabilia, the museum also displays Premier Zhou Enlai's 1969 US-made Belair automobile.

If not for war-preparation considerations, the place selected for the steel plant, a hillside called Nongnongping, would hardly have been a logical site for a factory. In designing previous steel plants, the Chinese had used a Soviet model that specified 'three greats, one person' (*san da yi ren*) – a great plain, a great factory district and a great railroad, all laid out in the shape of the character for 'person'. Nongnongping was a cramped 2.5 square-kilometre area surrounded on three sides by high mountains and on the fourth by the Jinsha River. The slope of the land varied from 10 to 20 degrees and in some places was as steep as 50 degrees, with cliffs, boulders and other geographic challenges (Panzhihua, 1997, p49). There was as yet, of course, no railroad. But at the end of 1965 a design team of 1300 specialists drawn from throughout the country arrived and, by the beginning of 1966, they had come up with a plan.

This plan was immediately thrown into disarray with the onslaught of the Cultural Revolution. Radicals propagated the notion that 'the workers are the masters of design; technicians can only be consultants' (*gongren shi sheji de zhuren, jishu renyuan zhi neng dang canmou*). They claimed that the plan's costs were too high and that there was no need for a roof on the sintering plant, since 'if peasants can farm under the open sky, why can't workers make steel under the open sky?' Because of the 'dispersed' element of the 'in mountains, dispersed, in caves' slogan, they recommended that the stages of the steel-making process should be separated out and the various components concealed in valleys throughout the region. Presumably, this greatly complicated production. Ultimately, through clever reporting, the technicians were able to minimize the most damaging of these proposals. However, many design flaws remained because of this interference (Panzhihua, 1997, p51).

Meanwhile, 20,000 road-builders and mine-diggers assembled from around the country were hard at work. Eighty per cent of these workers were completely inexperienced. In addition to their dangerous and difficult work, they were also required to conduct political study, criticizing Liu Shaoqi even as they struggled to open roads to the mines. They are said to have 'demonstrated a spirit of arduous struggle', a spirit (like that expressed in Mao Zedong's youthful poem) of 'boundless joy at struggling against the heavens'. When ventilation was inadequate for using dynamite, they persisted, using wet cloths pressed against their faces. Their heroic efforts soon produced martyrs and model workers such as Tang Dahei, who is said to have emerged from his work cut and bleeding, his pants in shreds (Panzhihua, 1997, pp59–60). Strategic considerations made hard work even harder. In accordance with the mandate to hide critical installations in caves, for example, a tunnel was burrowed into the mountains to house an electric generator, its coal chimneys poking out just above ground level where no bomber would notice them. The death rate in 1965 was 13 per cent of the work force, an extraordinary figure. For the period between 1965 and 1975, the death rate averaged 5.42 per cent, still exceedingly high (Sichuansheng, 1994, p131).[8]

As various 'battles' of design and road-building were declared, planners turned urgently to sintering, coking and smelting in Nongnongping itself. Steel workers arrived from Angang and Wugang, the huge steel mills of the city of Anshun in Liaoning province in the northeast and the city of Wuhan in central China. Large numbers of workers from Hunan had been sent first to Angang for training. In all, 700 factories were mobilized to help build Panzhihua (Naughton, 1988, p357). The goal was to 'speedily construct the Number One furnace system and make the Number One furnace quickly produce iron, so as to let Mao Zedong rest easy, let the Central Committee rest easy!' (Panzhihua, 1997, p87). A woman whose steelworker parents came from Liaoning told me:

A huge group of steelworkers came from Angang in 1969. Of course, no one wanted to come. But in those days it was impossible to say how you really felt. Of course, there may have been a few motivated by idealism. But if Chairman Mao said he couldn't sleep at night, that was because of the international situation with the Soviet Union, India, the US, even Japan. He felt surrounded by enemies. In fact, building the railroad or producing steel in Panzhihua wasn't going to give him any sleep. It was all for political considerations, nothing else. The wishes of the people were never part of it.

The official *Panzhihua Record* notes that this 'immigrant city' was characterized by 'mechanical' population changes (due to policy fiat), uneven distribution, many more males than females, lots of ethnic minorities and a small population (Sichuansheng, 1994, p129). In 1965, Panzhihua (then Dukou) administratively assimilated several great people's communes from Yunnan and Sichuan, comprising 80,836 people. In the first year, 41,407 immigrants arrived, for a total of 122,243. From 1965 to 1971, 373,639 more people arrived, for an average of 53,337 immigrants per year, or an average annual increase of 263.84 per cent. During the same period, 158,840 people left, reflecting the short-term nature of certain assignments, for an average of 22,691 people per year. When the influx and outflow of people are considered together, from 1965 to 1971, the total increase in the city's population was 214,799 people, an average of 30,686 people per year, and the mechanical increase, or increase due to administrative relocations, was as high as 151.68 per cent. Not surprisingly, the *Panzhihua Record* tells us that the majority of immigrants were young men. In 1965, 62 per cent of the population was male; by 1970, the figure was almost 70 per cent (Sichuansheng, 1994, pp130–131). This must have been the source of another kind of suffering beyond the harsh struggle with the land, as these young labourers would have been unable to find wives and establish families.

Premier Zhou Enlai set a target date of 1 July 1970 for Panzhihua to produce iron and for the railroad to be completed. This date is said to have been a powerful motivating goal that focused everyone's energy and attention (Sichuansheng, 1994, pp89–90). Meanwhile, as the Cultural Revolution raged on, some experienced technicians spent their daylight hours submitting to political criticism while continuing to oversee steel plant construction by night (Sichuansheng, 1994, p101). The goal was met: in July, Panzhihua turned out its first furnace of molten iron. The following year, it turned out its first furnace of molten steel.[9]

The Chengdu–Kunming railroad, built to transport Pangang's steel and primarily constructed by People's Liberation Army Unit 7659, was also completed, with great fanfare, in 1970. An extraordinary engineering feat of bridge and tunnel building, the railroad has played a huge role in opening up China's southwest to development. Some 300,000 labourers built 427 tunnels, with an accumulated length of 340 kilometres; the tunnels cover about one third of a rail line that totals just over 1000 kilometres. In all, 1999 bridges were built (Wan, 1990, pp141–142; Naughton, 1988, pp357–358). Rail links through the difficult terrain of the Third Front averaged double the cost of normal construction: the Chengdu–Kunming railroad cost 3.3 billion yuan (Naughton, 1988, pp157–158). Testaments to the great loss of life during construction accidents can be glimpsed today in the form of memorial markers near tunnels and ravines.

Environmental costs

Siting Panzhihua at the foot of high surrounding mountains, where emissions from the plant were trapped, caused severe pollution problems. Prevailing winds blew polluted air out of the valley during the day and back in at night. To exacerbate matters, temperature inversions often trapped pollution beneath warmer air masses, so that not even the tallest chimney could carry emissions out of the area. Moreover, for economic and political reasons, the 274 pollution and wastewater control devices that the plans originally called for were never installed. In 1975, after environmental monitoring began, the steel mill's particulate emissions were 2,197.5 milligrams per cubic metre, more than 218 times above the national recommendation, and those of the sintering plant were more than 320 times above it. A 1984 medical investigation showed that nearly 3 per cent of workers had lung diseases (Sichuansheng, 1994, pp157–158).

Water pollution was also severe. Because human health was not considered during the design phase, the steel plant was situated upriver from human settlements, and toxic wastes spewed directly into the river to become part of household water supplies. Eventually, more than 400 factories, 51 of them with heavy industrial output, were sited on the Jinsha River. During the 1970s, when water pollution was largely uncontrolled and sanitary conditions poor, infectious diseases were rampant; the official *Panzhihua Record* states that dysentery and hepatitis were common (Sichuansheng, 1994, pp328–330). One man who arrived in 1973 recalled that the Jinsha River had been yellow with pollution.

There were other environmental issues, as well. Panzhihua's enduring soil pollution by toxic metals is not surprising in an environment in which chemicals and metals were so heavily and carelessly used. Moreover, the extent of deforestation increased steadily, leaving the area surrounding Panzhihua almost completely barren. Under the influence of the Leap and 'learning from Dazhai', according to the official *Panzhihua Record*, deforestation climbed from lands at 1300 metres to those at 1500 metres above sea level. After Panzhihua was founded in 1965, three unnamed foreign countries were permitted to log heavily, extending deforestation to 1700 metres above sea level and reducing overall forest cover in the region to 24.22 per cent. 'From dense, to sparse, to barren', comments the *Panzhihua Record*. The result was terrible erosion (Sichuansheng, 1994, pp131, 331). A high-ranking planning official acknowledged past mistakes: 'In 1965, everything was in the service of producing steel. There was no environmental bureau in Panzhihua until 1979. In the early years, we were surrounded on all sides by enemies. War-preparation was the only consideration.'

A local Environmental Protection Bureau employee spoke more specifically about Panzhihua's location as the source of a host of problems:

The main plant should have been in a more open place, a less densely concentrated place. At the time, transport and politics were the only considerations. The main problems come from the [location] of the plant. Now, the coking factory is the main polluter. We had two benzene spills in 1995. The water tasted strange for a week or so each time, and we put out an alert that the people should not drink it. This year, the oldest electricity generating station [the one built in a tunnel] was shut down for pollution. Now we have a new one. The biggest problem is our reliance on coal. Panzhihua is fourth in the nation in steel production after Shanghai, Wuhan and Anshan. It is so rich in resources. Everything we need to produce steel is right here in the mountains. But it wasn't necessary to place it in a mountain valley.

It is extremely unlikely that the Panzhihua steel mill will be able to meet new pollution remediation requirements, mandatory since the millennium. It is equally unlikely that a major industrial operation of such national importance, employing tens of thousands of workers, will be shut down. As it is, the city has been sharply affected by the mill's recent layoffs of several thousand steel-workers. However, a second steel production base, with a projected output of 3–4 million tonnes of steel per year (compared with Panzhihua's current 1 million tonnes), is being built in Dechang in Liangshan Prefecture to Panzhihua's north (Information Office of Sichuan Provincial People's Government, undated, p54). More attention is being given to location and pollution issues, and some of Panzhihua's operations could shift there in the future.

Panzhihua's pollution problems were typical of those caused by other Third Front industries; industrial pollution in excess of what might have been expected with better planning and more suitable locations was a major consequence of the policy. Qu and Li (1994, p40) describe the 'in mountains, dispersed, in caves' formulation as 'direct[ing] many factories to remote mountains and gorges where they subsequently discharged large amounts of pollution. If conditions for diffusion and dilution were poor, serious air and water pollution resulted.' They characterize the Third Front as an example of irrational distribution of industry, with serious environmental consequences because mountain gorges often trapped industrial air pollution, while mountain streams frequently could not assimilate and dilute the influx of large quantities of chemicals.

Today, the Panzhihua steel mill and other factories remain sources of serious pollution of the Jinsha and Yalong rivers, which are among the headwaters of the Yangzi River. Deforestation has contributed to serious soil erosion and water siltation, and location problems and inadequate investment in pollution remediation have created ongoing health problems for local residents. Panzhihua hopes to become a major tourist destination and economic powerhouse for the region. If these goals are to be realized, environmental concerns must be a major priority.

The human and cultural tolls remain. Even today, Panzhihua's residents often retain a deep sense of affiliation with others from their home province. A journalist told me: 'After all these years, we Wuhan people still have a special connection. We spend the holidays together, more than 30 years after our arrival. We eat together and commemorate those who died because of the heavy work.' However, the younger generation may be losing this sense of connection to their parents' homes. A young woman whose parents came from another part of Sichuan province told me that the people of Panzhihua have blended into something that is not quite Sichuanese, not quite anything else. She seemed to take her connection to Panzhihua for granted in a way that her elders did not, indicating that, for a new generation, the deep Chinese sense of place may be dissipating. She and other young people to whom I spoke also complained vocally about Panzhihua's environmental problems and seemed deeply concerned about resolving them.

As the Panzhihua story demonstrates, locating heavy industry in remote mountainous valleys is obviously unwise from an environmental perspective. Air pollution is trapped in mountain basins and valleys; chemical effluents all too often seriously pollute river headwaters and streams. Ecosystems can be harmed when roads and railroads are built through rugged territory to facilitate transport of supplies and workers, as they can when land ill suited to agriculture is converted to farmland to feed relocated workers. Creating transportation routes through wilderness areas can extensively degrade ecosystems, as the heated controversy over the International Development Bank's funding of a highway through the Amazonian rainforest suggests. Similar debate rages over the propriety of US Forestry Service road-building activities in government-owned wilderness areas. In China, the Third Front policy opened up formerly inaccessible areas through the construction of railroads and roads. The propaganda of the time boasts that the effort resulted in human footprints left everywhere.

Conclusion

Today, Panzhihua is a city with great ambitions. An airport is under construction nearby, and the enormous Ertan Dam on the Yalong River, a few hours' drive from the steel mill, was completed in 1998 with a huge World Bank loan of US$1.2 billion. At 240 metres tall, it is the highest dam in China (until completion of the Three Gorges Dam) and the third highest in Asia. Despite the enormous human and environmental costs, some may see Panzhihua as one of the few Third Front success stories in that it did, indeed, give China access to a wealth of mineral resources, while the Chengdu–Kunming railroad associated with the project opened up a great section of the country. Mobilizing so many people to realize such difficult goals may seem to speak for the strengths of Maoism. Yet these achievements were won through the involuntary participation of thousands, through great suffering and loss of human life, and through the diversion of precious resources that other areas of China needed for development.[10]

Most of the hundreds of Third Front factories were impractical and ineffi-cient. Out of four large steel mills built as part of the Third Front, only Panzhihua ever approached its intended capacity, and several others were com-plete failures. In 1985, well into economic reforms, China adopted a plan for dealing with these problematic Third Front dinosaurs. Some were closed down or merged into other units, and 121 were moved back to medium-sized cities or whence they came, including 24 slated for removal to Chongqing. Even so, as many as half of Third Front projects are still in place (Naughton, 1988, p83), the most famous of which, in addition to Panzhihua, are the Mianyang Television Factory and the Shiyan Number Two Automobile Factory. Many people relocated to the interior with the Third Front have not gone home. In Guizhou, as in Panzhihua, for example, such resettlements have left a diverse population unusual in an insulated inland province; for such a poor area, the region has unusual capacity in such high-tech products as optical instruments and precision bearings (Liang and Shapiro, 1986, p181; Naughton, 1988, p356, 377). These industries and their employees, struggling with a legacy of poor location and irrational investment, and having endured great hardships for many years because of Third Front demands, are now under immense pres-sure to become profitable against huge odds.

As Third Front architects boasted in 1970, there are now human traces in almost all of China, and few ecosystems have been left unaltered. The legacy of the Third Front can be seen in oddly situated factories and in railroads through mountain regions that under other circumstances would have been bypassed. While any country might eventually have wished to open up interior regions and exploit the mineral resources of places such as Panzhihua, the strategically driven Third Front development was premature and came at an unnecessarily high economic and environmental price, much of which is still being paid today. During the Cultural Revolution, China was not ready to develop and industrialize its interior in a responsible and sustainable fashion. However, at the time the incursions into inland China must have seemed to Mao the very definition of national transformation, since the Western coun-tries he sought to equal had been engaged in unfettered development as well.

With the easing of military tensions after the visit of US President Richard Nixon in 1972, the 'prepare for war' slogan was replaced with a milder for-mulation: 'seize revolution, promote production, promote work, promote war preparation' (Zhang and Li, 1998, p356). Mao grew increasingly infirm, and his 'war against nature' went into retreat. Motivated, in part, by several cases of severe industrial pollution, in 1972 China participated in the United Nations Conference on the Human Environment (UNCHE) in Stockholm. This marked a turning point in China's attention to environmental issues and a departure from the official position that environmental problems could occur only in capitalist countries. Environmental institutions were established and gradually strengthened, regulations were issued and principles such as 'polluter pays' and reuse of the 'three wastes' (liquid, gas and residue), briefly propounded during the early 1950s, were revived and promulgated (Qu and Li, 1994, p3). However, the Communist Party did not relinquish Mao's notion that with will, all difficulties could be overcome. In 1974, the Environmental Protection Leading Group under the State Council set targets to control pollution within five years and eliminate it within ten (Xie, 1999). Of course, such problems have only become worse.

Under the reforms – despite the high priority assigned to environmental issues, the impressive group of environmental laws and regulations promulgated, and the integration of 'sustainable development' goals within national planning – China's environmental difficulties have increased. Environmental measures have not kept pace with rapid economic growth, population pressures and rising consumer expectations. However, devastating floods and some of the world's worst urban pollution have strongly focused the nation's energy on environmental issues. China has made enormous investments in pollution remediation, phasing in international environmental standards and shutting down polluting factories; new nature reserves are being created and existing ones are being more seriously respected; and anti-logging laws are not only being enacted, but are being enforced. It remains to be seen whether these efforts will turn China's environmental situation around.

One source of wisdom that is not being tapped, however, is an honest evaluation of the Mao era's environmental mistakes. These include, as we have seen, the perceived urgency of the security situation during the war preparation campaign, which induced Mao and his followers to shift resources away from basic needs in order to develop remote parts of China in environmentally and economically inappropriate ways. These choices were made without public discussion, and even dissent within the Communist Party was suppressed. The implementation of the Third Front campaign involved a high degree of coercion, forcible relocations, great human sacrifice, and widespread human suffering. It also polluted river headwaters, established industrial settlements in mountainous regions where air pollution would always be chronic, and exploited mineral resources where supporting infrastructure was extremely difficult and expensive to establish. The case thus provides a starkly cautionary example of the environmental and human repercussions of a set of policy decisions based purely on security concerns, open discussion of which might be instructive as China seeks a way out of its environmental predicaments.

Chapter 6

The 'Troubled Modernizer': Three Decades of Chinese Environmental Policy and Diplomacy

Yuka Kobayashi

Introduction

Since China opened its doors in 1978, it has become a more active participant in international environmental protection regimes. However, governments of the North and non-governmental organizations (NGOs) criticize China as a laggard and an obstructive, uncooperative actor in environmental regimes. Some analysts attribute this to the fact that China is a problematic 'realist' actor in foreign relations, which does not adhere to the liberal assumptions upon which environmental regimes are based. Against this, however, one needs to consider the extensive domestic implementation efforts that China has been making in order to comply with international environmental agreements. To criticize China as an uncooperative actor in international environmental regimes risks being simplistic.

While being polemical and using recalcitrant rhetoric in international negotiations, China has recognized the fact that environmental protection is important. Awareness of its importance has increased at the leadership level, resulting in a heightened profile for environmental issues in China's foreign relations. This has led to a proliferation of domestic environmental organizations, especially since the late 1980s. However, while implementing many measures to comply with environmental protection at the domestic level, China still does not have the capacity to enforce environmental protection.

Moreover, China does not want to be formally constrained in its domestic policies, nor does it want to be perceived by developing countries as being weak in its dealings with developed countries. As a result, China has adopted a strategy of becoming the unofficial leader of the Third World in international environmental negotiations, where a large divide has emerged between the North and South. Aligning with India, China has been advocating the interests of developing countries by refusing any kind of commitment that would impede economic development. The role China has taken as leader of the developing world and its domestic constraints have sometimes forced it to be more uncooperative in international environmental affairs than it would actually like to be.

This chapter outlines the main impediments that prevent China from being as proactive as it needs to be in environmental protection. These constraints at both the international and domestic level, and their interplay, explain Chinese cooperativeness in environmental regimes.[1] In order to place China's environmental problems in context, the evolution of China's environmental predicaments are first analysed. This is followed by a history of China's environmental diplomacy from 1972. Finally, the chapter analyses China's implementation of international environmental agreements, and explains why China is a 'troubled modernizer' rather than the recalcitrant actor in environmental regimes that Northern governments and NGOs make it out to be.

The evolution of environmental protection in China

China's leaders have always had regard for the environment. However, their source is different from the Western notion of environmental protection. According to the *Tian Ming* (Mandate of Heaven), emperors were judged according to whether there were natural disasters (for example, floods) during their rule (Ross and Silk, 1987, p1). The emperor's main concern was how to feed a growing population with limited resources, which is still true of leaders today. For example, the Communist Party and the *danwei's* (work unit's) top priority is feeding the population.

In order to understand China's environmental situation, it is useful to appreciate inherent physical problems and historical legacies. Physical problems with China's environment, such as resource availability, geographical make-up and demographic factors (for example, rising population) are timeless and fixed. These factors have always posed problems for China in environmental protection, irrespective of which political regime was in power. Historical legacies have also imposed serious constraints upon addressing environmental protection. Mao Zedong's influence still remains strong and presents serious impediments to environmental protection. This was exacerbated by post-1978 Deng Xiaoping reforms that promoted economic efficiency. These factors provide the foundation and shape the context for China's environmental stance today.

Physical problems

China has an unusually low endowment of natural gas, and clean energy sources are located in inaccessible regions in the northwest. Thus coal – the primary cause of indoor air pollution and acid rain – is the basic source of fuel for China. High-quality coal is exported, leaving the poor-quality coal for domestic use that accounts for 75 per cent of China's energy.[2] Demographic factors exacerbate the situation. Traditional Chinese culture advocated large families, and Maoist encouragement of pro-natalist policies helped to double the population from 1949 to 1979, adding even greater stress on the environment (Faust and Kornberg, 1995, p231). Because of the extensive over-farming needed to feed the population, policies such as *yi liang wei gang* (make grain the primary crop) for increased grain production were introduced. Moreover, most of the population is concentrated in the coastal regions, putting further pressure on the environment.

Historical legacies

Many of China's environmental problems are embedded in historical precedents that have shaped Chinese attitudes and activities. Although some studies show that environmental problems existed before the founding of the People's Republic of China in 1949, this problem intensified with Mao (Edmonds, 1998; Elvin and Liu, 1998).

Maoist views and policies

When China opened its doors in 1978, the view given to the capitalist states was that the centrally planned economy had improved environmental protection since there was less competition within industries compared to market economies (Kitagawa, 2000, p35). In reality, Maoist views and policies had little regard for the environment, with devastating effects upon it. Although one could argue that the low personal consumption policies advocated by Mao – the prohibition of private cars and his efforts to curtail urbanization after 1961 – had the effect of saving the country from environmental damage, they were not designed specifically to protect the environment, and any positive effects were externalities (Lieberthal, 1995, p282). Isolationism had kept the outside world oblivious to China's environmental problems until the 1980s, and the Cold War resulted in communist countries giving capitalist countries the impression that environmental degradation was an evil of capitalism (Sanwa Sougou Kenkyujyo, 1997, p192). This view was expressed by

Chang Hsien-Wu, Chinese delegate to the 1972 United Nations Conference on the Human Environment (UNCHE) in Stockholm, who blamed atmospheric pollution on capitalists, imperialists, colonialists and the neo-colonialism of the superpowers (UN, 1973).

Mao's worldview was so powerful that, despite some of Deng's modifications, it remains to a large degree China's worldview today. Mao suffered through China's history of foreign domination, and thus developed an obsession with sovereignty, a fear of intervention and a suspicion of foreigners. This 'victimization complex' conditions the thinking of many Chinese. Mao also took a very particular view of the environment. He saw the environment as a 'common good' that could be put to positive use. This is in contrast to the dominant Western view of the environment being a 'common heritage' or private property that needed to be preserved (Lu and Walsh, 1992, p16). As a result, most of China's forests were claimed by the state, with the remainder being collectivized (Ross and Silk, 1987, p2). According to Mao, nature was seen as something to be conquered, and this materialist attitude towards nature still remains strong among government officials (Edmonds, 1998, p726).

Mao's environmental views resulted in a number of other legacies that have posed serious problems for environmental protection in China. These legacies fall into the general categories of reckless development policies, weak rule of law and lack of awareness.

Reckless development policies

Mao copied the Soviet-style centrally planned economy, which emphasized heavy industry, forced industrialization and media censorship (Tang, 1993b, pp89–103), and which focused on maximizing industrial output without regard for environmental impact (Ross and Silk, 1985, p67). Thus, 'at the local level, factory managers were judged by their ability to increase productivity, and therefore they had no incentive to engage in the non-productive diversion of resources into installing pollution-control equipment' (Ross and Silk, 1985, p67). Development was important, and economic growth was one vital source of legitimacy for Mao (Breslin, 1997, pp497–508).

Examples of such policies include the First Five-Year Plan of 1953–1957, which put eight times as much investment into heavy industry as into light industry (Smil, 1984, p195). This was followed by the Great Leap Forward (1958–1967), in which Mao was 'fantasizing about a world being shaken by 60 million tonnes of Chinese steel by the year 1962' (Smil, 1984, p195). The strength of such a system was in its ability to mobilize resources for rapid economic development (Lieberthal, 1995, p280). Strong industrial ministries looked after their own interests and paid little attention to externalities or to the effects of their decisions on other issues such as the environment (Shirk, 1993, p24).

Mao's ideas were also found in the 'Four Modernizations', one of the pillars of developmental policy in China to this day (Shirk, 1993, p65). The Four Modernizations stress the development of agriculture, industry, science and technology, and the military, with no attention under these headings given specifically to the environment (Dreyer, 2000, pp111, 145). This developmental policy was pushed further after the Cultural Revolution (1966–1976) in order for China to recover as speedily as possible from the economic and social chaos of that period. Following the Cultural Revolution, China developed rapidly, with an average annual economic growth rate of about 10 per cent that continues to this day. However, this has meant that environmental degradation has occurred at a fast pace.

During the Maoist era, not only were there rapid growth programmes that indirectly worsened environmental degradation, but there were additional factors that directly damaged the environment: environmental and safety regulations were lax; inefficient production technologies were adopted; and pricing policies systematically encouraged waste of natural resources. This trend is still strong, with insufficient investment in energy efficiency, delayed price reform and heavily subsidized energy prices (Society for Environmental Economics and Policy Studies, 1998, p221).

Rule of law

Although Article 46 of the Environmental Protection Law stipulates that international treaties should take precedence over domestic law, the effect of such an article is nullified because law does not have much weight in China. If environmental protection is an interplay between 'politics', 'economics', and 'law', with all three having equal importance, this is problematic because 'law' is weak in China. In China, 'law' refers to a loose collection of 'ideas' (Greenfield, 1979, p29). This approach sees law as an instrument of state policy, which is in contrast to the Western notion of law, upheld by the principle of the 'rule of law' based on the strict separation of powers of administration, legislation and the judiciary.[3] As in the proverb *'Shang you zhengce, xia you duice'* ('With policy above, there is solution below'), policy comes before law and is given more weight. China has traditionally been ruled by men rather than by law (*renji*), and today is ruled by the leaders of the Communist Party (Ross and Silk, 1987, pp4, 10). During the Great Leap Forward and the Cultural Revolution, ideology took priority over law, and today policy interests continue to receive more attention than adherence to the law.

As a result, it has been difficult to build respect for environmental law in China. A recent Chinese environmental awareness report stated that although the Chinese public was becoming more aware of environmental degradation, actual knowledge of legal requirements is still lacking. In 1996, only 0.5 per cent of the general public had an understanding of environmental law, while

70 per cent of the population had, for the most part, 'only heard of' or 'not even heard of' environmental law or regulation (Kitagawa, 2000, p160). Since the late 1980s, China has passed many environmental laws. However, improvements remain superficial because the problem of environmental protection lies at a fundamental level in the very concept of law.

Lack of public awareness

One of the most fundamental environmental problems from the Maoist era is the lack of public awareness. During the Maoist years, the country was under strict government control, with very little room for freedom of speech and environmental rights to develop (Ross and Silk, 1987, p12). The media was censored, with only information about rapid industrialization being reported. Data on pollution was rarely available, making grassroots organizing almost totally constrained (Tang, 1993b, p91). Moreover, environmental consciousness was low among China's leaders under Mao, and with such a top-down societal structure there were no environmental protection groups to motivate environmental protection, unlike in democratic societies (Ross and Silk, 1988a, p136).

The Cultural Revolution worsened the situation by increasing chaos and isolation. Most Chinese were totally unaware of the international environmental movement, which was beginning in the industrialized world. China dismantled educational institutions, discouraged knowledge and debate, and the intelligentsia – referred to as the *chou lao jiu* ('stinking ninth category') – had been converted into a despised outcast group with no social standing. China was behind the West in technology and science, and relied on outside assistance. However, isolationism impeded the acquisition of information about environmental protection. The outside world was oblivious to China's environmental problems, and China's inability to obtain a seat in the United Nations (UN) before 1971 meant there was little outsiders could do.

Post-1978 Deng reforms

Deng Xiaoping's policies were pragmatic, open and market oriented. Deng believed that bureaucratic control stifled change and efficiency, and sought to decentralize power, allowing the economy to develop outside the non-competitive sector of the state economy, while also consolidating the rule of the Communist Party (Lieberthal, 1995, p127). Some of Deng's market mechanisms have increased environmental damage, while others have increased incentives to utilize resources more wisely, thus limiting environmental damage. Decentralization gave officials at the provincial level the means and incentives to develop their local economies, often increasing environmental problems. At the same time, the move away from the centralized economy made the industrial ministries and the State Planning Commission far less powerful (Jahiel, 1998, p757). Profitability and market prices for natural resources to some degree increased incentives to have efficient and environmentally less harmful production (Lieberthal, 1995, p282).

The environment was still not the highest priority in China during the 1980s, but the Sixth Five-Year Plan of 1982 (Chapter 35) and the Seventh Five-Year Plan of 1986 (Chapter 52) did devote one entire chapter each to the discussion of the environment (Ross and Silk, 1988a, pp3–4, 291–295). There was also some modification in media and NGO control during the 1978 reforms. However, these modifications were limited, and the state still controls much of the media. NGOs have to conform to governmental regulations and lack the ability to criticize environmental policy.

Deng's reforms have had some impact on environmental protection; but its overall effect is too early to assess. However, Chinese leaders still stress development and put raising the output of the economy as their highest priority. This makes it difficult for protective means to keep pace.

China's environmental diplomacy

Maoist views and reckless policies worsened the already existing geographical and demographical constraints on environmental protection. Deng's reforms accelerated development, exacerbating environmental degradation even more. China, as a developing country, must continue to feed its growing population, and believes that development and the eradication of poverty must come before environmental protection. Environmental protection with 'Chinese characteristics' means sustaining the environment for development. Song Jian, former chairman of the National Environmental Protection Agency, or NEPA (State Environmental Protection Agency, or SEPA, since 1998) and leader of the environmental movement in China, stated at the 1992 UN Conference on Environment and Development (UNCED): 'To talk about environment in isolation from ecological development and technological progress means an environmental protection devoid of environmental policies' (Jian, 1992, p12). In China, protecting the environment and development are two sides of the same coin (Guowuyuan Guoji Jishi Yanjiusou, 1996, p5). However, as was made clear in the 1998 National People's Congress, the primary goal for Chinese economic policy has been, and remains, rapid economic growth, with environmental protection being secondary (Jahiel, 1998, p787).

China's problems with environmental protection have geographical, demographical, ideological and historical origins that affect its level of cooperation. This results in the particular Chinese definition of 'sustainable development', which becomes an impediment in the negotiations for environmental cooperation. Environmental values and economic growth are related (Hishida, 1998, p11) and, in the case of China, the traditional and cultural importance of agriculture emphasizes the correlation. Thus, locally observable impacts of water supply, sewage and local pollution such as air pollution have become major concerns for China, while global environmental problems such as climate change are still deemed relatively unimportant. The Chinese stance has been one that balances geographical, demographical and historical constraints, as well as the tension between economics and Chinese environmental values. These factors have strongly shaped China's negotiating behaviour on the environment.

Beginnings of environmental diplomacy

In October 1971, at the same time as its entry into the UN, China first introduced environmental issues at the policy level. It convened a small governmental committee under the State Planning Council to prepare for the country's participation in the 1972 UNCHE at Stockholm (Ross and Silk, 1998b, pp810–81). Premier Zhou Enlai saw the conference as another means of re-establishing political and economic ties with the rest of the world, and arranged for a delegation to participate in UNCHE (Economy, 1997a, p267). China was viewed as a laggard participant since it opposed inclusion of the Vietnam War and nuclear testing in the conference declaration. However, it was active in the debates, and its vocal contributions comprised the Ten Cardinal Principles on Amending the 'Declaration on [the] Human Environment'.

The Ten Cardinal Principles argued that imperialist and capitalist policies of developed countries, population growth, development, war and nuclear weapons cause environmental pollution. Due to this historical responsibility, developed countries should pay compensation for international pollution (the 'polluter pays' principle), assist economic advancement, establish an 'international environment' and buy advanced technology to provide to developing countries at less than market price. On the other hand, developing countries reserve the right to shape their own environmental policy and exploit and utilize their natural resources in accordance with their own conditions, since economic development is indispensable for conservation. China also called for international cooperation and exchanges in scientific/technological knowledge on environment as long as it did not interfere with another country's internal affairs (*Peking Review*, 3 June 1972, pp8–11, 16 June 16 1972, pp4–8, 13).

At UNCHE, China became a voluntary leader of the developing world, advocating the Ten Cardinal Principles in support of developing countries' interests. While acknowledging the seriousness of environmental problems and the need to look after the environment, it placed the responsibility for pollution on the industrialized countries. China took an independent approach to its international relations – forming a Group of One – and has been apprehensive about entering into formal developing world coalitions (Kim, 1994, p407). However, it also recognized that siding with other developing countries would ensure Chinese interests, and promote China in the international arena. There was also a shared history of imperialist invasion among developing world countries, which generated cordial relationships and also resulted in China negotiating many international agreements as the 'Group of 77 [developing countries] and China' (Snow, 1994).

China sided with other developing countries to have the headquarters of the UN Environment Programme (UNEP) headquartered in Nairobi (Kim, 1992, p118). Since most developing world countries were newly independent, nation-building was their primary concern, and they were sensitive to the issues of sovereignty and 'eco-colonialism', where powerful countries supposedly imposed their environmental ideals on the struggling economies of the developing countries (Easterbrook and Palmer, 1997). The developing countries viewed development as being harmonious with nature and saw poverty, underdevelopment and overpopulation as root causes of environmental problems (UN, 1973).

After Stockholm, China became increasingly active in international environmental affairs, particularly at the rhetorical level. It participated in international dialogue and treaty-making processes, played prominent roles in several international environmental organizations, and accepted various environmental norms, provided there were no strong enforcement measures. One incentive was to become the legitimate representative of China by driving Taiwan out of negotiations during the early stages of China's re-entry into international organizations (Economy and Oksenberg, 1998, p353). Beijing's leaders were also increasingly concerned about their international image, reputation and credibility, especially given their growing dependence on financial aid, technological transfer and trade with the global economy (Hao, 1992, pp155, 166). By 1997, Beijing relied on 80 per cent of its environmental protection budget from abroad (Economy, 1997a, p278). Today, it is the largest recipient of environmental aid from the Japanese and the World Bank, and receives extensive resources from the Global Environmental Facility (GEF), the Asian Development Bank and the United Nations Development Programme (UNDP).

Change or continuity? The 1980s and beyond

During the 1980s there were three developments that accelerated Chinese activism in international environmental protection. First, environmental problems became more transboundary and global in character. Compared with earlier environmental problems that were deemed to be relatively local, global environmental issues such as ozone depletion and global warming required international cooperation. China's leverage increased, since its sheer size and population gave it tremendous influence over these issue areas. The Chinese government's realization of this 'environmental power' resulted in increased

Chinese activism. The international community also recognized China's importance, and in 1997 the Worldwatch Institute's annual *State of the World* report stated that the 'fate of the earth' lies with 'environmental heavy weights', including China (Flavin, 1997, pp7–10). Second, as a result of increased participation, China learned that active participation in regime formation could be to its own interest. China desired to take part in formulating international environmental regimes. Rather than keeping a low-key presence and complying with rules made by other states, by participating in the early stages of regime formation, it could have more of its interests reflected and set the rules of the game.

Third, China was increasingly turning towards the developing world, especially after the isolation imposed after the Tiananmen bloodshed of 4 June 1989. The ending of the Cold War had decreased China's leverage in the Washington–Beijing–Moscow relationship and this became even more pronounced after Tiananmen (Hao, 1992, p160). Fear of isolationism came to dominate Beijing's priorities in foreign relations, resulting in increased exchanges with developing world countries. Newly established international environmental regimes provided an opportunity for China to appeal to the developing world by way of advocating rules favourable to developing countries. Normalization of relations with India, helped by Rajiv Gandhi's 1988 visit to Beijing, also provided China with a basis for cooperation with India in forming developing world coalitions (Xinhua, 1999). The developing world coalition led by China and India was key for the success of the South's position during the late 1980s' ozone negotiations, and became the negotiating approach in the biodiversity and climate change regimes during the 1990s.

Recently, Chinese officials have summarized China's objectives in environmental diplomacy as follows:

- gain international status;
- develop environmental industries;
- advance sustainable development;
- gain aid and technological transfer;
- increase national security;
- push for developing world equity; and
- exercise leverage over the US (Cao et al, 1998, pp171–181).

Environmental diplomacy has started to receive attention due to its potential benefits as elucidated above. Domestic scholars have been encouraged to further research on how environmental diplomacy can be utilized to China's best interests (Cao et al, 1998; Zhao and Li, 1998). As developments at the international and domestic level paved the way for increased participation in international environmental diplomacy, China has entered into many international environmental regimes, followed by related domestic environmental legislation and regulations (Wang et al, 1999). These measures have gradually built up China's capacity to participate in international environmental diplomacy, resulting in increased involvement.

China played a key role in negotiations leading to the 1987 Montreal Protocol on ozone depletion and its 1990 London amendments. It aligned with India to advocate developing countries' interests, arguing that since developed countries were responsible for most of the damage, they should bear the cost of solving the ozone problem. This strong developing world coalition resulted in the establishment of a multilateral ozone fund to support the development and implementation of chlorofluorocarbon substitutes in developing countries (Economy, 1998, p272). China and India cooperated in bargaining for US$80 million during the first three years after their accession to the Montreal Protocol, to be followed by larger sums in the future (Rajan, 1997, p265). By 1998, China had launched 173 projects on ozone depletion with the help of US$105.6 million from the multilateral fund (Economy, 1998, p279).

The success in ozone had the effect of promoting China's drive for developing world coalition-building. The Chinese aspiration manifested itself in the convening of the 1991 Beijing Ministerial Conference of Developing Countries on the Environment and Development, where 41 developing countries gathered to create a united bargaining front for UNCED. The resulting Beijing Declaration was a reiteration of the Ten Cardinal Principles from UNCHE (Economy, 1998, p279). These principles also constituted China's position on climate change, established during the 1990s (Johnston, 1998a, p581). This highlights that the Chinese stance in environmental negotiations has not changed since 1972.

At UNCED, the Chinese delegation was largely engaged in polemics and reflected support for developing country interests over those of the developed countries. However, China was the first major state (and fifth overall) to ratify the Convention on Biological Diversity (CBD) and the Framework Convention on Climate Change (UNFCCC). These framework conventions (which set out broad guidelines in the beginning, leaving the specifics to be negotiated later) were suited to the negotiating style of China, which preferred to sign general, aspirational agreements (Kreisberg, 1994).

China learned from the ozone negotiations that it should not be a latecomer to a regime, so in contrast to ozone, where the South allowed the North to set the agenda and then fought a rearguard action to secure its interests, China participated from the beginning in the establishment of biodiversity and climate change regimes (Rajan, 1997, p264). As such, China would have more say in formulating the regime and greater opportunities to have its interests reflected. Due to its long history of isolationism, China was quite sensitive to the fact that it came late to defining rules in international relations, and thus has been proactive in stating its place in international forums. However, China's level of participation differs when comparing the environmental issues of biodiversity and climate change. It was more active in biodiversity, since it did not impose as much of a constraint on economic development. Developing countries are generally more reluctant to see the imposition of any binding or even voluntary obligations on themselves, especially where these might impede economic growth (Ross and Silk, 1998b, pp817–818). Showing these characteristics of a developing country, China was the 37th state to sign the Kyoto Protocol to the UNFCCC.

China's *de facto* leadership of the developing world forces it to represent the greater interests of the South, sometimes jeopardizing its own interests. This is most evident in the case of climate change, where the clash between North and South is most apparent. China pushed hard for *voluntary* reporting of greenhouse gas emissions, and opposed all efforts to require publication of regular progress reviews of greenhouse gas emissions (Economy, 1997, p273). One NGO observer commented that India, China and Brazil were often referred to as the 'Gang of Three', since they were difficult to get along with and had a poor attitude (Economy, 1997a, p273). However, despite its uncooperative international behaviour, in 1994 China was the first country to develop a domestic version of the UNCED's Agenda 21 on sustainable development. This reiterated China's position of economic development being in harmony with the environment and the importance of international cooperation as long as it was respectful of sovereignty.

Although combating climate change would impose great restraints on the economy, if China did not implement environmental protection measures, then it would be much affected by global warming. Sea-level change would alter a vast proportion of its invaluable coastline regions, resulting in a mass displacement of its citizens. Many of the domestic measures that were taken point to a desire to be proactive in climate change policy. However, China's international rhetoric in negotiations shows a very recalcitrant actor. On the much disputed point of mechanisms under the UNFCCC, China – which seemed well aware that technological transfers would be in its interests – pushed a stance that was against mechanisms, in general, due to pressure from the South to do so (see Kobayashi, 2003).

Compared to the Indians, the Chinese were more traditionally pragmatic, and were willing to sacrifice their principles for financial and technological assistance and 'were willing to cut a deal' (Economy, 1994, p190, and Rajan, 1997). However, throughout international environmental negotiations, there were cases where China had to ignore its immediate self-interest in order to secure its longer-term interest in retaining support from the developing states. But, in domestic actions, China does not have to lead the developing world, and thus we are able to see the other side of China, which is not the recalcitrant trouble-maker in environmental protection, but, rather, one trying to keep its development in step with environmental protection.

Domestic implementation of international conventions

Since the 1972 UNCHE in Stockholm, China's rhetoric in multilateral negotiations has continued to be polemical. However, China has become a signatory of international environmental conventions, and domestically has introduced implementation measures to comply with international environmental requirements as long as they do not constrain its interests. In 1971, China established an environmental body under the State Planning Commission (Wang et al, 1999, p104). After exposure to the international environmental movement, China convened the 1973 First National Environmental Protection Conference in Beijing, and additional environmental protection agencies were created at central and local levels.

After the reforms of 1978, China was more engaged internationally; as a result, it came under greater pressure to be cooperative in environmental protection. Deng's 1982 structural reforms established the new Ministry of Urban and Rural Construction and Environmental Protection, the main domestic environmental institution (Wang et al, 1999, p104). Many laws were passed during the 1980s and 1990s (Foreign Ministry of Japan, 1997), and by 1997, China had promulgated 6 environmental laws, 9 resource conservation laws and 28 environmental regulatory laws (Palmer, 1998, p798). These domestic environmental laws were passed so that China could comply and become signatory to the many environmental regimes.

Beijing held the Second National Environmental Conference during 1983–1984, and subsequently the State Council issued a 'Decision on Strengthening Environmental Protection' and established the *Zhongguo Huanjing Bao* (*China Environmental Report*), a monthly publication exploring environmental issues and exposing environmental wrongdoings (Economy, 1998, p278). During the same year the Environmental Protection Commission (EPC) was set up under the State Council to coordinate all agencies involved in environmental protection. The EPC became the National Environmental Protection Agency (NEPA) in 1983, being responsible for all aspects of environmental policy development and implementation. Later, in March 1988, NEPA was elevated to the vice-ministerial level directly under the State Council. While China kept its recalcitrant rhetoric at the international level, domestically it was doing much to keep up with environmental protection requirements. UNEP's executive director even declared that 'China is on the right track. I think it is taking environmental issues very seriously'(Xinhua, 1997).

Although China has introduced many measures domestically, enforcement continues to be a problem due to weak environmental laws and implementing institutions. NEPA was a sub-ministerial organ that was overpowered by the industrial ministries and provinces that it was supposed to supervise. Since 1985, the responsibility of environmental protection was given to the mayors of each city (or county administrators and governors of each province), while the making of national policy remained a highly elite-driven process (Lu and Walsh, 1992, p3). Technical guidance was given by NEPA, but administrative direction was the responsibility of the local governments (Shirk, 1994, p82). This structure of dual leadership by NEPA and local governments meant that environmental officials were unable to discipline the actions of local governments.

Increasing international concern for the environment did have some bearing on environmental protection in China. Though initially a low priority compared to local pollution, China has responded to the external pressure to address climate change. In 1990 the multi-agency National Coordination Panel on Climate Change was established, and in 1992 the State Council's EPC issued a document entitled *Woguo Guanyu Quanqiu Wentide Yuanze Lichang* (*Our Country's Fundamental Policy Towards Global Environmental Problems*) (restricted circulation document on file with author). This was a result of a domestic consensus reached between the various ministries involved in environmental protection and increased activism on part of the Chinese government.

There was also an increased motivation for the many powerful governmental agencies, such as the State Planning Commission and the Ministry of Science and Technology, to get their share of the 'environmental pie' (Jahiel, 1998, p786). From 1992 to 1997, 5 per cent of all World Bank loans to China were concerned with the environment, and other development agencies such as the Asian Development Bank and foreign governments have also been increasing their loans for environmental projects. The World Bank made China the biggest recipient of its total environmental aid, and began to insist on environmental impact statements as part of the documentation for its projects (Lieberthal, 1995, p283). As part of China's endeavours to signal to the international forums its pro-activeness in environmental protection, it held the Third National Environmental Conference in 1989 and the fourth in 1996, with both the head of the Communist Party (Jiang Zemin) and head of state (Li Peng) in attendance (Jahiel, 1998, p773). The investment in environmental projects was increased from 0.7 to 1.2 per cent of gross domestic product, and fuel subsidies were lowered by 50 per cent after 1990 (WRI, 1997). In addition, China established a vast network of governmental institutions to deal with environmental problems at the national, provincial and local levels, and in 1998 NEPA was replaced by the State Environmental Protection Administration (SEPA) with full ministerial power.

However, SEPA is essentially still a domestic ministry with the international dimensions of the environment primarily dealt with by the Ministry of Foreign Affairs (MOFA). MOFA is one of the more conservative ministries. It still weighs economic development and other foreign policy issues, such as security and human rights, over the environment. Thus, we see more recalcitrant rhetoric from MOFA delegation members in international environmental negotiations than we might anticipate from SEPA's efforts at the domestic level.

Conclusion

Since China opened its doors, it has become more active in international environmental regimes. Generally, awareness at the leadership level has increased, resulting in a heightened profile for environmental issues in Chinese foreign relations. In keeping with this, Li Peng repeatedly stressed importance of environmental protection in the 1993 *Eighth National People's Congress Report*. There has also been a proliferation of domestic environmental organizations and extensive legislation since the late 1980s. Considering the domestic constraints imposed on China by its population, geographic situation and powerful historical legacies, China's domestic efforts are significant. Criticisms from the governments of the North and NGOs that China is an environmental laggard do not seem valid. One must not forget that it also took the developed countries time and economic development to reach a higher environmental standard. It is only natural that China, still a developing country, is behind in environmental protection in comparison to developed countries.

However, it is clear that while trying to implement domestic measures to comply with environmental protection, China does not want to be formally constrained in its activities, nor does it possess the necessary capacity for implementation. China is also reluctant to pay for environmental protection since it believes that it is the responsibility of the developed countries to do so. It is also problematic that top-level leaders, who still view the environment as being secondary to economic development, can and do overrule environmentally proactive leaders. Moreover, in international negotiations, China's strategy of uniting with the developing world has been pushing it to take a more uncooperative stance and to be more recalcitrant than it would actually like.

Looking at Chinese cooperation in environmental regimes at the international and domestic levels shows that Chinese behaviour is more complex than one would assume from the simple label of 'recalcitrant'. When we examine the complex forces at work in environmental protection, we find an image of China as a 'troubled modernizer', trying to balance rapid development with environmental protection. As the Chinese proverb '*Qiongguo bu neng wai jiao*' ('Poor countries are not good at diplomacy') would have it, China is both *Zhongguo* ('China') and a *Qiongguo* (poor country).

Chapter 7

'Panda Diplomacy': State Environmentalism, International Relations and Chinese Foreign Policy

Jonathan Harrington

Introduction

During the past 20 years, Chinese domestic and international environmental policy has taken on increasing importance in relation to China's other policy priorities. Between 1990 and 2000, China almost doubled its environmental spending to over 1 per cent of gross domestic product (GDP) (Xinhua, 2000). Almost 200,000 government workers contribute in some capacity to environmental policy-making and implementation (Ma and Ortolano, 2000). Environmental topics are widely covered in the Chinese press. On the international front, China plays an important role in global environmental conventions and protocols.

What are the factors that have engendered such interest in environmental problems on the part of the Chinese government and larger society? This chapter offers answers to this question. In doing so, it provides a framework for understanding the diverse interactions of international and domestic forces that influence China's environmental diplomacy. Following a brief introduction to theoretical approaches in the study of environmental foreign policy, the chapter argues that one way to frame the Chinese case is to think in terms of 'state environmentalism'. State environmentalism comprises the environment-related activities of governmental and state-sanctioned non-governmental organizations (NGOs). Special focus is placed on the rise of state environmentalism, the impact of changing situational contexts on policy outputs, and the roles of senior Chinese leaders and their strategic use of global environmental politics to bolster and legitimize their rule.

During the 1970s and 1980s, international forces were important in shaping China's environmental foreign policy as environmental technocrats interacted with their overseas peers. As environmental issues took on greater salience, higher-level officials saw them as a means of promoting broader Chinese interests – for example, garnering international aid and bolstering China's diplomatic position among developing countries. By the 1990s environmental diplomacy was viewed by China's leaders as an important issue area, one that could help them to escape the diplomatic isolation that resulted from the political crackdown following the Tiananmen Square massacre in 1989.

Foreign policy approaches and the environment

One of the central debates in the foreign policy literature focuses on the importance of domestic versus international factors as primary explanatory determinants of the foreign policies of states. 'Realist' international systemic approaches emphasize the anarchic nature of the international system, relative gains and security-dominated self-help strategies that motivate the actions of states. In this anarchic system, each state uses various strategies to further its power vis-à-vis other competing polities (Waltz, 1979; Keohane, 1986). Critical approaches also focus on systemic factors as major determinants of international interaction. For many writers, international class conflict is the primary driving force behind change in the international system (Wallerstein, 1980).

Neo-liberal thinkers emphasize the effect that global economic relations have on state interaction. While they accept the 'realist' assertion that the international system is essentially anarchical, they point out that self-interested state actors frequently pursue cooperative approaches when short- and/or long-term joint gains are possible. Over time, state and sub-state cooperation leads to the development of numerous institutionalized and non-institutionalized regimes that provide benefits to, and place constraints on, the actions of states (Young, 1989; Keohane et al, 1994). Another body of literature focuses on the domestic determinants of foreign policy. These approaches examine a myriad of different causal phenomena that affect foreign policy, including the psychological and operational codes of individual actors, historically based cultural traditions, bureaucratic rules and norms, and social conceptions of national identity, regime type and so forth (Katzenstein 1996; Allison, 1971; Kim, 1994).

One common shortcoming of these various theoretical orientations is that they often 'lean to one side'. They either focus on external or internal forces as primary determinants of foreign policy. Some scholars that are working to overcome this bifurcation of causal explanations emphasize the idea that foreign policy-making processes in individual states are not monolithic but, rather, follow different trajectories depending upon the situational contexts (crisis/status quo) and issue areas (high politics/low politics) involved. They also assert that policy causation is a two-way street. Domestic contexts affect the international system and vice versa (Hermann, 1969; Hagan, 1995; Gourevitch, 1978; Schraeder, 1994).

State environmentalism

The first step that must be taken to understand the diverse forces that influence Chinese environmental diplomacy is to develop a framework for analysing China's environmental policy-making and implementation apparatus. The concept of *state environmentalism* provides a useful starting point. State environmentalism refers to 'environmental activities carried out by either individuals or groups of individuals within officially sanctioned, environmentally oriented public organizations both within and outside of the official government bureaucracy that have either direct or indirect effects on the evolution of environmental politics or policy-making and/or policy enforcement' (Harrington, 2000a, p129). In China, state environmentalism:

> *... includes activities carried out within bureaucratic organs such as the State Environmental Protection Bureau, policy-making within the State Council or the Politburo, or environmental activities at various other levels of the bureaucracy, including state and local environmental protection bureaus (EPBs). It also includes environmental activities that are carried out directly under the purview of officially sanctioned environmentally oriented professional, party and mass organizations, including state autonomous organizations* (Harrington, 2000a, p129).

State environmentalism, as it is formulated here, is not a social movement in the traditional sense. There is no presumption that state environmental actors are 'united by their communication, actions and goals around a certain set of issues or vision about changing society' (Hicks, 1996, p41). Actions and not ideology are the determining factor with regard to whether or not actors are engaged in state environmentalism. There are essentially two types of state environmental actors. The first type of actor is the 'true believer'. True believers' interest in environmental policy is driven by more than their job descriptions. True believers *care* about environmental issues and share many of the characteristics of environmental social movement participants. True believers provide the moral guidance and energy behind environmental policy initiatives.

Epistemic community theory provides a useful guide to understanding how true believers organize themselves and attempt to influence foreign policy. Haas has defined an epistemic community as 'a network of professionals with recognized expertise and competence in a particular domain and an authoritative claim to policy-relevant knowledge within that domain or issue area' (Haas, 1993, p151). The logic of epistemic influence focuses on three dynamics: uncertainty, interpretation and coordination. Uncertainty creates more demand for information. As demands for information increase, epistemic communities proliferate. As policy-makers become increasingly dependent upon epistemic communities for information and interpretation of complex issues, their influence expands (Haas, 1993). However, expert status and control over information do not guarantee substantive epistemic influence. Larger systemic forces, as well as internal politics – for example, competition from communities who share different aims and goals and changing issue saliency in relation to other issue areas – all affect the potential influence of environmental epistemic communities on policy outcomes.

State environmentalism and 'careerists'

True believers are indispensable to the growth of state environmentalism. However, most bureaucrats who draft and implement regulations within the environmental bureaucracy are not true believers. Rather, they are engaged in environmental activity because, simply, it is their job. These 'careerists' care about the environment because it is in their personal interest to do so. Two driving forces behind careerist environmental activity are entrepreneurialism and standard operating procedures. Well-established procedures govern each bureaucratic unit's interaction with other units. Few alternatives are considered, uncertainty is avoided and problems are factored down in such a way that they allow organizations to 'satisfice'. Furthermore, the goals of each organizational unit are rarely integrated (Allison, 1971). Bureaucracies, however, are not completely closed to change. True believers are most likely to want change. Careerists, however, also sometimes favour incremental change if it enhances their personal power or organizational prestige (Comisso et al, 1998). When the interests of these two groups meet, positive environmental policy outcomes are more likely to occur.

State environmentalism and global eco-politics

International actors of all types, intergovernmental organizations (IGOs), large non-governmental organizations (NGOs), academic institutions and research institutes are the 'third rail' of state environmentalism. Global eco-politics is characterized by 'many heterogeneous yet interrelated social and ecological factors that have become endogenized into collectively shared and empirically researchable visions of international environmental politics' (Alker and Haas, 1993). The influence of global eco-political actors can often be felt most profoundly in polities that lack the domestic political, social and economic structures normally associated with the rise of environmental movements. In some ways, global eco-political actors can take the place of domestic environmental movement actors by providing the agenda and the technical, financial and moral support that domestic state environmental advocates so desperately need to push their policy agendas. They can also provide selective incentives to careerists to encourage them to cooperate with environmental initiatives (Young, 1989; Ross, 1998).

A multilevel analysis

A combination of changing situational and issue contexts, and the interaction of state environmental and allied international actors, has had a profound influence on the rising salience of Chinese environmental diplomacy. During the 1970s and most of the 1980s, environmental issues were relegated to the backwaters of Chinese foreign policy. This, however, did not stop the proliferation of state environmentalists and linked global eco-political issue networks. This interaction was fostered by the general atmosphere of openness to foreign influence in a wide range of policy areas, which was brought about by Deng Xiaoping's popular reform policies. Foreign organizations' access to significant technological and financial resources and China's need to adapt to increasingly stringent strings that were attached to various types of development aid also helped. The low salience of environmental issues, which increased the fractured and decentralized nature of environmental policy-making processes in China, also gave domestic state actors a freer hand in moulding China's domestic environmental laws and regulations and bureaucratic growth. Despite these trends, however, Chinese environmental policy remained on the outer fringes of foreign policy-making. The onset of a legitimacy crisis, nevertheless, created new demands for creative innovation among China's foreign policy elites. One aspect of this innovation process was the strategic use of environmental issues to enhance China's international prestige and domestic legitimacy after the crushing of student protests in Tiananmen Square on 4 June 1989.

China's pre-1989 environmental policy

The modern advent of Chinese environmental foreign and domestic policy awareness is most commonly traced back to the China's participation in the 1972 United Nations Conference on the Human Environment (UNCHE) in Stockholm, Sweden. This meeting had an important catalysing effect on the rise of global eco-politics, in general, and was especially important to increasing environmental awareness in the developing world (Ross and Silk, 1987; Palmer, 1998). In preparation for this meeting, the Chinese government formed a small leading group for environmental protection under the State Council. This began the first of many early to mid 1970s' contacts that this cadre of engineers and scientists made with international environmental organizations.

Between 1971 and 1976, China joined 20 major IGOs, including the United Nations Development Programme (UNDP) and the United Nations Environment Programme (UNEP), which provided numerous opportunities for China's 'first generation' environmental experts to meet with their foreign counterparts. China's first representative to UNEP, Qu Geping, later became the head of China's National Environmental Protection Agency (NEPA), a post he held until 1996 (Bartke, 1991). Another major early leader in the environmental field who exemplifies this first generation is Song Jian. In 1974, he was appointed as the chair of the newly created State Commission on Environmental Protection (SCEP) and held a concurrent post as the chair of the State Science and Technology Commission (SSTC) (Ross, 1998). During the mid 1980s, he was appointed to the post of minister of the SSTC. These two organizations and NEPA formed the early core of China's environmental policy-making apparatus.

Having come into existence partly as the result of international engagement, these bureaucratic institutions were open to foreign influence from the beginning. China's environmental experts were among the most travelled of China's bureaucratic elite. This greatly enhanced their ability to establish long-term relationships with top officials from numerous environmental IGOs, who later became valuable allies and suppliers of technology and resources (Jacobson and Oksenberg, 1990).

Despite the expanding 'conference diplomacy' that existed among Chinese and foreign experts, environmental issues did not really enter the lexicon of domestic policy priorities until the early 1980s. Probably the most important step in this evolutionary process was a successful campaign by Song Jian and other environmental experts to conceptually package environmental protection with China's new population control policy. Another environment awareness-raising activity that was packaged under the auspices of public image-building was China's 'panda diplomacy'. It is not certain whether or not China's state environmental lobby was behind China's penchant for having giant pandas tag along with senior officials on state visits, but there is little doubt that environmental advocates used pandas to increase domestic awareness of environmental issues. Protecting pandas quickly became both a domestic and international priority. This issue served as a catalyst for a whole range of biodiversity protection programmes, many of which were funded by foreign institutions (Harrington, 2000a).

Foreign actors not only funded projects and provided technology, but they also had a significant influence on China's environmental laws and regulations. Chinese legal experts had little experience with environmental issues. This opened up opportunities for Chinese environmental experts, drawing from Western models, to put their imprint on environmental legislation (Ross and Silk, 1987).

Western models mingled with Chinese bureaucratic traditions in the construction of China's environmental bureaucracy (Sinkule and Ortolano, 1995). The growth of China's environmental bureaucracy significantly increased the influence of China's true believers and led to the creation of a wide-ranging environmental educational, training and research infrastructure. Between 1984 and 1990, environment-related bureaus popped up in a number of government ministries. The National Environmental Protection Agency expanded in size and staff and environmental protection bureaus were established at the provincial, county and village levels of government (Sinkule and Ortolano, 1995).

The expansion of environmental bureaucracy had a profound effect on the growth of state environmentalism. First and foremost, it expanded the ranks of careerists at various levels of government (China Statistical Publishing House, 1991). Second, as more people were asked to get involved with environmental management, government organs at various levels were compelled to provide environmental management training to their employees (Jahiel, 1998). Third, it forced local governments to think about environmental management.

The growth of China's bureaucratic and legal frameworks did not happen in isolation from larger changes in the economy. Another motive force behind growing interest in the environment was environmental policy-makers' ability to convince some senior policy-makers that double-digit economic growth was taking its toll on China's environment. Some late 1980s' estimates of the cost of environmental destruction ranged from 8 to 13 per cent of China's total GDP (Zhang et al, 1999).

Environmental policy-makers did not only care about convincing the leadership of the need for more stringent environmental policies. They also fought to increase press coverage of environmental issues. The same themes of efficiency, cost and population control that resonated with government officials were also effective in raising the awareness of the masses (Qu and Li, 1994).

'Formal' environmental foreign policy during the 1980s

While China's state environmentalists made much progress in pushing their international and domestic agendas during the 1970s and most of the 1980s, environmental foreign policy received relatively little interest from foreign policy-makers in the Ministry of Foreign Affairs (MOFA) or from other members of the senior leadership (Li, 1997; Xinhua, 1998). However, one example of formal environmental experts' interaction with foreign policy elites involved China's preparations for global warming negotiations (see Chapter 9). China was a relative latecomer to climate change discussions. In 1987, it decided to put together a team of officials to participate in the meetings of the Intergovernmental Panel on Climate Change (IPCC). This group included members from the SSTC, NEPA, the State Meteorological Administration (SMA) and MOFA (Chayes and Kim, 1998). The primary purpose of this initial grouping was to study the problem of climate change. Environmental experts also played an important role in other environmental negotiations, such as in negotiations that led to China's signing of the Convention on International Trade in Endangered Species (CITES) and the Law of the Sea.

Despite these cooperative efforts, Chinese environmental engagement with global environmental regimes and domestic policy-making activity were constrained by long-standing concepts that broadly defined China's overall foreign policy approach. In her discussion of the influence of environmental experts on foreign policy, Economy notes that traditional 'themes that predominate in the realm of high politics – traditional Chinese values of sovereignty, Third/First World dichotomies and image – continued to dominate all aspects of foreign policy-making including environmental policy' (Economy, 1998, p264). This has led to the emergence of what Economy calls a *bifurcated* foreign policy in which 'the actors, institutions and beliefs promulgated at international negotiations have remained consistent; but a second set of actors advancing a different set of interests and operating at a relatively distinct level of diplomacy has emerged' (Economy, 1998, p265). The policies that have grown out of this bifurcated situation show the continued dominance of traditional approaches, albeit combined with new environmental content.

Tiananmen Square and the road to Rio

Near the end of the 1980s, some progress was made in building up China's ability to confront the environmental costs of high economic growth; but significant challenges remained. China's new legal and bureaucratic infrastructure lacked depth. The environmental bureaucracy lacked ministerial status. General institutional capacity was low, and while the national bureaucracy had some strong leaders in place, this was not often the case at other levels of government. While the senior leadership welcomed the positive public relations and resources that low-level environmental diplomacy generated, environmental protection was seen to be more of a future rather than a present problem. China was a poor country that could not afford to sacrifice economic development for the sake of environmental protection (Zhang et al, 1999).

Interestingly, a seemingly unrelated event – the 1989 Tiananmen incident – had a major effect on changing the direction of China's domestic and international environmental policies. The potential effects of the Tiananmen Square incident on China's domestic and foreign environmental policy have received little attention in the literature. This is a bit surprising given many socialist governments' use of symbolic environmental politics to prop up their domestic and international legitimacy during the 1980s. In fact, it seems that there are some interesting similarities between China's post-Tiananmen environmental policies and strategies implemented by a number of Eastern European states that used environmental issues to help their lagging popularity at home and to diffuse international criticism from abroad.

One case in point is Hungary. Like post-Tiananmen China, Hungary suffered from a dual legitimacy crisis. While 'goulash communism' had gone much farther than most Eastern bloc states in allowing the growth of civil society, the floodgates of discontent were opening just below the surface (Jancar-Webster, 1998). On the international front, Hungary's human rights record was openly criticized by the West. The Hungarian regime responded to these dual threats to its legitimacy by trying to mollify domestic demands for more political and social openness and to deflect international criticism by allowing more open discussion of what the government believed was a salient 'low politics' issue: environmental protection. During the early 1980s, Hungarian scientists and government officials became active participants in 'conference diplomacy'. The government encouraged the development of 'autonomous' mass organizations, which it believed could be used to satisfy increasing demands for civil society participation (Lipshutz, 1996). It also hoped that these organizations would draw away support from non-sanctioned groups. The environmental issue was especially suited to 'symbolic politics' because the government held a virtual monopoly over environmental information and it was relatively easy for the government to carry out activities such as holding conferences or passing legislation to show that it was 'responding' to the desires of the masses (Harrington, 2000b). The main problem with the Hungarian model was that the overall process of political liberalization created new avenues for members of its growing environmental movement to pursue their environmental agendas outside of state institutions. For instance, by the mid 1980s, most of the government's environmental 'true believers' had moved on to civil society organizations, which largely destroyed Hungary's own developing 'state environmentalism'.

On the surface, one might think that the Hungarian experience would discourage the Chinese government from using the environmental issue as a tool to enhance its domestic and international legitimacy. However, there are two important differences between the Chinese and Hungarian experiences that made the use of the environmental issue more appealing to the Chinese government. First, China did not have an organized environmental movement or any intrusive environmental NGOs to worry about. Almost all of China's prominent environmental advocates worked within the government. Second, few of China's environmental true believers have shown the stomach for openly calling for regime change. The same is true for the great majority of China's newly minted NGOs, which resemble public service organizations more closely than advocacy groups.

Global eco-politics and the search for legitimacy

The Tiananmen incident created dual foreign policy and domestic legitimacy crises of a severity not seen in decades. World leaders, responding to both domestic and international demands to 'punish' the Chinese leadership, greatly curtailed their high-level diplomatic contacts with Chinese leaders. On the domestic front, Chinese as well as foreign observers were surprised by the extent of the government's crackdown during and immediately following 4 June 1989. Tens of millions of people in all of China's major cities had participated in anti-government demonstrations (Oksenberg et al, 1990). Government pursuit of many democracy movement leaders received heavy international coverage, further sullying China's image (Baum, 1994).

China's international situation did not appreciably improve in the months following the incident. Leaders of the industrialized world repeatedly rebuffed public high-level contacts. Domestically, China's economic reforms were put on hold and political reforms openly discussed in the press earlier that year were relegated to more private realms. Under these circumstances, the Chinese leadership needed some creative thinking in order to overcome these dual crises. It is during this period that it seems that the Chinese leadership began to realize that the environment issue could provide an opportunity to end its domestic isolation.

This line of reasoning follows from the fact that while high-level contacts had been drastically reduced, 'conference diplomacy' continued to function, albeit at a lower level. Suddenly, the extensive but relatively low-level international policy networks that sustained Chinese environmental policy-makers took on added importance at MOFA and other central government foreign policy-making centres. Conference diplomacy offered a diplomatic lifeline to the outside world. Environmental diplomacy was especially appealing because foreign governments had a harder time justifying their denial of China's right to engage in efforts to save the global environment. Maintaining this lower level of diplomatic contact was also appealing to China's major international partners because China was just too big to ignore. Environmental diplomacy offered a useful 'fallback' issue area that industrialized states could use to continue engagement with the world's most populous state (Gibbons, 1997; Economy, 1999).

On the domestic front, allowing public discussion of environmental issues offered a relatively safe way to 'open up' social space for the masses. The leadership was aware of latent interest in environmental issues on the part of the public and wanted to capitalize on it. All of the multi-pronged approaches used by environmental advocates in the government to push the development of legislative and bureaucratic infrastructures, and to focus on the growing shortages of arable land and petroleum, as well as the increasingly serious pollution problems brought about by a decade of double-digit GDP growth, were beginning to gain critical mass acclaim by the end of the 1980s (Chao, 1993; China Statistical Publishing House, 1988, 1998). This new interest in opening up environmental discussions is evidenced by increasing coverage of environmental stories in the Chinese press, beginning in 1991. A content analysis of the *China Daily* index reveals that environmental coverage steadily increased starting in 1991, reached an initial peak in 1992, and then stabilized in 1993 and 1994 at a much higher level, only to renew its upward rise in 1995 (*China Daily* indexes 1990–1995).

On the diplomatic front, the launch pad for China's new international and domestic environmental push was the 1992 United Nations Conference on Environment and Development (UNCED) in Rio de Janeiro. The first step in this strategy involved an intensifying of international activity relating to major international environmental regimes. Between 1990 and 1994, China hosted at least 18 major international environmental conferences (Johnston, 1998a; SEPA and UNEP, 1999). Many of these meetings were co-hosted by long-time friends of Chinese environmental policy-makers, including UNEP, the World Bank and the World Wide Fund for Nature (WWF) (Johnston, 1998a). Most of these conferences occurred before the Rio Earth Summit. From a diplomatic standpoint, probably the most important meeting was the Ministerial Conference on Environment and Development, which was attended by over 40 developing states. This meeting resulted in the signing of the Beijing Declaration, which traced out the Group of 77 developing countries (G77) and China's major negotiating positions for Rio. This conference received heavy coverage in the domestic press (*China Daily*, 1992).

Another important step taken by the Chinese leadership was a softening of its stance in ozone-layer negotiations. Much has been written about why China decided to sign the Vienna Convention and the London amendments to the Montreal Protocol on protecting the ozone layer. This literature mainly focuses on developed nations' agreement to create a funding mechanism in order to help developing states comply with emission reductions standards, which had been a central demand of the G77 and China. It seems reasonable to assume, however, that in the context of China's overall international situation, China's signing was also a kind of 'peace offering' to the industrialized world, which legitimized its active participation in global eco-politics (Chayes and Kim, 1998).

China's changing participation in global warming negotiations in the run-up to the Rio Earth Summit also exemplifies China's post-Tiananmen 'upgrading' of environmental diplomacy. As mentioned before, prior to 1989, most of China's international environmental contacts, with a few exceptions, were maintained by environmental advocates and bureaucratic actors outside the Chinese leadership. In 1989, however, the composition of China's climate negotiating teams became increasingly dominated by MOFA and State Planning Commission representatives, while participation by SSTC and NEPA representatives was drastically reduced. NEPA suffered the most. In 1995, only one NEPA representative was on the negotiating team at the first Conference of the Parties (COP1). This downgrading in status of traditional centres of international environmental engagement also signalled a partial victory for the leaders of the industrial and mining bureaucracies who were wary of the potential negative effects that new, more stringent international greenhouse gas controls might have on their operations (Economy, 1994; Chayes and Kim, 1998; Carpenter et al, 1995). The global warming negotiations also signalled China's strategic decision to strengthen its leadership, and weaken Indian influence, over the G77 bloc at the negotiations.

Li Peng and a host of other senior leaders headed China's Rio delegation. Li and Song Jian both made environmental policy speeches at the Earth Summit. This outward activity, however, was just a sideline to more important events going on at the summit, which included numerous high-level meetings with G-7 leaders, including George Bush, John Major and Helmut Kohl. These visits 'broke the ice' for more high-level contacts in the future. After going to Rio, Li Peng seized the initiative by visiting a number of Middle Eastern states and Finland (*China Daily*, 1992). China's diplomatic isolation was fast fading into history.

Post-crisis environmental acceleration

Following the Rio UNCED meeting, one policy strategy carried out by the Chinese government that exemplified its commitment to environmental diplomacy was the push to be the first country to produce a sustainable development national action plan. Consequently, China was the first country to complete an Agenda 21 planning document. This had an important catalysing effect on its environmental planning process, resulting in numerous environmental planning documents being formulated after 1993. China's Agenda 21 was different from previous government planning documents because it proposed a much more comprehensive approach to environmental management. It called for the integration of policies relating to natural resource management, population control, industrialization, education, consumption, social services, poverty and healthcare in ways that increase the sustainability of China's long-term development (Xinhua, 1994). While this document was largely symbolic in nature, those that followed included more concrete steps to deal with a host of environmental problems. The 1996 fourth National Environmental Protection Conference led to proposals that were enshrined in China's Ninth Five-Year Plan (1996–2000) and its Long-Term Development Plan (1996–2010) (Ross, 1998).

'Green freedom'

China used the Rio Earth Summit to launch a major environmental publicity campaign. While most of this coverage emphasized all of the good things that China was doing domestically and internationally, increasingly open critical discussion of China's environmental problems also surfaced. This rise in press coverage of environmental issues was welcomed and encouraged by environmental policy advocates. The press was the environmentalists' primary tool for stimulating popular support for their policies. These efforts were supported by a growing number of environmentally minded journalists and publishing houses.

Interest in environmental issues was not limited to foreign and domestic experts. In 1996, President Jiang Zemin made the keynote speech at China's fourth National Environmental Protection Conference. Jiang, Li Peng, Zhu Rongji and many other senior government officials have become much more public in expressing their interest in environmental issues (SEPA and UNEP, 1999). Jiang has acknowledged the severity of environmental mismanagement by publicly stating that one of the reasons for the severity of China's 1998 summer flooding season was poor land management practices and excessive deforestation. During that same year, the environmental bureaucracy was upgraded to ministerial status, even while more than ten other ministries were shut down (Jahiel, 1998).

Increasing press coverage of environmental issues and symbolic involvement by senior leaders has greatly increased popular awareness of environmental problems. Local governments now publish weekly reports on air pollution in major cities (daily reports are issued for Shanghai and Beijing). There are real-time noise pollution indicators at some major intersections in Shanghai and Beijing. Most educated people have a basic understanding of the concepts of global warming and ozone-layer depletion. In fact, it was widely accepted among the populace that global warming was the reason for China's destructive 1998 floods, which were responsible for almost 200 billion RMB in destruction and damaged over 1 million homes (SEPA and UNEP, 1999; Li, 1997).

Another example of China's opening to environmental discussions has been the rise of environmental NGOs. Like many formerly socialist Eastern European states, China has long maintained a number of so-called autonomous mass organizations, such as the China Greening Association; but the appearance of NGOs that are not officially under the umbrella of the state is a recent phenomenon. Liang Congjie, the founder of one of the first of these independent organizations, Friends of Nature, spent years trying to get permission to set up his organization. Now, Liang has become one of China's most influential environmental advocates (Ng and Turner, 1999; Liang, 1999).

The limits of Green freedom

While coverage of environmental problems, both good and bad, has greatly expanded, there is one high-politics issue that China's leadership has refused to budge on: China's much criticized Three Gorges Dam project. After decades of debate, this massive undertaking was finally approved in 1993. Its strongest champion, Li Peng, steadfastly defends the environmental benefits of the project. However, many other government representatives seem to disagree. Overall, opposition was dramatically displayed in the final National People's Congress (NPC) vote on the dam, during which about one third of the delegates either abstained or opposed the dam. The public debate on the dam, however, has been mostly relegated to Chinese academic journals, foreign conferences and publications. More strident activists, such as Dai Qing, have been either jailed or exiled (Dai, 1994).

China's independent green NGOs, which now number in the hundreds, are also severely constrained in the scope of their political activities. NGO leaders realize that while their cooperation, criticism and investigative work is generally welcome, there are political lines that they cannot cross. On more than one occasion, overzealous members of China's growing environmental press corps have been detained or harassed for making overtly political criticism of government policies (Delsi, 2000).

The limits of China's environmental diplomacy

After the political crisis of the early 1990s following the Tiananmen incident, interest in environmental diplomacy on the part of central government's foreign policy-makers continued. Conference diplomacy continues unabated today, and China still clamours for the right to host major international environmental meetings. In 1999 China hosted the 11th Meeting of the Parties to the Montreal Protocol. This was the largest international environmental conference ever held in China. China received credit for a draft proposal, widely referred to as the 'Beijing Declaration', which called on the parties to 'demonstrate a stronger political will and take more effective action to fulfil their obligations under the convention and the protocol' (Oberthur, 2000, p40). However, this symbolic act did little in the way of increasing China's concrete commitment to reducing the production of ozone-depleting substances.

China's participation in the Kyoto Protocol on global warming exemplifies an even more forceful example of its strategic use of global eco-politics to serve its national interests. Until recently, the Chinese leadership has shown little flexibility on the issue of global warming. In 1995, it carried out a failed attempt to stop the parties to the Framework Convention on Climate Change (FCCC) from moving on to discussions of a protocol that was expected to lead to firm commitments on the part of developing nations to decrease greenhouse gas emissions. The Chinese leadership has been very public in its insistence that fighting global warming is a problem for developed states to fix first. This rhetoric has helped to solidify China's leadership in the developing world. In the climate change meeting at The Hague in November 2000, China's opposition to asking developing nations to make firm commitments regarding greenhouse gas (GHG) reductions remained largely unchanged (Churie et al, 2000).

However, since The Hague meeting, China has adopted an increasingly cooperative stance towards the Kyoto Protocol. China's latest 'strategic' use of the global warming issue has won it much support at home and abroad. The spokesman of G77/China at the sixth Conference of the Parties (COP6) in Bonn, Germany, during July 2001 clearly articulated China's main reason for supporting the political agreement that came out of that meeting: it amounted to a 'triumph for multilateralism over unilateralism' (Hanks et al, 2001, p14). The US withdrawal from the Kyoto Protocol has significantly redrawn the fault line of global eco-politics. G77/China's move towards the European Union (EU) position is a classic act of geopolitical 'balancing' against US hegemony. China inched closer towards protocol ratification at the seventh Conference of the Parties (COP7) in Morocco by committing to help 'sell a deal that would ensure sufficient ratifications for entry into force of the protocol' before the World Summit on Sustainable Development (WSSD) in September 2002 (Boyd et al, 2001, p15).

China's actual timing for ratification of the protocol was clearly planned for maximum diplomatic effect. Furthermore, China was forced to make a quick decision given the fact that India formally ratified the protocol in August 2002 and offered to host the eighth Conference of the Parties (COP8) in October 2002. Zhu Rongji's speech at the WSSD, during which he stated that China had formally ratified the protocol, contrasted sharply with US Secretary of State Colin Powell's address to the assembly, which was met with jeers and heckling by some delegates. The ratification was also a major victory for China's 'true believers', who worked for more than a decade to firmly commit China to a cooperative stance towards the global warming regime.

Unfortunately, China's ratification of the Kyoto Protocol, like its commitment to the ozone regime, places few requirements on the Chinese government to take concrete steps to deal with the greenhouse gas and ozone atmospheric threats (because of China's 'developing country' status). In all fairness, China has made some progress in both areas. Greenhouse gas emissions probably decreased during the 1990s. However, China's use of global eco-politics provides political cover for symbolic policy responses to its worsening environmental problems.

Conclusion

China continues to face numerous domestic and international environmental challenges. However, the overall trend is a positive one. According to Chinese sources, spending on environmental remediation increased during the 1990s (Xinhua, 2000). The leaders of China's newly upgraded and growing environmental bureaucracy continue to consolidate and expand their influence. Environmental issues receive daily national coverage. Conversations with educated urban Chinese reveal their increasing awareness of environmental issues. Since 1990, China's legal and bureaucratic environmental infrastructure has greatly increased in size and importance. The State Environmental Protection Administration (SEPA) was recently given ministerial status. China now has over 360 environmental laws and regulations, including over 30 major laws, which focus on environmental issues (SEPA and UNEP, 1999). There is also growing evidence that environmental law enforcement is improving (China Statistical Publishing House, 1995, 2000).

Environmental diplomacy offers numerous benefits to China. On the one hand, Chinese leaders can use the issue of global warming to chastise the US's poor greenhouse record, while at the same time using environmental engagement as a fallback issue during times of tense Sino–US relations. China's climate change diplomacy has also helped to solidify its self-proclaimed leadership of the developing world. Chinese policy-makers are developing a clearer understanding of how symbolic global eco-politics can be used to serve the national interest. China's ratification of the Kyoto Protocol scored points everywhere except in the US, whom China sees as an increasing threat to world peace and stability. Ratification of the protocol provides further evidence to the rest of the world of China's intention to be a responsible partner in creating an evolving multilateral international system.

China's expanding environmental diplomacy suggests that senior Chinese policy-makers do not view domestic and international aspects of disparate policy issue areas to be isolated from one another. Analyses of China that 'lean to one side' may mask important domestic and international events, situational characteristics and policy actors that contribute to the country's environmental diplomacy. Using a multilevel approach to understanding environmental foreign policy-making offers many opportunities for understanding foreign policy determinants in developing countries. China's experience is illustrative of the many challenges that large non-democratic developing countries face as they struggle to balance the dual requirements of economic growth and environmental protection.

Chapter 8

Taiwan's International Environmental Policy: Balancing Trade and the Environment

Wen-chen Shih

Introduction

The development of international environmental law and the proliferation of multilateral environmental agreements (MEAs) took off after the 1972 United Nations Conference on the Human Environment (UNCHE) held in Stockholm (Malanczuk, 1997, p241). During the two decades between the Stockholm conference and the 1992 UN Conference on Environment and Development (UNCED), held in Rio de Janeiro, international environmental regulatory regimes began to take shape in the form of various MEAs and other soft law instruments, such as policy statements and declarations. Various MEAs to encourage the implementation of, and compliance with, these agreements have employed novel techniques such as trade-related environmental measures (TREMs). The negotiation of MEAs, such as the 1987 Montreal Protocol on ozone protection, the 1992 Framework Convention on Climate Change (FCCC) and the 1992 Convention on Biological Diversity (CBD), also led to growing interest in the field of 'environmental diplomacy' (Tolba et al, 1998).

In the UN, the People's Republic of China replaced the nationalist-led government of Taiwan in 1971. Taiwan's membership in various international organizations was also replaced by China after 1971. Therefore, during the two decades when international environmental regulatory regimes took off, Taiwan completely broke off from international society, retreating to build up its export-led economic development. As a result, the government was unaware of the rapidly developing international environmental regimes. In 1990, Taiwan applied for accession to the General Agreement on Tariffs and Trade (GATT), the predecessor to the World Trade Organization (WTO). After more than ten years' negotiation, Taiwan became a WTO member in 2002. Contrary to the successful experiences in participating in the international trading community, Taiwan's first encounter with the international environment regime seemed like a nightmare. During the early 1990s it was threatened with trade sanctions under the Convention on International Trade in Endangered Species (CITES). Since then, the perception of the international environmental regime has often been associated with how it might affect Taiwan's international trade or affect its reputation. Though not a party to any MEA, Taiwan has nevertheless adopted the policy of voluntary compliance with major MEAs since the early 1990s. It is possible that trade restrictions or sanctions might not be imposed on Taiwan if it complies with obligations prescribed under these MEAs. In other words, the *raison d'être* of the policy of voluntary compliance with major MEAs is based on Taiwan's economic and trade interests.

There seems to be no coherent foreign policy framework in Taiwan that responds to the international environmental regime, except the poorly implemented policy of voluntary compliance with major MEAs. On the other hand, in the GATT/WTO membership application process, Taiwan has already had extensive experiences in trade negotiations, and it has carried out the necessary legislative reform in trade-related laws and regulations. Foreign policy has often been geared toward trade and economic issues in the past because it is these areas in which Taiwan – the top 20 trading country – has a 'comparative advantage'. It is therefore not difficult to speculate on the true reasons behind Taiwan's adoption of its present policy of voluntary compliance with MEAs.

One of the flexible foreign policies that the Taiwan government is adopting is an 'environmental foreign policy', although the content and meaning of this policy are still evolving. Considering the leverage Taiwan might have in the global debate on trade versus environment, particularly in the context of compatibility between the WTO and MEAs containing trade measures, will the government take advantage of this new leverage and reorient its international environmental policy? This is the central theme of this chapter.

The compatibility between trade-related environmental measures and obligations under the GATT was first raised in the famous 1991 tuna/dolphin case between the US and Mexico.[1] Since then, free traders and environmentalists have debated whether TREMs will be used as a disguised trade barrier and whether the GATT is undermining global and national efforts to protect the environment. In this trade-versus-environment debate, questions regarding the compatibility between MEAs containing TREMs and the GATT/WTO particularly worry several secretariats of MEAs and concerned states, as TREMs have been perceived as an effective tool to implement MEAs or to attract membership (Charnovitz, 1996, pp174–175). As for now, no TREM authorized by an MEA has been challenged under the GATT/WTO. The reason for this might be that memberships between the WTO and major MEAs containing TREMs largely overlap. However, Taiwan has been, and will continue to be, unable to become a party to any major MEA due to its ambiguous status under international law.

Taiwan has, in the past, been threatened by CITES with possible trade sanctions for its weak conservation work, and was actually subject to trade sanctions by the US between 1994 and 1995 under the US Fisherman's Protective Act of 1967 (the so-called 'Pelly Amendment'). Both the government and local non-governmental organizations (NGOs) have been very frustrated in trying to participate in the international environmental regulatory regime as a way of helping with Taiwan's domestic environmental problems. In addition, more and more MEAs, such as developments under the climate change and biodiversity conventions, attempt to regulate economic and trade aspects of their parties relevant to the objectives of the conventions. This development worries the government even more as Taiwan is highly dependent upon imported energy and is now trying to build up its biotechnology industry. Hence, it will undermine Taiwan's trade and economic interests if TREMs are employed under the climate change and biodiversity regimes.

After Taiwan joins the WTO, will the government, out of frustration and aware of the economic and trade interests at stake, bring complaints to the dispute settlement body (DSB) of the WTO and give substance to the conflict between the WTO and MEAs? In other words, will the existing international environmental policy of voluntary compliance with major MEAs be revised in the face of economic- and trade-oriented foreign policy after Taiwan becomes a member of the WTO? If the answer is yes, what are the implications for Taiwan's domestic environmental protection efforts? And if the answer is no, how will the government carry out implementing or improving the existing policy of voluntary compliance with major MEAs? All of these questions are analysed in this chapter.

The remainder of this chapter is organized as follows. The next section outlines Taiwan's environmental foreign policies, including interaction with the international environmental regulatory regime since the early 1990s, and the adoption and implementation of the current policy of voluntary compliance. The third section of the chapter discusses the core theme: Taiwan is in a unique position in the trade-versus-environment debate, especially in the context of the compatibility between MEAs and the WTO, and of Taiwan's potential challenge, before the WTO's DSB, of MEAs containing TREMs. The section also discusses several policy implications resulting from these issues and suggests some possible future directions for Taiwan's environmental foreign policy.

Taiwan's environmental foreign policy: Practice and implementation

As mentioned above, in 1971 Taiwan retreated from international society after its seat in the UN was replaced by mainland China. As a result, the government was unaware of the development of an international environmental regulatory regime comprised mainly of MEAs. On the domestic front, environmental protection only gained momentum when the Environmental Protection Administration (EPA) was established in 1987 (Tang, 1993a, p523), despite the enactment of various pollution control regulations during the mid 1970s. The government only began to feel the pressure from international society with regard to environmental issues in the early 1990s (Yeh, 1999, p360). This section examines Taiwan's interaction with MEAs during the 1990s and how that experience has influenced the adoption of the main (and probably the only) international environmental policy by the government: the policy of voluntary compliance with MEAs.

Taiwan's interaction with international environmental regimes since the early 1990s

Two key events during the early 1990s brought Taiwan closer to the international environmental regulatory regime. During 1992 and 1994, Taiwan was suddenly under the spotlight of the international conservation community – namely, CITES and international environmental NGOs – for its use of rhino horn and tiger bone in traditional Chinese medicine. CITES asked Taiwan to adopt its standards in regulating international trade in endangered species. But this might be legally flawed, as Taiwan is not a party to CITES and is therefore not bound by it (Shih, 1996, pp122–123). Nevertheless, sensitive to pressure coming from the international media, Taiwan took measures, including revising the 1984 Wildlife Conservation Act in 1994 to bring it into compliance with CITES, thereby avoiding trade sanctions or restrictions as a result of CITES. Nonetheless, Taiwan suffered trade sanctions by the US, under the Pelly Amendment, after it was certified by the president in 1995 as 'diminishing the effectiveness of' international environmental agreements like CITES (Berger, 1999, p396).

Another less publicized incident involved the 1987 Montreal Protocol. The Montreal Protocol specifically sets down trade-restrictive provisions between parties and non-parties concerning international trade in ozone-depleting substances, unless the Conference of the Parties (COP) has certified that such non-parties have adopted measures comparable to those in the protocol. As certain chemicals used in Taiwan's computer manufacturing industries were identified as having an ozone-depleting effect, the government was extremely worried that the Montreal Protocol might authorize its parties to restrict or prohibit trade with Taiwan. As a result, between 1989 and 1995 a series of administrative regulations – in line with the regulatory schedules of the Montreal Protocol and its later amendments – were adopted by the Ministry of Economic Affairs of the Executive Yuan. Consequently, Taiwan has not been subject to trade restrictions under the protocol (Brack, 1996, p50).

Two more interactions with the international environmental regime have been less direct and confrontational than those with CITES and the Montreal Protocol. In January 1997, Taipower, Taiwan's power utility, signed a contract with North Korea to export 60,000 barrels of low-radioactive nuclear waste for storage within two years to North Korea. This project attracted media attention and was strongly opposed by South Korea and environmental NGOs, and was later postponed for an indefinite period. The second incident involved the illegal dumping in December 1998 of mercury-tainted cargo at the Cambodian port of Sihanoukville by Taiwan's biggest conglomerate, the Formosa Plastics Group. The toxic cargo roused suspicion and panic in the local village and put Taiwan in the international spotlight. In April 1999 the Cambodian government ordered the Formosa Plastics Group to ship the cargo back to Taiwan. Proposals to send the cargo to the US or Europe failed. Consequently, the toxic waste was shipped back to Taiwan to be processed in the Formosa Plastics Group's own processing site in south Taiwan.

Both of these incidents involved the conduct of Taiwanese private business behaviour that nevertheless brought adverse international attention to Taiwan. The government's response was to rely upon the international environmental regulatory regime to clarify and deal with the issues. During the nuclear waste incident, the government instructed (or at least urged) Taipower to comply with all of the International Atomic Energy Agency's regulations.[2] In the hazardous waste controversy, the government stated that the regulations of the Basel Convention on the Control of Transboundary Movements of Hazardous Wastes and Their Disposal should be respected and observed.[3]

From these experiences, Taiwan's interaction with the international environmental community in both public and private sectors has not been well perceived. The government's reaction to these encounters has centred on how it might cause Taiwan's trade interests to be harmed (for example, in the CITES and Montreal incidents) or how it would affect Taiwan's reputation (for example, in the hazardous waste incident). International environmental policy-making was near impossible as the government adopted a piecemeal approach, dealing with environmental problems that had international or global dimensions as they came along. In addition, Taiwan's status under international law or under the UN system only compounded environmental problems because the government was unable to deal with them via diplomatic means. This is the background leading to the adoption by Taiwan of the policy of voluntary compliance with MEAs during the early 1990s.

Voluntary compliance with multilateral environmental agreements

In his message to the 1992 Earth Summit, then President Lee Teng-hui stated that: 'The Republic of China [Taiwan] … had voluntarily indicated to adopt all measures in observance of the agreements of the Montreal Protocol and the Framework Convention on Climate Change.' This was the earliest official statement from the president regarding Taiwan's international environmental policy of voluntary compliance with the MEAs. Compliance with international agreements requires the government to transform obligations under the agreements into domestic laws and regulations. In line with the phase-out schedules of the Montreal Protocol and its various amendments and adjustments, the Ministry of Economic Affairs promulgated and revised a series of administrative notes in 1989, 1991, 1993 and 1995. According to Article 4.8 of the Montreal Protocol, trade with non-parties will only be permitted if that non-party is determined, by a Meeting of the Parties (MOP), to be in full compliance with the phase-out schedule of the protocol. Taiwan's regulations of ozone-depleting substances controlled under the protocol were adopted to demonstrate Taiwan's compliance with the protocol so that Taiwan would be permitted to continue exporting to parties to the protocol. The division chief of the Chemical Industry Division of the Bureau of Industry, Ministry of Economic Affairs, was quoted in an interview before attending the fourth MOP to the protocol that 'whether Taiwan can become a party to the Protocol is of less concern; the main purpose of attending this meeting is to make sure that Taiwan will not be subject to trade sanction' (Sun, 1993, p24). But it is important to note that these regulations are not legislation adopted by the Legislative Yuan and promulgated by the president. They are rules of an administrative nature adopted by the Executive Yuan without delegation from any relevant laws. As a result, the legality of these regulations is questionable.[4]

In the CITES case, Taiwan was subject to trade sanctions by the US in August 1994. The agency in charge of wildlife conservation, the Council of Agriculture (COA), contemplated that if the amendment to the 1989 Wildlife Conservation Act could be adopted in the Legislative Yuan before the ninth session of the COP to CITES, to be held in November 1994, the chances of being sanctioned under CITES would be greatly reduced.[5] The Legislative Yuan adopted amendments to the 1989 Wildlife Conservation Act at the end of October 1994. The resolutions reached at COP9 did not impose sanctions on Taiwan. The sanctions imposed by the US were lifted in June 1995 after the Clinton administration was satisfied with conservation work undertaken by the government, including amendments to the Wildlife Conservation Law (Blank, 1996, p63).

As far as domestic applications of MEAs are concerned, the aforementioned are probably the most concrete examples of implementing the policy of voluntary compliance. The implementation of this policy is driven by the fear of being sanctioned by the MEAs in question. In fact, the whole reason behind adopting the policy of voluntary compliance is driven by economic and trade interests (Shih, 2002b). To illustrate this phenomenon, the following discussion illustrates the superficial implementation of Taiwan's policy in the case of the 1992 climate change and biodiversity conventions.

During the second half of the 1990s, the government closely followed any developments associated with the climate change and biodiversity regimes. Both the FCCC and the CBD require their parties to prepare and submit national reports containing, respectively, national inventories of emissions and removal of all greenhouse gases (GHGs), and measures adopted to implement the conventions. Considering the framework nature of these two MEAs, the reporting obligations are probably the most concrete treaty obligations required for their parties. In line with the policy of voluntarily compliance with MEAs, the government started to prepare the required reports as a way of 'implementing' the conventions.

The preparation of national reports has its merits in terms of harnessing, through the process of drafting regulations and holding public hearings, consensus among the government, NGOs, relevant industries and the public. Nevertheless, the government has not taken up adoption or revision of applicable domestic legislation in line with the FCCC and the CDB. For example, the EPA prepared draft legislation on the control of GHGs in 1999. This legislation, however, was not even submitted to the Cabinet for discussion as of 2004. Much focus has been put on the economic and trade implications of these two MEAs when discussing how the government should take action in response to the development under the climate change regime and the biodiversity regime (Shih, 2002b). Since trade measures were not adopted under these two MEAs, the government does not seem to be in a hurry to implement obligations under the climate change regime and the biodiversity regime. In other words, when trade interests were not in immediate danger, the policy of voluntary compliance with MEAs was not carried out to the extent that the government was willing to revise or enact laws to implement the agreements.

The new Taiwanese government, led by the Democratic Progressive Party (DPP), came into power in May 2000. President Chen Shui-bian published a series of white papers on various policy issues during his presidential campaign in February 2000. In the White Paper on Foreign Policy, one of the 'cross-century strategies on foreign policies' is so-called 'environmental diplomacy'. One of the campaign pledges in this 'environmental diplomacy' is to encourage the government to participate actively and to comply with international environmental norms and agreements.[6] No further elaboration on the content of this 'environmental diplomacy' has been made since the new government took office in May 2000. It is therefore not yet clear whether the new government will continue to adopt the policy of voluntary compliance with MEAs. This increases the potential importance of another question: will Taiwan's WTO membership influence the government's international environmental policy?

The trade-versus-environment debate and the WTO

Trade-versus-environment debate: Taiwan's unique place

The compatibility between TREMs and GATT/WTO has attracted immense and controversial debate since the first tuna/dolphin case in 1991 (see, for example, Hurlock, 1992; Mayer and Hoch, 1993; Parker, 1999). Several disputes concerning the use of TREMs have been brought forward to the GATT/WTO since 1991.[7] None of the TREMs has been held to be compatible with obligations under the GATT or any of the multilateral agreements under the WTO, such as the Agreement on Technical Barriers to Trade (TBT Agreement) and the Agreement on Sanitary and Phytosanitary Measures (SPS Agreement).[8] TREMs adopted unilaterally – that is, adopted according to a member's domestic laws – have been generally condemned as undermining the effectiveness of the WTO. For example, the failure of the US to exhaust multilateral efforts, such as raising the relevant issues in the CITES Standing Committee, has been criticized by the Appellate Body of the WTO in the recent dispute concerning a US embargo on certain products from countries who have not used turtle excluder devices in their nets (the so-called 'shrimp/turtle case').[9] Suggestions have been put forward to reconcile the conflict between TREMs and GATT/WTO, or between MEAs containing TREMs and GATT/WTO (Crawford, 1995; Nissen, 1997; Rutgeerts, 1999).

Potential conflicts between MEAs containing TREMs, such as CITES and the Montreal Protocol, have long been debated (Brunner, 1997). In the 1998 'shrimp/turtle' case, the Appellate Body made several references to MEAs, such as the 1982 UN Convention on the Law of the Sea (UNCLOS),[10] CITES and the CBD. This suggests the gradual acceptance of MEAs within the WTO, at least in terms of giving effect to interpreting relevant provisions of GATT in disputes involving TREMs, and of affirming the importance of multilateral approaches to environmental problems (Berger, 1999, p369). The relationship between MEAs and WTO has taken up two out of ten items in the working programmes of the WTO Committee on Trade and Environment (CTE),[11] and is now subject to the current WTO Doha negotiation round. It seems that TREMs authorized under MEAs are getting more sympathy within the WTO and the DSB (Shih, 1996, p135).

About 20 or so MEAs contain TREMs with varying degree of trade restrictions, and none has been challenged under the GATT and the WTO

(Crawford, 1995, p579). In addition, as memberships between the WTO and the MEAs overlap, conflicts between such MEAs and the WTO might not necessarily be settled under the WTO. As perceived by the WTO itself, CTE took the view that 'problems are unlikely to arise in the WTO over trade measures agreed and applied amongst parties to an MEA'.[12] Problems are more likely to arise when MEAs require or encourage parties to adopt trade measures against non-parties. Taiwan, as the following analysis will show, will probably be the most qualified WTO member to bring a case to the WTO, forcing the DSB to examine the compatibility of MEAs with obligations under the GATT/WTO.

Taiwan is regarded as a province of China under the UN system. According to the UN Environment Programme (UNEP), which has aided the negotiations of many MEAs, ratification of MEAs is mainly limited to sovereign states and regional economic organizations, and 'the UN recognizes the Government of China as the sole representative of the People's Republic of China, including Taiwan'.[13] In line with UNEP's position, Taiwan may not become a party to any MEA in its own right. But, legally speaking from the UN perspective, it is nevertheless bound by those MEAs to which China is a party. This interpretation is impossible to work, in practice, as China does not have *de facto* jurisdiction over Taiwan. In addition, this interpretation might undermine the effectiveness of MEAs that differentiate their parties according to their different stages of development and impose different sets of obligations accordingly, simply because Taiwan is in a more advanced stage of development than is mainland China (Shih, 1998, p44). Furthermore, this UNEP interpretation has not been observed in practice, as is demonstrated by Taiwan's dealing with the Montreal Protocol and CITES during the early 1990s.

Therefore, MEAs that lay specific trade measures against non-parties can adopt TREMs or authorize their parties to adopt TREMs against Taiwan. The purpose of MEAs of this nature is to encourage non-parties to become parties. Taiwan, however, is probably the only non-party that wants to but is unable to become a party. If Taiwan feels its trade interests are being affected or jeopardized, it cannot choose to become a party. The only legal remedy the government can seek when its trade interests are undermined is to bring a complaint to the WTO's DSB against WTO members (also party to such MEAs) who adopt TREMs against Taiwan in compliance with their obligations under such MEAs.

In the case of CITES, the convention itself does not impose trade measures against non-parties. As a non-party, Taiwan is not required under international law to comply with obligations under the convention. In this incident, however, Taiwan was required to comply with the CITES regulations if Taiwan did not want to be subject to trade sanctions. At the Standing Committee meeting in September 1993, a decision was adopted recommending that parties are to consider implementing 'stricter domestic measures up to and including prohibition in trade of wildlife species'.[14] Despite this finding by the Standing Committee, the convention itself did not mandate that the US impose trade sanctions. Nevertheless, the certification authorized by the president that Taiwan should be sanctioned for its lack of progress in eliminating its illegal trade in tigers and rhino was 'authorized by the Pelly Amendment and specially recommended by the relevant international body' (Blank, 1996, p72) – namely, the CITES Standing Committee. Under the circumstance, if Taiwan had already been a GATT Contracting Party and had brought a complaint to the GATT, the US would justify its decision by referring to the relevant international body, such as the COP or the CITES Standing Committee. The panel would, in that case, have to examine the compatibility of CITES, or resolutions or decisions reached by organs of CITES, with GATT.

This discussion demonstrates Taiwan's unique place in the current debate on the potential conflict between MEAs and GATT/WTO because it can 'substantiate' such 'potential' conflict and force the DSB to review the GATT/WTO compatibility of MEAs or TREMs authorized under MEAs. Will Taiwan bring such complaint to the WTO when it is trade-sanctioned under similar circumstances now that it is a member?

Trade sanctions and MEAs: Will Taiwan complain to the WTO?

Compared to its relatively successful experiences of applying for membership in the WTO, Taiwan's encounters with MEAs during the early 1990s have engendered substantial negative sentiments among its people. In the CITES incident between 1992 and 1994, the media was full of titles such as 'Trade sanctions', 'Taiwan threatened by the CITES with possible trade sanctions', 'Taiwan in danger of being sanctioned by the US' (Shih, 2002b). As a non-party, Taiwan is not required to adopt CITES regulations in its wildlife trade. However, during 1992–1994, not only was Taiwan required to comply with the CITES standard, even the non-binding decisions of the Standing Committee seemed to compel Taiwan to comply if trade sanctions were to be avoided (Shih, 1996, pp122–123). The obstructive attitude of China in opposing any type of participation of Taiwan in either the Standing Committee or the COP complicated the situation even further (Shih, 1996, pp121–124). Following the US sanctions, it was even more firmly believed that failure to comply with environmental standards of MEAs would harm Taiwan's reputation and, more importantly, its trade interests.

Suggestions on how to respond to similar cases in the future mostly focus on how Taiwan can bring such cases to the WTO when it becomes a member.[15] It thus seems plausible that Taiwan might abandon its policy of voluntary compliance with MEAs after it becomes a member of the WTO if trade interests are again greatly at stake or threatened because of TREMs imposed by MEAs. In addition, the constant shutting of doors by MEAs to allow Taiwan to participate in any capacity in their decision-making, while requiring it to comply with their decisions, only aggravates the problem. Essentially, it leaves the DSB the only legal tribunal to which Taiwan can legitimately claim to be discriminated against. What will be the benefits and costs for Taiwan of bringing such cases to the DSB?

Legitimate trade interests are, indeed, jeopardized if Taiwan, as a non-party, is required to comply with obligations from certain MEAs, particularly if those obligations have economic implications. For example, as a non-party Taiwan is not required to reduce its GHGs emissions under the Kyoto Protocol. However, because some newly industrialized country parties to the FCCC might become the next group to be required to observe substantive obligations to reduce GHGs emissions, countries that are in direct competition with Taiwan might seek to have it comply with the same obligations (Shih, 2002a). If this scenario does happen, which is not wild speculation (as the CITES incident showed), Taiwan might be subject to trade restrictions if it does not comply with a set of obligations whose negotiating process did not involve Taiwan. Taiwan's legitimate trade and economic interests might thus be affected. Under the circumstances, bringing a case to the DSB might assist Taiwan to seek legal remedy and to guard its legitimate interests as a WTO member. This is the first and probably the most important benefit of Taiwan's bringing an MEA-induced TREM to the DSB.

Moreover, Taiwan's move to bring MEAs to the DSB would force the DSB or the Appellate Body to rule on the GATT/WTO compatibility of MEAs in dispute. The potential attention this might stir within both the trading community and the international environmental regulatory regime could be used as a bargaining chip to ask MEAs to develop special sets of rules applicable to Taiwan. At the moment, Taiwan cannot even obtain a non-party observer status at official meetings of MEAs, nor can Taiwanese NGOs obtain observer status. Only international NGOs headquartered in Taiwan can participate as observers in these meetings, and this form of participation was even challenged by China as it insisted that Taiwanese officials were amongst the NGO delegation that violated the 'One China' policy. 'Frustration' is the first and only word you hear from Taiwanese officials, NGOs and academics regularly attending meetings of MEAs. Against this sentiment, and out of frustration and desperation, the likelihood of urging MEAs to take Taiwan's interests seriously through the most extreme means of bringing MEAs to the DSB may be viewed as an attractive option in Taiwan.

Does this mean that Taiwan will definitely abandon its policy of voluntary compliance with MEAs and bring cases to the DSB when TREMs authorized by MEAs are being imposed upon Taiwan? Despite the potential benefits of doing so, the following considerations might suggest otherwise. First, under the current controversial trade-versus-environment/MEAs-versus-WTO debate, Taiwan will draw immense adverse publicity by bringing the MEAs to the DSB. Environmentalists might feel especially outraged. This negative publicity will no doubt damage Taiwan's reputation. Campaigns to boycott products made in Taiwan, as the UK conservation NGO Environmental Investigation Agency did in 1992 as a protest against Taiwan's weak conservation work, has the potential to harm Taiwan's trade interests as well.

Second, the tactic of threatening to bring MEAs to the DSB, in order to persuade MEAs to adopt specific rules applicable to Taiwan, might be less effective than the government believes. Taiwan, contrary to its economic and trade strength internationally, is not an 'environmentally important' country in the sense that failure to secure compliance from Taiwan will not bring a complete breakdown of any single MEA (Shih, 2002b). For example, although rich in biodiversity, Taiwan does not have natural resources, such as rain forests, the destruction of which have global implications. In spite of its advanced stage of industrialization accompanied by a relatively high level of GHGs emissions, Taiwan, unlike China and India, does not have the potential to substantially offset efforts made by developed countries to combat global warming. Therefore, failure to bring Taiwan in line with MEAs does not carry the same implication as would failure to bring large developing countries into the agreements. As a result, it is doubtful whether MEAs, considering the minor role Taiwan plays in influencing the effectiveness of their respective objectives, will be willing to craft a separate set of rules to suit Taiwan's interests. If prescribing rules that allow Taiwan to participate agitates China or even leads to China's withdrawal from membership, MEAs can afford to ignore Taiwan's 'threat' to bring them to the DSB.

Third, and most important, what will be the consequences if the DSB or the Appellate Body decides that TREMs authorized under the MEAs are compatible with the GATT/WTO? As the previous section indicated, TREMs are gradually gaining more acceptance within the WTO. Suggestions have been put forward in the CTE to exempt TREMs authorized by MEAs from GATT/WTO rules.[16] If such suggestions are to be adopted by the GATT/WTO, Taiwan will be unable to bring a complaint to the DSB in situations where the TREM in question is mandated by an MEA. Furthermore, references to MEAs have also been made in the recent Appellate Body report in the 'shrimp/turtle case'. One commentator noted that the 'acceptability of conservation measures like the sanctions against Taiwan may now be improved by the Appellate Body's willingness to consider the importance of CITES and other multilateral treaties in the sea turtle case' (Berger, 1999, p397). In other words, Taiwan might be unable to successfully challenge TREMs mandated by MEAs if such TREMs were applied in a GATT/WTO compatible manner (that is, in a non-discriminatory manner). Under this circumstance, Taiwan would be placed in the most difficult situation. It could be required in the future to comply with obligations of MEAs, especially those that authorize or encourage parties to adopt TREMs against non-parties, if it does not want to undermine its trade interests. Taiwan will then be unable to seek any legal remedy if economic and trade interests are in real jeopardy.

To sum up, the abandoning of the policy of voluntary compliance with MEAs and bringing the MEAs to the DSB might not be, in the long run, an ideal environmental foreign policy for Taiwan. In addition, such actions do not seem to fit with the rhetoric of 'environmental diplomacy' the new government proclaims. What are the alternatives?

Policy implications and suggestions

It does not seem to suit Taiwan's long-term interests to bring TREMs mandated by MEAs to the DSB. This policy will not only harm Taiwan's reputation, it may also fail to protect Taiwan's economic and trade interests. In addition, such a policy, and the abandonment of the policy of voluntary compliance with MEAs, would undermine efforts to protect the domestic environment. At the moment, the policy of voluntary compliance with MEAs is not implemented to the fullest extent. Domestic environmental NGOs sometimes rely upon pressure and cooperation from the international environmental community to urge the government to adopt stricter environmental standards or legislation. With the policy of voluntary compliance with MEAs in place, regardless of how it has been loosely implemented, domestic environmentalists can find legitimate reasons to persuade the government to comply with international environmental standards that are appropriate to Taiwan's local environmental condition. Therefore, even in the context of trade- and economic-oriented foreign policy, this chapter does not recommend that Taiwan adopt a new international environmental policy of bringing TREMs authorized by MEAs in front of the DSB. Doing so would not protect and promote Taiwan's interests.

The current policy of voluntary compliance is not without drawbacks. Unilateral declarations and acts of states can, under certain circumstances, create international obligations for the declaring state. This was demonstrated by cases involving nuclear testing brought before the International Court of Justice (ICJ) in 1974.[17] The ICJ stated that unilateral declaration should become binding upon the declaring state according to its terms if such declaration is given publicly and with an intention to be bound. The government thus needs to be cautions of the overall circumstances in which the policy of voluntary compliance is stated and implemented (Shih, 2002a). Judging from the selective and loose implementation of this policy, however, it might be difficult to prove the 'intention' of the government of Taiwan to be bound by, for example, provisions of the FCCC and the CBD. Nevertheless, the potential legal effect of creating international legal obligations from the policy of voluntary compliance with MEAs needs to be taken into consideration.

The current environmental foreign policy of voluntary compliance with MEAs will likely continue, regardless of Taiwan's WTO membership. Abandoning this policy and choosing to bring TREMs authorized or mandated by MEAs to the DSB, when such TREMs are imposed on Taiwan, could prove to be too costly in the long run. In addition, this chapter also recommends that when making statements concerning the policy of voluntary compliance, the government should take into account the potential legal effect of such unilateral declarations. They could create international legal obligations for Taiwan. The government should be clear in stating the special circumstances and background leading to the adoption of its policy, and it should declare its objection to bearing the same obligations as parties do but without enjoying the rights conferred to parties.

Conclusion

This chapter set out to examine the following question: will Taiwan's existing environmental foreign policy of voluntary compliance with major MEAs be revised, in the face of economic- and trade-oriented foreign policy, now that Taiwan is a WTO member? After weighing the benefits and costs of bringing the MEAs to the DSB when TREMs are imposed on Taiwan, the answer to this question is that it probably will not. One of the main reasons is that, considering the gradual acceptance of the multilateral approach by the DSB, the Appellate Body and the WTO, at large, the chances of winning such a complaint have been diminished. The consequences of losing such a complaint (the acceptance of TREMs authorized or mandated by MEAs under the WTO) would cost Taiwan its reputation, as well as legitimate trade and economic interests, and this would compel Taiwan to comply with MEAs if it wishes to avoid trade sanctions in the future. Another main reason for maintaining the current policy is to help bring more stringent domestic environmental regulations in line with international environmental standard.

This chapter therefore recommends that Taiwan continue to follow the existing international environmental policy of voluntary compliance with MEAs. Nevertheless, the policy needs to be adjusted to take into account the potential international legal obligations this policy – a form of unilateral declaration or act of state – might create for Taiwan. In the process of arriving at this recommendation, this chapter has shown that motivations for Taiwan's environmental foreign policies are complex. They must be weighed against domestic trade and economic interests, as well as international factors, such as environmental agreements, international economic institutions and the policies of other states. Balancing trade and environment in the context of the compatibility between MEAs and WTO, as the case study of Taiwan illustrates, also involves complex weighing-up of various interests of individual states and of the international community at large.

Part 2

Eco-Politics, International Relations and Strategies for Sustainable Development in East and Southeast Asia

Chapter 9

China and the Climate Change Agreements: Science, Development and Diplomacy

Ho-Ching Lee

Introduction

Signs of global warming are already apparent. Measurements indicate that the average surface temperature of the Earth has increased by 0.4 to 0.8 degrees Celsius (0.7 degrees to 1.5 degrees Fahrenheit) over the last century. About half of this warming has taken place during the last 20 years, and the last two decades have been the hottest on record – perhaps the hottest during the last 1000 years. Sea level is rising, glaciers are melting and precipitation patterns are changing. Furthermore, many parts of the world have experienced heat waves, floods, droughts and weather extremes. The frequency and intensity of severe weather events such as El Niño seem to be increasing (Lemonick, 2001; Lane and Bierbaum, 2001). Most important, perhaps, the warming is not distributed evenly around the globe, meaning that some areas are experiencing much greater change.

China is one East Asian country affected by global warming, and there have been many recent signs of these effects. The summer of 2001 arrived early in Beijing, with temperatures climbing to as high 37 degrees Celsius in mid May, after weeks of sandstorms (Central News Agency, 2001). Most notably, the Yangtze River region of China suffered a severe flood in 1991 and an even more devastating one in 1998, leaving thousands of residents dead and millions of people homeless. And Qomolangma Mountain in the Himalayas, known as the 'roof of the world', has lost some of its ice cap (*China Times*, 2000, p10).

These climate-related events in China and elsewhere have caused countries around the world to realize their vulnerability to climate change. Scientists from various disciplines have conducted climate research to assess climatic impacts related to social and economic activities. Internationally, the United Nations (UN) initiated a process of environmental negotiation and cooperation to curb global greenhouse gas (GHG) emissions. Governments have made efforts to launch mitigation and adaptation projects. However, curbing GHG emissions will have adverse effects on the economic growth of many developed and developing countries, although the effects will vary. For China, given its vast reserves of coal, which are a major source of cheap and reliable energy, joining the international effort to reduce GHGs may hinder its economic growth. But the intense pressure from the international community for active participation in GHG limitation efforts, as well as the opportunity of gaining financial assistance and technology exchanges through the international agreements, cannot be ignored.

This chapter explores the evolution of China's participation in the 1992 Framework Convention on Climate Change (FCCC) and its 1997 Kyoto Protocol. It illustrates how climate science provides a stimulus to an international treaty, and also how national participation influences the foreign policy process. Given China's size, its population and economic growth, as well as its intense reliance on domestic coal, it would seem unlikely that China would take part in a treaty that might one day require it to limit energy use. However, China was among the first ten countries to ratify the FCCC. Why, then, does China involve itself in an international environmental treaty to achieve a collective goal, even if that treaty may not be consistent with its best interests? In what ways does China see itself as an important player in international environmental negotiation and cooperation?

China's participation in the United Nations environmental agreements is largely motivated by China's interest in foreign affairs. For example, in the climate change regime, China speaks frequently for the developing countries and has become the spokesperson for the developing world. Furthermore, China's negotiating stand comes largely from its perceived right to development and to parallel economic growth with environmental protection. By engaging itself in climate negotiations, China can influence the process and gain access to foreign assistance and technology. To China, environmental diplomacy helps to raise its international profile and bolster its international reputation. Domestically, climate diplomacy has resulted in expanded climate research, energy conversion and efficiency, an emerging legal framework, and institutional capacity for environmental management. Thus, there are myriad benefits for China of involving itself in international environmental negotiations

This chapter begins with a summary of recent advances in the science of climate change. Next, it reviews the climate change negotiations and China's participation in the processes of the FCCC and the Kyoto Protocol. It derives lessons from China's environmental policy-making before proposing a set of recommendations for not only 'negotiating' but also 'managing and implementing' the climate change regime.

Recent advances in climate science

Research findings and perceived risks of climate change have motivated all stakeholders in the climate negotiations. Science has played a vital role in policy debates on global warming and climate change (see Table 9.1). When it comes to climate problems, scientific questions have been focusing on whether the climate is changing, and if so, whether humans and human activities are causing it.

Table 9.1 *Chronology of Climate Science Policy Evolution*

Year	Scientific activities	Policy process
1988	IPCC created by UNEP and WMO	In response to UN resolution, scientific assessment conducted on an international basis
	Toronto Conference on the Changing Atmosphere	Called for a 20% CO_2 emission reduction by 2005
1989	Noordwijk Declaration on Atmospheric Pollution and Climate Change	US Global Change Research Program established
		Advocated 20% reduction goal
1990	IPCC first assessment report	
1991	Second World Climate Conference in Geneva	INC process began
1992	IPCC supplementary report to the IPCC scientific assessment	Climate convention (FCCC) signed at the UNCED Rio Earth Summit
1994		FCCC entered into force
1995	WMO report on ozone research and monitoring	First Conference of the Parties (COP1) held in Berlin; national emission reduction plans developed

1996	IPCC second assessment report	COP2 held in Bonn; secretariat and subsidiary bodies established
1997	*Regional Impacts of Climate Change: An Assessment of Vulnerability (*IPCC, 1997*)*	COP3 held in December in Kyoto
1998		COP4 held in December in Buenos Aires
1999	IPCC special report on *Aviation and Global Atmosphere (*IPCC, 1999*)*	COP5 held during October–November in Bonn
2000	IPCC special reports on *Technology Transfer*, *Emissions Scenarios* and *Land Use, Land-Use Change and Forestry (*IPCC, 2000*)*	COP6 held in December in The Hague
2001	IPCC third assessment report	COP6 part two reconvened in July in Bonn COP7 held during October–November in Marrakesh
2002	IPCC special report on *Climate Change and Biodiveristy*	COP8 held during October–November in New Delhi
2003		COP9 held in December in Milan
2004		COP10 to be held in December in Buenos Aires

Source: Adapted and updated from FCCC (2002)

The IPCC process

Among climate research scientists and groups, the UN-sponsored Intergovernmental Panel on Climate Change (IPCC) is the most authoritative. The World Meteorological Organization (WMO) and the UN Environment Programme (UNEP) jointly established the IPCC in 1988. Serving as a scientific advisory body to provide policy-relevant information, the IPCC was set up to assess climate change and its impacts. It also develops response strategies and explores the social and economic aspects of climate change. The IPCC has three working groups (WG): WG I on scientific assessment, WG II on impacts and WG III on cross-cutting issues and policy responses. WG I has been the most active and visible, producing scientific assessment reports in 1990, 1992, 1995 and 2001 (see IPCC, 2001).

IPCC reports are generally viewed as the best foundation for the scientific understanding of global warming and resulting climate change. They are widely cited and represent interdisciplinary scientific assessment and science-policy dialogue. The IPCC prepares special reports and technical papers on specific topics in response to requests from the parties to the FCCC. In 1997, a special report on the regional impacts of climate change was published by the IPCC to explore the potential consequences of climate change and vulnerability assessment for ten regions (IPCC, 1997), and other detailed reports have been issued periodically. The importance of these scientific assessment reports and special reports to the policy debate cannot be neglected. The 1990 assessment report provided scientific input into the policy process, arguably leading to the FCCC, a framework convention setting general emission guidelines. Furthermore, the 1995 report contributed to the Kyoto Protocol at the third Conference of the Parties (COP3), which set specific national emissions targets and timetables. In November 1998, when the fourth Conference of the Parties (COP4) was held in Buenos Aires, there was a recommendation made by many nations to link further reviews of commitments to the scientific assessment cycle of the IPCC.

The IPCC's 1995 second assessment report concluded that 'the balance of evidence suggests that there is a discernible human influence on global climate' (Houghton et al, 1996, p4). It anticipated that warming associated with human-induced carbon dioxide (CO_2) and other GHG emissions in the future will be greater than any warming rate seen in the last 10,000 years (Houghton et al, 1996, pp3–7). According to the 2001 third assessment report, global mean surface temperatures are projected to increase by 1.4 to 5.8 degrees Celsius (2.5 to 10.4 degrees Fahrenheit), about 50 per cent higher than projected in the second assessment report. This higher estimate was mainly due to the lower projected emissions of sulphur dioxide resulting in less offset of the warming effect of GHGs. What is more, IPCC scientists found that 'there is new and stronger evidence that most of the warming observed over the last 50 years is attributable to human activities' (Watson, 2000, pp2–3). This newest scientific finding is particularly alarming, when considering a 5 degree Celsius shift was enough to end the last ice age. Even the impact of the lower 1.5 degree increase would have broad negative implications upon water resources, agricultural productivity, ecosystems such as forests and coral reefs, energy strategies and human health.

Regional climatic impacts in China

Based on the IPCC findings, the Earth is warming and will continue to warm, largely due to human activities such as the burning of fossil fuels and deforestation. The scientific questions have shifted from whether the climate is changing to how much (magnitude), how fast (the rate of change) and where (regional trends). Moving from the global to a regional scale, China, the largest developing country and second largest CO_2 emitter, is worthy of special discussion. What will be the climatic impacts on China? How will the government of China address climate change?

While recognizing that scientific uncertainties exist, the IPCC estimated in its regional impact that temperate Asia, including China, will confront decreased water supply, change of agricultural output, erosion, flooding, saltwater intrusion in coastal areas, sudden migration and potential impacts on human settlements, public health concerns such as infectious diseases, and pollution hazards (Watson et al, 1998, pp355–379). General circulation models (GCMs) have found substantial climatic effects on China (Wang et al, 1994). Large wintertime warming (greater than 5 degrees Celsius) has been calculated for central northern plains and the northeast regions of China. There may be precipitation increases in central China, but substantial decreases in the southeast, with effects on monsoon rains. These changes will have serious implications for water supply systems. There may be changes in cloud cover and quite large changes in soil moisture, with much drier conditions found along the east coast during summer. These results may lead to the following impacts: longer and hotter summers and shorter and warmer winters, sea-level rise, changes in precipitation and hydropower generation (which accounts for 5.1 per cent of total power generation in China), and changes in agricultural practices and, perhaps, production.

Taken together, the climate impacts in China could be quite substantial, with largely adverse consequences for precipitation patterns, water supply, energy consumption, ecosystems, sea level, public health and human settlements. These adverse changes would undermine the very foundations of sustainable development. It is therefore particularly important to integrate potential future climate changes within long-term planning, especially given China's ambitious plans for developing the western part of the country in coming decades. Along with scientific advances in climate research, a call for international cooperation to combat climate change is underway in the context of the UN. The goal has been to achieve international agreement to reduce greenhouse emissions collectively. China has an important role to play in this process.

China and the climate change negotiations

China's participation in climate change negotiations can be understood in the broad context of Chinese foreign policy principles and development interests. Essentially, each country's negotiating stance is influenced by a variety of factors, including 'national interests, geography and existing national and international political coalitions, blocs and friendships' (Harris, 2000, pp9–10). As with most developing countries, China's primary national interest is economic development. In terms of population, China is the largest country in the world. In terms of global CO_2 emissions, China is equally a 'big' country, contributing 12 per cent of the world's CO_2 emissions, second only to the US. The success of any international effort to address climate change will therefore require the participation of China.

Furthermore, China is among the countries most vulnerable to the adverse impacts of climate change. It has limited capacity and flexibility to mitigate or adapt to changing climate conditions. In this regard, China sees participation in climate change negotiations as an opportunity to have access to new funds and technologies. Its desire (and demand) for assistance from the developed countries draws largely from its previous experience with the phase-out of ozone-depleting substances under the Montreal Protocol (National Environmental Protection Agency, 1993). Indeed, the notion of developed countries providing financial resources to developing countries for environmental purposes was incorporated into the FCCC, notably in Article 11.

During the climate change negotiations, China and the Group of 77 developing countries (G77) established the largest bloc (Wang, 1999, pp135–149). The so-called 'Group of 77 and China' emerged in November 1991 at the early stages of negotiations. This was an outgrowth of two milestone events and their resulting documents: UN resolution 44/228 in December 1989 and the Beijing Declaration in June 1991. Both documents established a more coherent and orchestrated developing-country stance for future environmental negotiations. More specifically, this bloc subsequently served as a united front for China to forge a common position on FCCC principles and other issues of interest to developing nations (Bodansky, 1994).

China's stand in the climate change negotiations is explained by its national interests and its approach to bargaining. First, China's position is rooted in self-interest as defined by its status as a developing country. Its first and obvious interest is economic development. Second, the Chinese view the climate change negotiations as a bargaining process in which they hold much of the leverage. Given China's current status as the second largest emitter of CO_2, and also the fact that its future emissions will increase rapidly, its participation in any successful climate change agreement is essential. Third, bargaining leverage is enhanced by establishing a strategic alliance with other developing countries.

Furthermore, China's participation in the FCCC provides access to financial assistance and technology transfers. And, in many respects, China has become the spokesperson for the developing world, thereby raising its profile and improving its international recognition and reputation. Since China joined the world in international environmental affairs during the early 1970s, China's international presence has increased on issues such as global warming, and it has also broadened the range of policy responses to environmental problems, such as expanded climate research, emerging rule of law and institutional arrangements (Economy and Oksenberg, 1999, pp35–36).

China's emissions trend and energy context

China's emissions of CO_2 have grown phenomenally since 1950, when it stood tenth among nations. Growth from the late 1960s has been fairly regular. Total CO_2 emissions since 1950 of countries with large emissions are (in billions of tonnes): US, 186.1; European Union (EU), 127.8; Russia, 68.4; China, 57.6; Japan, 31.2; India, 15.5; and Canada, 14.9 (Kluger, 2001, pp34–35). The life cycle of CO_2 in the atmosphere is 50 to 200 years, so these large emitters contributed to the current atmospheric concentrations of CO_2. In other words, the industrialized countries have a historical responsibility to address the current problem of global warming. To China, the developed countries collectively caused global warming, and they therefore 'owe China special consideration because of past injustices' (Economy and Oksenberg, 1999, p25).

A snapshot of major GHG emissions shows that the US still leads, producing 6503.8 million metric tonnes of CO_2 equivalent (MtC) in 1997, followed by China at 4964.8; India, 2081.7; Russia, 1980.3; and Japan, 1166.1 (Revkin, 2001, p12). Developing countries with large populations, such as China and India, have very low per capita emissions compared to those of developed countries. For example, China is the second largest total emitter after the US; but its per capita emissions are about one seventh of those in the US (see Table 9.2).

Table 9.2 *World Carbon Emissions from Fossil Fuels: the Top Ten (2001)*

	Total emissions	
Country	Percentage of world emissions	Emissions per capita (metric tonnes)
US	24	5.4
China	14	0.7
Russia	6	2.7
Japan	5	2.5
India	5	0.3
Germany	4	2.8
Canada	2	4.2
UK	2	2.5
South Korea	2	2.2
Italy	2	2.0

Source: Doyle (2002, p29)

These discrepancies further intensify the equity debate and give rise to the demands of developing countries for the 'right to development' and 'common but differentiated responsibilities'. Developing countries believe that the developed countries should take the lead in reducing GHG emissions. A Chinese delegate captured this sentiment underlying their negotiating position: 'What they [developed nations] are doing is luxury emissions; what we are doing is survival emissions' (Wang, 1999, p174; see Huber and Douglas, 1998).

As a general rule, a country's economic growth rate is closely associated with the growth in energy consumption. About three-quarters of the energy in China is generated by coal. Among the six largest energy-consuming nations, only China relies so heavily on this dirty and bulky source of fuel. This heavy reliance, however, is not a consequence of economic competition and choice, but rather results from centralized planning, subsidized low energy prices, and inadequate technology and management. Most worrisome, coal combustion has caused serious environmental pollution problems and adverse impacts on public health, agriculture and quality of life. Acid rain, in particular, has become a severe problem. Average annual sulphur dioxide concentrations are more than three times World Health Organization (WHO) standards, and neighbouring countries such as Japan and Korea have concerns about acid rain from China (Pacific Northwest National Laboratory, 2001).

China, like other developing countries (and transitional economies), uses energy inefficiently – meaning that there is room for improvement. There has been some progress over the past two decades. For example, a recent study by the National Committee on US–China relations argues that 'China has managed to uncouple energy growth from economic growth more effectively than even most developed countries' (Logan et al, 1999). In fact, China has experienced energy growth at half the level of economic growth, while for countries such as India, South Korea and Brazil the energy growth has surpassed the economic growth rate. A recent report issued by the Natural Resources Defence Council (NRDC) also suggests promising signs in China's efforts to cut its CO_2 emissions, pointing to reductions of 17 per cent between 1997 and 2001, even while its economy grew 36 per cent. In contrast, CO_2 emissions in the US increased 14 per cent during the same period. If these figures are reliable, this shows that China has surpassed the US in efforts to reduce CO_2 emissions (Lazaroff, 2001; Eckholm, 2001).

The NRDC estimated in 2001 that China's CO_2 emissions for 2000 were about the same as in 1992. By 2020, with a continued economic growth rate of 5 to 6 per cent, China's emissions will be twice its 1990 level (1100 MtC), but still below US emissions in 1990 (1300 MtC). The NRDC study found that China's lower emissions increases were due to decreased reliance on coal, phasing-out of coal subsidies, closures of coal mines and the implementation of energy efficiency programmes, showing that the government has recognized many of the problems associated with China's reliance on coal, and that it is taking steps to reduce this reliance.

International environmental linkages

With China's energy profile in mind, it is now useful to examine China's presence in international environmental agreements. The 1972 UN Conference on the Human Environment (UNCHE) held in Stockholm was China's first major appearance on the international environmental stage. It gave impetus to the development of environmental policy and bureaucracies around the world (Ross, 1998, pp87–90). Generally speaking, the process of China's international environmental participation can be categorized in three stages: an initial stage from 1972 to 1978, which focused on the UNCHE and its follow-up activities; a developing stage from 1979 to 1992, including negotiation of the Montreal Protocol on ozone depletion and China gradually taking a leading role in the bloc of developing countries; and an ongoing stage, which began with the 1992 UN Conference on Environment and Development (UNCED, or the Rio Earth Summit) and a growing number of international environmental regimes (Wang, 1999, pp100–179).

To many observers, international environmental policy and politics can be viewed as a winding road from the Stockholm conference. For China, this road has turned out to be both a challenge and an opportunity. China's involvement has been developed or constrained by the primacy of its economic development and national sovereignty. At the same time, it heralds a new era of China's engagement and cooperation where *huanjing waijiao* (environmental diplomacy) has emerged as a policy alternative. Since 1979, China has been actively participating in international environmental activities launched by UN-related organizations such as UNEP, the UN Development Programme (UNDP), the World Bank and the Asian Development Bank. Internationally, because of the increasing salience of the environmental problems and policy responses, China has signed and participated in nearly 30 multilateral treaties addressing issues such as ozone depletion, biodiversity, whaling, wetland protection, transboundary movement of hazardous wastes and, of course, global warming and climate change. In terms of bilateral relations, China has signed environmental protection cooperation agreements with the US, Japan, Canada, Germany, Korea, India, Australia, Mongolia, Russia, Ukraine, Finland, Norway, Denmark and the Netherlands (Information Office of the State Council, 1996; Wang, 1999, pp180–210).

China wishes to be appreciated as an active and constructive member of the international community. According to a White Paper on its environmental policy, it therefore has taken vigorous action to promote international cooperation in environmental protection. For example, in April 1992 it set up the China Council for International Cooperation on Environment and Development, which was designed to promote international cooperation in sustainable development. This advisory council, made up of more than 40 scientists, government representatives and advisers from overseas, makes policy proposals on areas such as energy and environment, resource accounting and pricing systems, and environmental laws and regulations (Information Office of the State Council, 1996).

China's participation in the climate change agreements

China is now a party to the FCCC and its Kyoto Protocol. Two important documents – the 1991 Beijing Declaration and Li Peng's 'Five Principles' of 1992 – illustrate the bases for China's negotiating stance on climate change.

A principled negotiating stance

The Ministerial Conference of Developing Countries on Environment and Development, proposed by China and held in Beijing in June 1991, was attended by 41 developing countries. This forum resulted in the promulgation of the Beijing Declaration. It set forth a 'principled' negotiating stand asserting the need for international cooperation, the right to development, opposition to interference in the internal affairs of states, and demands for financial assistance and technology transfer. The timing of the conference was critical, coming just before related formal UN negotiations were launched. The Chinese government attached major significance and visibility to this gathering. One consequence of the conference was the establishment of China as a spokesperson or advocate for the developing world (Wang, 1999, pp143–144).

Chinese Premier Li Peng attended the Rio Earth Summit in 1992. During a speech he outlined five principles guiding China's future course of economic development and environmental protection, reflecting the priorities of developing countries declared in the Beijing Declaration:

1   Environment and development should be integrated, but environmental protection should not be achieved at the expense of the economy. Environmental protection can only be successful when development has been attained.
2   From an historical perspective, the developed countries are responsible for global environmental degradation and the current problems with GHG emissions. We [China] should not talk about responsibility.
3   Developed countries should provide resources for implementation of agreements or declarations signed. This financial resource should not be considered as assistance, but as the responsibility of the developed states. China believes that this assistance should be viewed as compensation.

4   The developed countries should find suitable mechanisms to develop sub-
    stantial programmes. In order to accommodate national intellectual
    property rights, the governments of the developed countries should buy
    the technology from companies at less than international market prices.
5   The sovereignty of national resource rights must be respected. No country
    can interfere with the decisions of another with regard to the use of its
    natural resources (Economy, 1997b, p32).

In international environmental negotiations, China officially reiterates its commitments to these principles: sovereignty, opposition to interference in internal
affairs, development rights, responsibility of the industrialized countries, and
demands for financial assistance and technology transfer. In practical terms,
the primacy of parallel economic development and environmental protection
seems to be meshed into an overall balance of economic, social, environmental
and foreign affairs interests (Ross, 1998, pp90–91). Looking ahead, the level
and extent of China's participation in the climate change regime depends upon
a long-term policy trend in which these interests are balanced. Over time,
resistance to certain treaty commitments may be reduced.

China's commitments under the FCCC and the Kyoto Protocol

The FCCC was signed by more than 150 nations at the Rio Earth Summit and
entered into force in 1994. As of mid 2004, more than 190 countries were sig-
natories. The basic elements of the Beijing Declaration and Li-Peng's Five
Principles have, for the most part, been incorporated within the FCCC. For
example, principles included in Article 3 of the convention include 'common
but differentiated responsibilities', whereby developed countries take the lead
in combating climate change, and full consideration of specific needs and special circumstances of developing countries (Harris, 2001a, pp48–51).

In general, there are three types of commitments as elaborated in the
FCCC text:

1   those to be undertaken by all parties;
2   those applied to parties in Annex I (all Organisation for Economic Co-
    operation and Development (OECD) (that is, developed) countries except
    Mexico, the EU and countries in transition, such as Russia, Ukraine and
    Poland; and
3   those to be undertaken by parties listed in Annex II (all OECD countries
    except Mexico and the EU).

Under this framework of commitments, China, as a non-Annex I country, is to
prepare national inventories of GHG emissions caused by human activities;
develop programmes to mitigate and adapt to climate change; integrate climate

change considerations with other domestic policies; and conduct research to reduce uncertainties concerning scientific knowledge of climate change. China's commitment under the FCCC is therefore relatively minimal, with no emissions reduction targets. By comparison, Annex I countries were called upon to individually or collectively return to their 1990 CO_2 emissions levels by 2000, as specified in Article 4.2(b). Annex II countries were also called upon by the convention to provide new and additional financial resources and to transfer technology to meet the costs incurred by developing countries in complying with their obligations, as specified in Article 4.3-5.

Prior to negotiation of the FCCC, the most closely related international treaties were the 1985 Vienna Convention for Protection of the Ozone Layer and the associated 1987 Montreal Protocol (which has been amended several times). The Vienna convention was a framework convention setting out general policy goals and research objectives, whereas the Montreal Protocol dealt with actually reducing chemical pollutants that deplete the stratospheric ozone layer. In terms of treaty formation, the FCCC negotiations took a similar convention-protocol approach. This two-step process first uses a framework convention that identifies what has to be done, gathers scientific information to arrive at greater scientific consensus, and calls for general emissions guidelines without binding commitments. A subsequent protocol sets more specific emission commitments with targets and timetables (Susskind, 1994, pp30–37).

Parties to the FCCC agreed to the Kyoto Protocol at the third Convention to the Parties (COP3) in 1997. The protocol calls upon Annex I countries to reduce their emissions of GHGs by an average of 5.2 per cent below 1990 levels during 2008–2012. Article 4 allows a group of nations to form a 'bubble' in which the group has an overall target to meet. Article 3 allows for carbon sinks, such as land and forestry practice that would absorb CO_2. Article 17 stipulates that emissions trading (ET) is permitted among industrialized countries, and participating nations can issue domestic GHG emission permits. Articles 6 and 12 allow for joint implementation (JI) and the Clean Development Mechanism (CDM). JI provides for the transfer of emissions reduction units between Annex I parties. The CDM enables Annex I parties to take emissions credits through projects in non-Annex I (developing) states if these joint projects produce a reduction of emissions relative to a 'business-as-usual' emission scenario.

During the Kyoto negotiations, China and the G77 resisted the imposition of any binding emissions targets on developing countries. They met with great success, and the developing countries are exempt from any emissions reduction obligations. This is reflective of their declarations on the right to development. They also gained provisions for access to financial assistance and the technology necessary for capacity-building. China views ET, JI and the CDM as domestic emissions reductions through alternative or 'out-of-country' implementation. China thinks that there should be a strict 'cap' placed on these alternative methods of emissions reduction, and that these alternatives should only serve as supplements to real reduction within each developed country (Ministry of Foreign Affairs, 2002).

Climate change and China's environmental diplomacy

Linking environment and foreign policy has become an emerging practice in world politics, and more and more agreements are concluded through a process of international environmental negotiation and cooperation. However, most global environmental problems are growing worse. This tendency of environmental diplomacy is reflected in the climate change negotiations.

China's negotiating principles – such as the right to development; parallel economic growth with environmental protection; industrialized countries' historical responsibility; and demand for assistance and technology – have almost all been incorporated within the text of the FCCC and the Kyoto Protocol. To China, climate diplomacy is conducted under the concept of *qui tong cun yi* ('approach the common ground and reconcile the differences') (Solomon, 1999, pp181–183). That is, engaging in a process of participation itself does not necessarily mean committing to any responsibilities. And it is paradoxical that participation in an international environmental agreement requiring emission reductions does not necessarily impose emissions commitment.

By 1998 China's environmental protection efforts had already used US$3.2 billion in foreign assistance (Wang, 1999, p178). China has received funding from the World Bank and the Global Environment Facility (GEF), and it has borrowed more money from the World Bank for energy-related projects than any other country. From 1984 to 1999, the World Bank funded about US$7 billion for 36 energy projects, and the GEF provided an additional US$90 million in co-financing for projects on energy efficiency and renewable energy (Martinot, 2001). This foreign assistance may have helped to shape or influence China's environmental protection policies, its development of legal frameworks, personnel training and general institutional capacity-building. China's greenhouse emissions, through efforts in energy efficiency and renewable energy projects, have been reduced accordingly.

China's climate diplomacy, as led by the Ministry of Foreign Affairs (MOFA), has been strengthened and integrated. When the IPCC was established in 1988, the lead agency in China's climate change affairs was the China Meteorological Administration (CMA). As climate negotiation developed and evolved, the State Development Planning Commission and then MOFA became the lead agencies. More specifically, all of China's delegations to UN climate change meetings are organized by MOFA. Negotiating stance is coordinated by MOFA. China's contact office and focal point for the FCCC secretariat is located in MOFA. Altogether, MOFA is therefore the lead agency in climate change negotiation and management. To China, climate change is seldom a 'scientific' issue. It involves national economic development and foreign affairs interests that are important diplomatically.

Conclusion

The enhanced greenhouse effect associated with human activities, such as the burning of fossil fuels and deforestation, are major factors causing global warming and climate change. As the atmosphere knows no national boundaries, the issue of global warming has to be addressed effectively through a global effort to limit GHG emissions. Consequently, the FCCC and the Kyoto Protocol were negotiated. Given its size, population, rapid economic growth and heavy domestic reliance on coal, China's development path will affect the world's environment more than that of any other nation. China now produces about 12 per cent of the global GHG emissions, second only to the US (which produces about 25 per cent of emissions). Any international agreement cannot be fully successful without support and participation of China. China is a party to the FCCC and signatory to the Kyoto Protocol. As a non-Annex I (developing country) party, it has 'common but differentiated' responsibilities; but it is not obligated to undertake any emissions reductions, nor will it be required to reduce emissions even if the Kyoto Protocol is fully enacted in the future. Developed countries have 'historical' responsibilities to take the initiative for emission reductions. To China, participation in the agreements is its contribution, and environmental protection should be balanced with its economic development while the developed countries should take the lead in addressing climate change.

Whether intended to meet the goals of the climate regime or not, China has taken steps to slow the growth of its emissions. Through financial assistance and technology transfer, China has built up its capabilities to combat climate change in the areas of energy efficiency and renewable energy. Contrary to many studies' forecasts that China's emissions would increase rapidly and surpass US emission as early as 2015, there is evidence that its emissions are increasing at a rate below the rate at which its economy is growing. Despite President George W Bush's assertion that China is not addressing global warming, it is, in fact, doing a much better job in this respect than is the US. The role of China in climate change seems to be more positive than the Western world perceives.

Nevertheless, China can play a more positive role. Since China is in the early stages of industrialization, it can still take a different development path than the historical path of Western nations. This could ensure economic growth commensurate with environmental protection. One barrier is a lack of recognition by each country about the activities and accomplishments of the other. In this regard, it is important that all countries *qui tong cun yi* ('approach the common ground and reconcile the differences'), allow common interests to gradually outweigh points in contention, and foster the growth of mutual trust. Despite unsolved differences on joint implementation, emissions trading and the Clean Development Mechanism, the FCCC and the Kyoto Protocol have established a foundation for continued dialogue. The protocol encourages non-Annex I countries to take voluntary action to reduce their emissions. For practical reasons associated with deteriorating domestic environmental conditions, a call for emissions reduction is not inconsistent with China's national interests, currently and in the long run.

Chapter 10

Thailand and the Convention on Biological Diversity: Non-governmental Organizations Enter the Debate

Jak Sangchai

Introduction

The Convention on Biological Diversity (CBD) was opened for signature on 5 June 1992 at the Earth Summit in Rio de Janeiro. It came into effect on 29 December 1993. By late 2002 nearly 190 countries were parties to the convention, with the most notable non-parties being the US and Thailand (Secretariat of the CBD, 2002). The CBD's three goals are to promote:

> ... *the conservation of biological diversity, the sustainable use of its components, and the fair and equitable sharing of benefits arising out of the utilization of genetic resources, including by appropriate access to genetic resources and by appropriate transfer of relevant technologies, taking into account all rights over those resources and to technologies, and by appropriate funding* (United Nations Conference on Environment and Development, 1992, Article 1).

Why has Thailand joined the US in resisting accession to the CBD? Debate about the convention has been very controversial in Thailand since it signed the agreement in 1992. The country's response to the CBD issue involves not only the government sector, but other sectors also participate in the debate.

For example, the media has continuously reported on news and issues concerning the CBD. Thailand's domestic actors have taken the CBD issue very seriously because they believe that the CBD presents imminent danger to the people's livelihood: food, lands and forests. These issues have long been debated in Thailand for years (see 'Debate 3: Bio-piracy, intellectual property rights and trade' later in this chapter).

Many Thai non-governmental organizations (NGOs) have actively protested against the government's attempt to ratify the CBD. While other countries and their NGOs view the CBD as an environmental agreement that promotes conservation and the protection of the nature, Thai NGOs see the CBD as more than just an environmental agreement; they see it also as a development and trade one. They argue that the Thai government is too eager to ratify it in order to receive funds and technology transfer from developed countries. They believe that Thailand would have to lose biological resources in return for any gains. They are also concerned about other issues – for instance, traditional medicine, community rights, farmers' rights and control over patents and intellectual property. In addition, the issue even caused a rift between government agencies.

This debate over the country's role in the CBD highlights many important attributes of contemporary environmental foreign policy in Thailand, including changes in Thai politics and society, the increasing influence of NGOs and civil society in Thailand, and the loss of administrative control by bureaucrats. Debates concerning the CBD in Thailand, examined in this chapter, illustrate conflicts between actors – particularly the government and NGOs (see Table 10.1). The debates revolve around:

- questions of sovereignty;
- the sufficiency (or insufficiency) of existing Thai legislation;
- the relationship between the CBD, intellectual property rights and international trade; and
- technical legal issues.

This chapter examines these debates, highlighting the actors and forces that shape Thai foreign policy on this important environmental issue.

These four debates are a direct result of political changes in Thailand in the aftermath of the 1997–1998 financial crisis. The Thai political system has been under public pressure to be more accountable and transparent. NGOs and civil society have criticized the Thai government for its failure to prevent the economic meltdown, and for allowing transnational companies from the West to cause the collapse of many financial institutions, thereby increasing unemployment and personal debts. Thus, the people feel threatened by foreign influences and their nationalistic sense is heightened. Thai NGOs have portrayed the CBD as a trap by transnational companies to steal the country's biological resources and intellectual property, and as a threat to the country's sovereignty. They point out that, since the CBD affects Thailand's sovereignty, its ratification requires parliamentary approval, like that of other trade agreements, in accordance with the country's 1997 Constitution. They have therefore gained considerable support from the public against the CBD. The upshot is that heavy campaigning by NGOs and academics against the CBD, particularly through the media, has prevented the government from ratifying the CBD.

Table 10.1 *Main Actors in the CBD Debate in Thailand*

Supporting ratification	Opposing ratification
• Ministry of Science, Technology and Environment (MOSTE)	• Ministry of Public Health (MPH), via the Institute of Thai Traditional Medicine
• Ministry of Agriculture and Cooperatives (MAC)	• NGOs, via the Thai Network on Community Rights and Biodiversity (BIOTHAI)
• Academics	• Academics

Debate 1: National sovereignty

The CBD itself incorporates two conflicting ideas: the 'common concerns' of mankind and 'national sovereignty'. These ideas were in profound conflict with regard to international environmental regimes long before the introduction of the CBD. On the one hand, a country would like to keep its jurisdiction over its territory and it wants resources to be used for the benefit of the country and its people, rather than the benefit of other countries and their peoples. On the other hand, the concepts of common concern, common heritage and common problems represent a more contemporary holistic ideology of the interconnectedness between lives and nature. Many environmental problems are transboundary, and the only solutions to tackle problems of this nature are through pooling the efforts of people all over the world. That is, international cooperation is necessary to solve these problems. However, international cooperation is itself a compromise because countries must give up part of their sovereignty and decision-making power in order to achieve the common environmental objective; but, in the end, the success of international cooperation relies heavily upon national implementation.

It is rather curious that it was Thai NGOs which brought up the question of sovereignty and sovereign rights, whereas NGOs in other countries urged their governments to ratify the CBD (Pookpakdi, 2000, interview; Lianchamroon, 2000, interview). The behaviour of Thai NGOs in the CBD debate on sovereignty appears to be inconsistent with many observers who cite proliferation of NGOs as evidence that state sovereignty is eroded from below, to the point where the power of the central government is transferred to local communities (Dryzek, 1987). It seems that Thai NGOs are concerned about transboundary environmental problems, but are confused about how to solve the problems. While Thai NGOs want the Thai government to maintain the country's sovereignty at the international level, they call for decentralization of power from the government and people's participation in the government's processes because they do not believe that the government truly represents the people. This means that Thai NGOs agree that the Thai government represents the country on the international stage, but that it does not represent the country within the country itself. However, it has been widely accepted that the bureaucrats dominate Thailand's direction and administration.[1] NGOs have challenged that the CBD benefits the government, not the people or the country as a whole.

In fact, the CBD affirms that 'States have sovereign rights over their own biological resources' and 'States are responsible for conserving their biological diversity and for using their biological resources in a sustainable manner' (United Nations Conference on Environment and Development, 1992, Preamble and Article 3). Article 15 of the CBD, which involves benefit-sharing and access to genetic resources, has caused ferocious arguments in Thailand about sovereignty and the sovereign rights of the country. NGOs in Thailand claim that the country would have to sacrifice sovereign rights in order to facilitate access to genetic resources for other countries, even though it is only conditional access: Article 15.2 states that member countries should try to set conditions to facilitate the access to genetic resources by other member countries without imposing restrictions that are against the objectives of the CBD. According to the NGOs' understanding, the country cannot decline a request to access resources, even though it can set conditions for the access, which means the country loses power in making decisions and, therefore, loses its sovereign rights. As a result, it is sensible from the NGOs' viewpoint that the country should have absolute rights to determine whether or not it provides access to genetic resources. The bottom line of this argument is about whether the environment is a national or an international matter. However, given that everyone, including NGOs, recognizes that environmental problems are transboundary, the problems should be solved by international cooperation. Otherwise, some countries would protect the environment while others – the free riders – would not.

The Thai government's answer to the question of why the country should join the CBD is simple and weak: 183 other countries have ratified the convention. If they could lose their sovereign jurisdiction, why did they ratify it? Why should Thailand opt out? So, in the government's point of view, Thailand should join the CBD in order not to be left out – that is, for reasons of image:

'Thailand is a small and developing country. It is always necessary to consider position and status when making decisions on international issues' (Poopatanapong, 1999, interview).

Surprisingly, further and better reasons for why Thailand should join the CBD come from the NGO side: since almost all countries have ratified the CBD, Thailand is indirectly forced to initiate policy and to conduct activities stated in the CBD. Otherwise the country might be accused of being a free rider, which could affect its economic interest (Subcharoen, 2000, interview; Lianchamroon, 2000, interview). Some NGOs, such as the Thai Network on Community Rights and Biodiversity (BIOTHAI), which changed its position from 'opposing' to 'not opposing' ratification, have admitted that they do not care whether or not Thailand joins the CBD. They previously opposed the ratification because they wanted the public to pay more attention to the issue, and to foster governmental accountability by being more involved in the policy process (Lianchamroon, 2000, interview).

Debate 2: Sufficiency of existing legislation

There are a number of arguments between the government, NGOs and academics over whether Thailand's existing laws are sufficient in this issue area. Although Thailand does not have a specific law concerning biodiversity conservation, the Ministry of Science, Technology and Environment (MOSTE) and the Ministry of Agriculture and Cooperatives (MAC) suggest that the country's existing laws are sufficient. Cumpeeraparp (1995, pp54–63) argues that there are many Thai laws which involve biodiversity, but they only relate to some aspects. For instance, the 1975 Plants Act concerns genetic diversity, the 1960 Wildlife Conservation and Protection Act concerns species diversity and the 1961 National Park Act deals with ecological diversity.

The main difference between Thai laws and the CBD is in the area of genetic resources. The CBD allows wide use of genetic resources (United Nations Conference on Environment and Development, 1992, Articles 6, 7, 10, 11, 15), whereas Thai laws prohibit such utilization. For example, Article 16 of the 1961 National Park Act sets conditions prohibiting human activities to use national park areas. Furthermore, Articles 7 and 8 of the CBD address activities that can have adverse impacts upon the conservation and sustainable use of biodiversity; but Thai laws do not pay much attention to this issue. More importantly, the laws give considerable authority to government officers to use conservation areas for other purposes, such as converting national parks into tourist attraction sites. As a consequence, it is necessary for Thailand to introduce new laws or amend existing laws for the country's own national environmental interests.

NGOs suggest that Thailand does not have sufficient laws to protect bio-diversity and local people, and farmers would be disadvantaged if the country fully joined the CBD without first having protection by domestic laws. However, their point is not that Thailand lacks adequate or effective environmental legislation, but that it lacks sufficient trade, patent and intellectual property legislation because NGOs link the CBD to the global economy, international trade, and patent and intellectual property rights.

Debate 3: Bio-piracy, intellectual property rights and trade

Thai NGOs perceive the CBD as a trap for developing countries which have most of the genetic resources in the world, set up by developed countries and transnational companies to gain access to the resources. Hence, ratifying the CBD means the first step to legalizing 'bio-piracy'. Lianchamroon (1998, p4) explains that:

> *Bio-pirates mean those who utilize the biological resources and traditional knowledge without permission and/or sharing equally benefits to the local community. Normally, the bio-pirates may use intellectual property to legitimize the exclusive ownership over the biological resources/knowledge and prevent others, including local communities, to make use from those developments.*

The government responds that resources in Thailand have always been taken out of the country by legal and illegal means. The CBD would help the government to reassert control over bio-pirates. Moreover, with cooperation between CBD member countries, it would be possible for the government to track down bio-pirates outside of its national jurisdiction, and – if they are used or modified for commercial purposes – the country would at least claim or share in the benefits.

Thai NGOs are anxious about bio-piracy because there have been examples of it in many countries. The classic case in Thailand is that of *Plau Noi* (*Croton sublyratus*), a local medicinal herb, from which the Sankyo Company of Japan extracts CS684 – an active substance for ulcer treatment. The company patented the substance under the name of Plaunotol in 1983, and produces and sells Plaunotol under the trade name of Kelnac. NGOs point out that the company has patents on the production process and products of Plaunotol, which is derived from the genetic resource and local wisdom of Thai people. And it closes the door to Thai research and development because Thai researchers cannot use the same processes and products for development (Lianchamroon, 1998, p40).

Thai NGOs considered that Thailand did not have sufficient legislation on the biodiversity-related intellectual property and patent issues. They pressured the government to introduce three new laws: the Plant Varieties Protection Act, the Thai Traditional Medicine and Local Knowledge Protection and Promotion Act and the Forest Community Act.

The Plant Varieties Protection Act

The 1999 Plant Varieties Protection Act aims to protect and patent both local and new plant varieties, including genetically modified plants. The objective of the act is to allow communities to register, protect and conserve plant varieties in their localities. At first, the law was drafted to protect only new plants; but NGOs protested, saying that this would mean that only plant breeders would have privileges and benefits. They suggested that farmers should also have privileges because they have traditional knowledge and methods that have improved plant varieties for years. NGOs asked the government to include themselves and farmers in the drafting committee, fearing that farmers' rights would have been ignored (Thitiprasert, 2000, interview; Lianchamroon, 2000, interview). The government officer in charge of the Plant Varieties Protection Act accepted the idea of having this new legislation was developed from debates about the CBD (Thitiprasert, 2000, interview). This was reinforced by Article 27.3(b) of the World Trade Organization Agreement on Trade-Related Aspects of Intellectual Property Rights, including Trade in Counterfeit Goods (WTO TRIPS Agreement):

> *Members may ... exclude from patentability: plants and animals other than micro-organisms, and essentially biological processes for the production of plants or animals other than non-biological and microbiological processes. However, members shall provide for the protection of plant varieties either by patents or by an effective* sui generis *['unique' or 'of its own kind'] system or by any combination thereof* (Genetic Resources Action International, 1997, p122).

Thai NGOs and some international NGOs are anxious about global trade and the influences of countries which have more economic power. They believe that the economic superpowers are trying to change the TRIPs Agreement by removing exclusions from patentability for plant and animal varieties, as well as biological processes for the production of plants and animals (Genetic Resources Action International, 1997, pp13–14). Thai NGOs fear that it would be disastrous for Thailand if the article were to change while the country does not have its own effective patent or other *sui generis* laws. In fact, Thailand has the 1979 Patent Act and the 1992 Second Patent Act, both of which do not allow plants, animals and micro-organisms to be patented. However, the 1992 Patent Act includes patenting on biotechnological matters, pharmaceutical products and biological processes for the production of animals, plants or micro-organisms. It seems that, from NGOs' perspectives regarding the TRIPs Agreement, they were calling for the patenting of plants and plant varieties. However, they called for different and separate types of patenting systems because they did not think that Thailand's current patent act and patenting system were adequate. The NGOs wanted a new law following the *sui generis* system as stated in the TRIPs Agreement. The result was the Plant Varieties Act, which took effect in 1999.

The Thai Traditional Medicine and Local Knowledge Protection and Promotion Act

NGOs were also concerned that medicinal herbs and local knowledge about traditional medicines would not be protected. They argued that it was necessary to have a specific patent law for traditional medicines, a law benefiting people and communities which have knowledge about them. In cooperation with NGOs, the Ministry of Public Health (MPH) introduced the second piece of legislation, the Thai Traditional Medicine and Local Knowledge Protection and Promotion Act. It is one of the most controversial laws in Thailand due to its underlying context and rationale, its origins and its related advantages (or disadvantages). The law caused a rift between government agencies. The act emphasized registration and patenting of traditional medicines used by traditional healers, so that they could claim benefits. The MPH feared that the CBD would give foreign researchers and companies easier access to genetic resources, including medicinal herbs. This would mean that if foreign researchers and companies genetically modify the herbs and patent them, traditional healers could not claim benefits. However, Thai government environmental officers believed that this issue had little to do with the CBD and the law that controls access to genetic resources was necessary (Pookpakdi, 2000, interview; Bunpapong, 2000, interview). Moreover, the objective of the CBD clearly points to equitable sharing of benefits from the use of resources. Article 8(j) of the CBD calls on member countries to:

> ... *respect, preserve and maintain knowledge, innovations and practices of indigenous and local communities embodying traditional lifestyles relevant for the conservation and sustainable use of biological diversity and promote the wider application with the approval and involvement of the holders of such knowledge, innovations and practices and encourage the equitable sharing of benefits arising from the utilization of such knowledge, innovations and practices* (United Nations Conference on Environment and Development, 1992, Article 8j).

Moreover, the First Secretary of the US Embassy to Thailand sent a letter to the Department of Intellectual Property, Ministry of Commerce, in 1997, expressing the US's concern about the drafting of the act, and stating that the registration system under the act could violate the TRIPs Agreement (Cumpeeraparp, 1998, pp31–36). Nonetheless, the act, in fact, follows the *sui generis* system under Article 27.3(b) of the TRIPs Agreement and Article 27.3(a), which states that member countries may exclude 'diagnostic, thera-peutic and surgical methods for the treatment of humans and animals' from patentability (Genetic Resources Action International, 1997, p122). The inter-ference of the US provoked Thai academics, lawyers and NGOs to send a letter of protest to the US Department of State. However, the draft act became law in 1999.

In addition to the concerns already described, some academics and govern-ment officers allegedly accused a senior officer of the MPH of rallying support from NGOs and using the act for personal interests because she actively pushed for introduction of the act and aggressively opposed the CBD.[2] Under the new act, her office would be elevated to a higher level, from division to bureau, and she herself would be promoted. More importantly, one observer suggested that 'this law is evil' because it gives enormous authority to a spe-cific MPH office (Mallikamal, 1999, interview). For instance, the director of the office is the registrar of traditional medicines. At the same time, if someone appeals for a review of the registration, the director is also a secretary and member of the appeals committee. Therefore, it would be easy for corruption to occur because there are no checks and balances (Mallikamal, 1999, inter-view). Arguments about this act became irrational during the later stages, with both sides adopting aggressive styles: those who supported ratification of the CBD were accused of being traitors to the country, while those who opposed it were accused of using the new act for personal benefit.

The promulgation of the 1999 Thai Traditional Medicine and Local Knowledge Protection and Promotion Act was succeeded by cooperation between officers of the MPH and NGOs. The whole drafting and legislative process was completed within only two years, from 1997 to 1999, which was unusually quick when compared with the normal law-making process in Thailand. This was due to massive pressure on the government, the NGOs' aggressive tactics and conflicts between government agencies. Furthermore, NGOs were able to expand the debate concerning this act, and the CBD, beyond the conservation issue to include community rights and local liveli-hood issues. More importantly, the most prominent and aggressive actors came from the government – namely, the MPH officers who sided with NGOs, which made it more difficult for the government to ignore the NGOs' con-cerns. In addition, an attempt to interfere in the legislative process by the US only caused more publicity. The US interference was immediately portrayed by

NGOs and academics as an example of a developed country trying to influence a developing country, which was exactly what Thai NGOs used in order to campaign against the CBD.

The Community Forest Act

The third piece of legislation, the Community Forest Act, has sparked debate in Thailand for the last 20 years – indeed, from the period before there was a CBD. The general idea of 'community forest' is to allow people in each community to manage their own natural and genetic resources. Conflicts concerning this act are related to differences over concepts, methods and measures concerning whether people can live within forests or should live outside of them. While the government criticizes people who live adjacent to the forests as being those who cause deforestation due to their encroachment, NGOs believe that local people and communities are those who know well how to treat and look after the forests because their livelihood depends upon resources acquired from the forests (Panyarachun, 2000, interview). As a result, from the NGOs' point of view, it is very difficult, albeit possible, to draw a borderline between forests and adjacent communities.

Previous drafts of the bill did not make it through the Thai Parliament. The current drafts, one proposed by the Royal Forest Department (RFD), and another proposed by groups of NGOs, are stuck somewhere in the legislative process. A push for the bill was reinvigorated by debates about Article 8(j) of the CBD concerning knowledge, innovations and practices of indigenous and local communities. Knowledge in this sense means knowledge that local people use for their livelihoods, and that has been passed from generation to generation in the community and is specially bonded with the natural environment surrounding communities. Therefore, local people and communities know best about their surroundings and should have rights to manage and look after surrounding natural resources, and to participate in the government's environmental and natural resource management policies.

Other questions followed the two new laws. Are these laws sufficient to accommodate the CBD or to protect the country against the disadvantages of the CBD? They are certainly related to the CBD, but they do not cover all of the issues in the CBD if the intention of NGOs was to prepare the country for its ratification. More importantly, it seems that the two acts are likely to have been direct responses to the WTO TRIPs Agreement, rather than the CBD (Institute of Thai Traditional Medicine, 2000, p19). In fact, these laws would not guarantee that Thailand would be free from CBD threats when it joins (or, in the opinion of those who want Thailand to ratify the CBD, that the country would gain opportunities). Moreover, the CBD is still being developed, and there will be new issues coming up in the future. New rules can be made by a vote at the Conference of the Parties (COP). The later that Thailand joins in, the more rules are made. And when Thailand joins in, it has to follow the rules made earlier. It will be too late to complain.

Another problem concerns the plants that NGOs seek to protect from acts of bio-piracy. Some plants are not native, but were introduced to Thailand a long time ago, such as *Choom hed tes* (ringworm bush), *Tarn* (Palmyra), papaya, grape and some species of rice (Thitiprasert, 2000, interview; Kutintara, 2000, interview). If some countries can find evidence that the plants originated in their countries and do not want to share the benefits with Thailand, the country would have a big problem. Moreover, the formulae of some traditional medicine are the same in other Asian countries. Thailand might be wrong if it claims that they belong to the Thai people because other countries which have evidence of origin may be able to patent the formula, so that Thailand would have to pay the price for their patent rights. This could be the real reason that NGOs do not want Thailand to ratify the CBD: as long as the country stays out of it, the country can continue to gain benefits from those plants and formulae. This would mean that the country itself might have committed an act of 'bio-piracy' (if other countries have sufficient evidence to that effect). It would be good only if those plants and formulae really belong to Thailand, and the country is a member of the CBD, so that it can claim or share benefits. Therefore, linking biodiversity issues with the intellectual property rights agenda might not always be beneficial.

Some Thai NGOs became silent on CBD issues after the two laws they asked for entered into force. Thitiphan Pookpakdi of MOSTE suggests that this is because those NGOs obtained what they wanted: not the two laws, but greater popularity and, hence, more funding. More importantly, Pookpakdi suggests that some NGOs opposed to the CBD are not environmental NGOs; they are actually development NGOs and social NGOs, and their environment-related activities are extensions of their development activities. What they are concerned with is not the state of biodiversity in Thailand, but the rights of farmers and the rural poor. They seem concerned about the effects of global trade, not (global) conservation issues. The CBD is only a means that they use to accomplish their objectives (Pookpakdi, 2000, interview).

Debate 4: Legal technicalities

The CBD debate has divided government agencies. MOSTE, which is responsible for conservation of biodiversity, has joined hands with MAC, responsible for utilization of biological resources, in pushing for early ratification of the CBD. Opposed to joining the CBD is the MPH, which is joined by NGOs and a sympathetic legal interpretation regarding the CBD from the Office of the

Council of State (OCS). The debates on sovereignty, intellectual property rights and bio-piracy have all come down to different legal interpretations of the CBD and Thailand's Constitution. For example, according to the OCS, Article 15.2 of the CBD (which says that 'Each Contracting Party shall endeavour to create conditions to facilitate access to genetic resources') affects the country's sovereignty because member countries 'have to' always allow access to genetic resources. Thai law enforcement would be changed, and approval from the Thai Parliament is therefore required under the second paragraph of Article 181 of the 1995 Constitution (currently Article 224 of the 1997 Constitution),[3] which states as follows:

A treaty which provides for a change in the Thai territories or the jurisdiction of the State or requires the enactment of an Act for its implementation must be approved by the National Assembly (Office of the Council of State, 2000).

Although OCS is a legal adviser of the government, MOSTE and MAC continue to insist that the CBD does not affect the national jurisdiction and that existing laws are adequate, so it is not necessary to take the CBD to the Thai Parliament for approval. Actually, MOSTE completely dismissed the interpretation of the OCS on Article 15.2 of the CBD. It stated clearly that the OCS was wrong because the interpretation of OCS contradicts the principle of the agreement ('States have ... the sovereign right to exploit their own resources pursuant to their own environmental policies'; United Nations Conference on Environment and Development, 1992, Article 3). Under Article 3 of the convention, a country can even completely forbid access to its resources because such a ban does not contradict the objectives of the CBD. In addition, it was already agreed at the CBD's 1996 third Conference of the Parties (COP3) that each country has the right to determine, under its own legislation, the definition and scope of the word 'access'.[4]

Another difference exists regarding interpretation of the area of jurisdiction, with the main agencies in opposition being the Ministry of Foreign Affairs (MFA), as adviser to the government on international law, and the OCS, as adviser to the government on national law. The MFA informed the Cabinet Secretary that none of the articles of the CBD would affect the sovereignty and jurisdiction of Thailand because the convention only states that member countries must 'try' to implement policies in accordance with the treaty. Furthermore, there is no binding obligation that members have to enact new legislation for implementing the convention, and there are neither articles contradicting existing Thai laws, nor any that directly affect the rights, freedom and duties of the Thai people.[5] Therefore, there is no need to get approval from the Thai Parliament.

Because the differences of opinion between these two agencies could not be resolved – the CBD had become a technical and political issue – the Cabinet decided on 27 October 1998 to have the MFA and the OCS bring the issue and their opinions to the Constitutional Court (Article 266 of the 1997 Constitution states that if there is a problem over the authority of agencies under the constitution, the agency or President of the Parliament can propose the issue to the Constitutional Court for consideration) (Office of the Council of State, 2000).[6]

It is commonly understood that when an international treaty is made, those countries which decide to join have to sacrifice part of their sovereignty to work under the direction of the treaty (consent to be bound) and accept its obligations. The CBD (and any other international agreements) are not right from the OCS's point of view because no one should tell the country what to think or do. Therefore, in the opinion of the OCS, words such as 'shall endeavour to facilitate access to genetic resources' in Article 15.2 of the CBD are not right. Nevertheless, MAC, MOSTE and MFA see the same article differently. They believe that the country retains decision-making powers over whether access can be granted. There is a difference between 'trying to do' and 'doing' something, in their opinion; but the OCS argues that it is not even right if someone is forced under the agreement's obligation 'to try', as if one cannot think by oneself. Actually, the OCS seems to forget that Thailand has already signed the CBD, which means the country is not told or forced to try, but it has already agreed in principle to try.

If Thailand wants to retain sovereignty at the level suggested by the OCS, it might not be able to sign any agreements with other countries or international organizations without first getting approval from the Parliament. In other words, the question is about how to interpret the meaning of 'jurisdiction area' of the country. MFA views it as a geographical area extending into the continental shelf and exclusive economic zone. OCS views it as a normative political sphere in which the country has complete decision-making power and freedom to think without foreign influences. However, if the principle of the bill (such as the first two Thai laws mentioned earlier in this chapter) is influenced by an international treaty, does that not mean that the country has already lost its jurisdiction?

The matter was sent to the Constitutional Court in the middle of 1999. Although it normally calls a press conference when delivering its decisions, in this case the court quietly stated on 5 October 2000 that CBD ratification requires parliamentary approval (Constitutional Court of Thailand, 2000). However, on 27 November 2001, the Cabinet agreed in principle to ratify the CBD without getting approval from the Thai Parliament and planned to ratify the agreement before the World Summit on Sustainable Development (WSSD) in September 2002 (Mekprayoonthong, 2002, p109). The Cabinet resolution clearly violated the Constitutional Court's decision; but the delay-and-silence tactics worked well – the Thai public hardly knew about this development regarding the CBD. Nevertheless, some NGOs and politicians started to voice their concerns again in 2002 and Thailand has yet to ratify the agreement.

Implications of the CBD debate in Thailand

There are several implications that arise from the CBD debates in Thailand. One of the most important implications concerns the connection between international and national politics. Whereas the environmental issue has intertwined these two levels of politics, arguments about the relationship between global environmental cooperation and state sovereignty raise basic, but powerful, questions regarding sovereignty's importance in the current era of globalization. The debate about the CBD issue in Thailand has exemplified a clash between two ideas. One might say that there has been no such thing as true sovereignty since the start of major world trade 100 years ago. Colonialism and imperialism resulted from powerful countries trying to find more space and resources beyond their own borders. The present could be viewed as being similar (Miller, 1995). Hence, many developing countries, NGOs and academics have branded global environmental cooperation as a new form of colonialism or imperialism organized by developed countries (Hempel, 1996; Kittiampon, 2000, interview). The OCS's interpretation of Article 15.2 of the CBD, in fact, applies to the whole convention. Its interpretation and Thai NGOs' questions about losing sovereignty when ratifying the CBD raise questions about national autonomy and highlight the limitations of international cooperation.

Another important implication of the CBD debate is that NGOs have confirmed their status and influence in Thai political and societal scenes. NGOs' increasing roles in the policy-making process, with assistance from the media, have made the government more vulnerable to the public and society. The legitimacy of the Thai government and bureaucracy (already contemplated in academic circles) is now questioned by the general public. The government's inclusion of NGOs in many policy-making and law-drafting committees is, on the one hand, a response to demands by NGOs and the people to let them participate in governing the country. On the other hand, the government's structural and behavioural changes can be viewed as an effort to retain power, even as the government's grip on power has been decreased substantially. The CBD debate is probably the first time that the Thai government was pressured by NGOs to introduce new laws.

The debate about the CBD has provided both opportunities and problems for the government and Thai society. It creates an opportunity for society to be educated about the importance of biodiversity; to become aware that environmental politics is related to many issues, such as development, agriculture and industry; and to participate in the country's political process and development. Nonetheless, the debate has also caused many problems. Disagreement between the government and NGOs in the debate could put more distance between the two sides, which would certainly not be good for Thai society. It is likely to take a very long time for the government and NGOs to truly work together. The MPH and NGOs cooperated in order to pressure the government to legislate the 1999 Thai Traditional Medicine and Local Knowledge Protection and Promotion Act. However, the alliance was short lived. Both sides fell out soon after the act was promulgated because NGOs were disappointed to find out that they would not play any continuing role under the act (Subcharoen, 2000, interview). Perhaps the MPH found that NGOs were no longer of any use. The MPH was accused by many academics, as well as by government officers from other agencies, of interfering in the CBD issue for its own interests.[7] This is evidence of an old problem in Thai government: coordination between agencies.

The government did not expect that the CBD could bring about such trouble. Neither did it expect a strong reaction from NGOs. Nevertheless, NGOs do not naturally see things in the same way as the government. From the NGOs' viewpoint, there are links between biodiversity, trade, intellectual property rights, social justice and equity between developed and developing countries. Indeed, NGOs opposed to the CBD ratification have concentrated heavily on these issues, rather than on conservation issues, which are the main objectives of the CBD. This is because many NGOs opposing the ratification are not environmental NGOs, but rather development and social NGOs which are primarily concerned about community rights and the rights of farmers and poor people.

Conclusion

The CBD debate, and particularly the role played by Thai NGOs in the debate, has widened Thai politics and society, making the government more responsive to the public. This is probably an act of self-defence by the Thai government to make sure that it remains in control of the country. The influence of NGOs was strong enough to cause paralysis in the government's process of CBD ratification. At the same time, one government agency (MPH) used NGOs to fight against other agencies (MOSTE and MAC); that agency gained additional authority from the new legislation. Therefore, one of the results of the CBD debate was that power and control remain with the government. In a way, NGOs became an instrument for one government agency to strengthen its power. They were also used in the power struggle between government agencies. Although some new government committees are composed of NGO representatives, they are only a minority in the committees. They are there merely to improve the image of government, and to show that the government has become more publicly accessible.

Thus, the debate has resulted in the opposite effect suggested by the erosion-of-state theory, which implies that state power is eroded from below by NGOs and civil society, and that the power of central government is transferred to local communities (Dryzek, 1987). On the contrary, local communities did not take power away from the Thai government after the CBD debate. In fact, the government gains more authority from the new legislation pushed by NGOs. The Thai government remains centralized.

However, this is not to suggest that NGOs did not achieve anything from the CBD debate. They have certainly succeeded in influencing the policy-making and decision-making processes. NGOs and their allies were able to draw support from the people, which made the government hesitate to take decisions on ratification. And politicians – the Cabinet – failed to take decisive measures to solve the stalemate, fearing the debate's political complications and consequences. Instead, they passed that responsibility on to the Constitutional Court. Furthermore, the role of NGOs, the media and academics in the debate has arguably made the people pay more attention to biodiversity issues and become more concerned about the environment.

The debate about the CBD in Thailand has missed the point of the CBD as an environmental agreement. The debate has been much more about the implications of the CBD and has, consequently, lost environmental focus. Global trade, intellectual property rights and the rights of the poor and farmers have been at the centre of the debate, not biodiversity. This is not to say that what some Thai NGOs and academics have claimed concerning the CBD is wrong, because those issues can, indeed, be direct implications of the agreement. However, the arguments made by NGOs to demonstrate the 'evilness' of developed countries and transnational companies occurred when Thailand was not a member of the CBD, and the CBD is still an ongoing process. The debates also showed that NGOs and their allies often try to prevent possible adverse effects arising from the government's activities and from forces outside Thailand. Rather than ignoring them or trying to dismiss their opinions and suggestions, particularly because they are the ones which are concerned and have knowledge, the government should respect and respond to their views. This is what has happened. NGOs and their activities have affected the work of the government; NGOs now work as a check-and-balance mechanism and fill a gap between the government and the people. The case of the CBD is one of the best examples to illustrate changes in how the Thai government works as well as demonstrate ongoing changes in Thai society.

Chapter 11

Mekong River Politics and Environmental Security

Peter Stoett[1]

Introduction

Shared resource use, sustainable development, human rights issues and regional power politics are all visible components in contemporary debates on the future of riparian states in Southeast Asia. This chapter argues that the foreign policies of states with a stake in the Mekong River will be greatly affected by the interactions that occur as plans – some of them nearing a half-century in age – for increased hydroelectric, irrigation and navigational uses of the river are gradually realized. This takes place within the context of a particularly conflict-prone region where external powers have played a key role affecting peace and war, as well as market development.

Shared resource cooperation in the region was often viewed as a positive foreign policy on behalf of both riparian and anti-communist states. This is of interest to international relations theorists devoted to the study of international resource domain management (Soroos, 1992). Inter-state cooperation on technical issues has been a staple of the functionalist (Groom and Taylor, 1975) school of thought, as well as studies linking environmental conservation to peace-building (Brock, 1991) and the prospects of 'transnational eco-governmentality' (Goldman, 2001, p499). Given the ideological domination of a utilitarian perspective of nature by external funding agencies, a propensity to equate regional stability with the taming of the wild forces of the river emerged and has survived despite the violence endemic to the region.

However, the enthusiasm for this regional functionalist approach is now saddled with increased knowledge of the detrimental ecological and social impact that large-scale hydroelectricity projects entail, and the complications related to a recalcitrant Burma and aggressive Chinese presence in the region. We are as likely to frame the Mekong question in terms of resource-driven conflict, eco-regions and sovereignty (Byers, 1991), and the power relations attendant to an upstream–downstream relationship (Lowi, 1993). From both a foreign policy and a human security perspective, continued river 'development' looks at least as troubling as it does promising, and the greatest concerns voiced by transnational non-governmental organizations (NGOs) relate directly to the environmental problems caused by various schemes to alter the flow of this interstate river.

Of course, it is inevitable that some environmental alteration will take place, especially in an area where energy needs are expanding along with the global economy. The Asian financial crisis certainly slowed this process down; but it continues with renewed vigour today, as Thailand, China and Vietnam engage in mass industrial and agricultural production for export. Of special interest, then, is what impact globalization is having on environmental security along the Mekong, the lifeblood of millions of riparian people, wildlife and several delicate ecosystems. This is, at heart, a question of *human security*, as large-scale hydro development has such a visible impact on those displaced for projects. China's involvement has become instrumental, as it continues to industrialize Tibet and Yunnan Province, where the Mekong begins its 4500 kilometre descent into the Lower Basin on its lengthy journey to the South China Sea. Indeed the only dams actually built across the span of the river itself are in Yunnan, though Laos has engaged in similarly controversial large-scale damming along its tributaries. As China has not joined the Mekong Development Commission, there are justifiable fears that it might proceed with recklessness, endangering the livelihood of the lower Mekong delta states and riparian peoples, millions of whom depend upon the Mekong for sustenance.

This chapter describes the Mekong River geography and related politics, and discusses the multilateral approaches that have been developed to deal with its common exploitation. The needs of each riparian state vis-à-vis the river will be examined, as will the environmental security questions raised by continued development. Finally, it concludes with a policy recommendation: though small-scale development can be quite healthy and productive, large-scale projects should be abandoned due to their long-term, often unpredictable, consequences. However, the increasingly visible role of upstream China in the region casts doubt on the ability of the international donor community to have a significant impact at this stage. Unlike most of the previous contributions to this volume, this chapter is more explicitly conjectural, suggesting possible policy responses. As such, it goes the next step by examining how to respond to the consequences of past and ongoing environmental diplomacy and foreign policy.

The Mekong River: Development and relations

The Mekong is an inescapable variable in the foreign policy planning of all the Southeast Asian countries. It takes many names along its path, such as Mae Nam Khong (mother of the waters), Tonle Thom (great river), Song Cuu Long (nine dragons river) and Lancang Jiang in China. It flows from the Tibetan plateau southward, through Xinjiang and Yunnan provinces in China, and the Lower Basin begins near the Burmese town of Ciang Saen, running by Myanmar, Laos, Thailand, Cambodia and Vietnam, before spilling into the South China Sea. Its many tributaries invade all of the riparian states, extending as far as the Gulf of Thailand, a criss-crossing mesh of water networks that colour the geophysical and cultural landscape of Indochina. Yearly floods bring such an abundance of water that it backs up into the Tonle Sap in Cambodia, filling the Great Lake and temporarily reversing the flow of the river.

By all accounts, the Mekong River has played a central role in the complex history of the region (see Thi Dieu, 1999). However, it was not until the advent of European colonization that the river became a point of border demarcation, initially between the English (in Burma in 1825) and the French (in what was termed Cochinchina in 1862). The river was certainly viewed as a prized possession within the French empire (the Union Indochinoise), fuelled initially with the overoptimistic dream that it could serve as a trade highway between the delta and China (navigation upstream the Mekong is notoriously difficult).

There is a deep historical linkage between political change and river use in the region, documented by archaeologists and historians, including the use of the river by indigenous peoples on small-scale tributaries and fairly extensive hydraulic systems imported from India and elsewhere (Thi Dieu, 1996; Brocheux, 1995; Van Liere, 1980). Large-scale commercial agriculture, centred mainly on rice production, began during the late 1800s. Following World War II, and in the midst of the colonial struggles germane to the region, US interest produced a series of plans for hydroelectric dam construction; this became known as the Mekong Project, intended to buffer the region from communist influence. The functionalist logic is apparent in early assessments of the Mekong, with their comparisons to the Tennessee Valley Authority (TVA) project in the 1930s. In fact, the Chairman of the TVA, David Lilienthal, helped Lyndon Johnson to develop a plan for the Vietnamese Mekong delta (Lilienthal, 1944). Meanwhile, the Eisenhower administration's failed bid to launch the Water for Peace plan in the Middle East during the

1950s was matched by Lyndon Johnson's support for the Mekong Project during the mid 1960s as an alternative to war. Of course, US involvement in Vietnam would become much more direct during the 1960s and 1970s.

The first multilateral treaty related to the Mekong was, in fact, the Convention on Fluvial and Maritime Navigation on the Mekong and on the Waterways Allowing Access to the Maritime Harbour of Saigon, November 1949. This convention was signed by the pre-independence 'associated states' of Vietnam, Laos and Cambodia, and created the Provisional Mekong Committee. The post-colonial Paris Convention of 1954 continued the quest for regional economic development. Thailand was not a participant at this stage; but subsequent development plans were, in fact, largely centred on Thailand, which was seen as the most reliable ally against the encroachment of Sino or Soviet influence in the region. A study conducted by the Economic Commission for Asia and the Far East, released in 1957 and supported by the French, emphasized the need for coordination amongst riparian states. In September 1957, the Statute of the Committee for the Coordination of Investigations of the Lower Mekong Basin was signed. Members included Cambodia, Laos, Thailand and Vietnam, with American C H Schaaf appointed in 1959 as the first executive agent. Companies involved in financing included Nippon Electric, Price Waterhouse, Shell and the Ford Foundation. Many Western states, including the US, France, New Zealand, Australia, the UK and Japan, joined the funding spree via the Colombo Plan. As Thi Dieu writes, though it was

> ... *ostensibly detached from political pressures, the MC [Mekong Commission] was a showcase of successful regional cooperation acting as a foil against communism ... [but] aid was, in fact, more bilateral than was immediately apparent ... it was eventually entirely up to the donor country to make the decision to finance either in its totality a project or several projects* (Thi Dieu, 1999, p67).

Canadian, Filipino and Japanese teams carried out research for the proposed Sambor Project in Cambodia, although the proposed Pa Mong Dam, between northeast Thailand and Laos, was to be the biggest (if it had been constructed as planned, it would have been the largest dam in the world at that time). Offers of technical assistance from the USSR were turned down by the Thais and the Republic of Vietnam.

Human rights activists have raised serious objections to the larger-scale projects. The Pa Mong Dam, as envisioned in 1970, would displace up to 500,000 people were it to be built today at a height of 260 metres; up to 300,000 individuals would be displaced at a height of 250 metres. In 1987 the Mekong Secretariat produced a revised regional plan that would limit the dam's height to 210 metres, lowering the total projected displaced individuals to 60,000 (and giving occasion to rename the project the *Low* Pa Mong). The Pa Mong would produce electricity and be used for extensive irrigation purposes, to Thai benefit, and it would also assert Bangkok's control over what has been difficult political terrain: the northeast. But local opposition to the imminent displacement has been a strong rallying cry for transnational human rights activists.

Cooperation fell to the vicissitudes of regional war for much of the 1970s and 1980s. In 1977, Khmer Rouge Cambodia (Kampuchea) withdrew from the MC, and the three remaining riparian states formed the Interim Committee for Coordination of Investigation of the Lower Mekong Basin, otherwise known as the Interim Mekong Committee. It was not until 1995 that Cambodia was back, in full, and the Mekong River Commission (MRC) formally replaced the 1957 MC and the 1978 Interim Mekong Committee. This was established with the signing and ratification of the Agreement on the Cooperation for the Sustainable Development of the Mekong River Basin in Chiang Rai, Thailand, on 5 April 1995. China and Myanmar were invited as observers. The MRC deals essentially with three interrelated programmes, funded through the World Bank and key bilateral donors: water utilization, basin development planning and protection of the environment and ecological balance. Critics charge that the latter is of least concern. One of the major proposed projects today is the 600 megawatt (MW) Nam Theun 2 hydroelectric dam in Laos, along the Nam Theun River. Construction would flood some 700 square kilometres of forest, including the Nam Theun-Nakai National Biodiversity Conservation Area, displace close to 5000 indigenous people, and it is difficult to predict the full range of downstream effects.

The 1995 agreement represented what may, in retrospect, be considered a substantive normative shift from the past in that it does not oblige the states to inform each other of any serious undertakings affecting the river. Negotiations resulted in 'tugs of war' between Thailand, eager to proceed with mainstream hydropower and irrigation schemes (in particular, its mun-Chi project of diverting water from the Mekong to irrigate the dry northeast), and Vietnam, anxious because of the potentially negative impacts of such projects on its delta (Thi Dieu, 1999, p205). Downstream, Cambodia and Vietnam were obviously less than pleased by this development, but were left without a choice in the matter. The Secretariat which employs over 100 people has been housed in Bangkok, Thailand, Phon Phem, Cambodia, and, most recently, Vientiane, Laos. Its primary challenge is to construct a 'system for coordinating water resource development activities and allocating dry season water, while protecting the environment and maintaining friendly relations among member states' (Bowder and Ortolano, 2000, p531) – a high order, indeed.

The Commission might be seen as the centre of environmental management in the area; but this would be a false impression. It has limited jurisdiction and operates largely as a funding valve. However, many states and external agencies have maintained an interest in the resource-rich region (rice, rubber and tin were three mainstays). The Australian presence has been strong; for example, the first bridge across the Mekong (Thai–Laos) was financed by Australia (see Hirsch and Cheong, 1996). The Asian Development Bank (ADB) is a regional investor, as is the World Bank, the Japanese and many others. The Association of Southeast Asian Nations (ASEAN) has launched its own Mekong Basin Development Cooperation initiative (Vietnam joined ASEAN in 1995; Laos and Burma in 1997; and Cambodia in 1999). The Global Environmental Facility (GEF), largely a World Bank enterprise, contributes funding toward the Mekong River Basin Water Utilization Project and the Mekong River Basin Wetland Biodiversity project. Other United Nations (UN) agencies involved include the UN Environment Programme (UNEP), the UN Development Programme (UNDP), the UN Educational, Scientific and Cultural Organization (UNESCO, which has responsibility for World Heritage listings), and others. Many bilateral agencies are engaged in the region, both through the MRC and through bilateral projects. Major players include Japan, Australia, Germany, Sweden, Canada, the European Union (EU), the US, the UK and Denmark. Increasingly, as we will see below, private capital is making inroads, especially through the so-called BOOT approach (build, own, operate, transfer).

What remains constant throughout this brief history is the attempt to alter the river's natural course in an effort to achieve the 'modernization' of the region. As Bakker suggests, by 'depicting the river as "under-utilized" or "uncontrolled", hydro-development of the Mekong basin is portrayed as the *creation* of uses and users, rather than the reprioritization or even displacement of uses' (Bakker, 1999, p220). The long-term goal of a harnessed river has met with fierce opposition from environmental and local groups, and many NGOs, discussed later, have dedicated their work to mitigating the impact of large-scale alterations; but they have limited political power. As China begins to alter river flows at source (from the Yunnan highlands), the political issues involving the consent of the affected become more complex; but it is the same modernization imperative that is driving ecosystem alteration. This chapter turns now to brief discussions of the riparian states, and outlines some of the foreign policy dilemmas they face.

Vietnam

We begin where the river ends. During the 1900s, the Vietnamese fought against foreign occupation by Japan, France, the US and China. Perhaps more than any other Southeast Asian state, Vietnam's foreign policy relations have undergone great change. Though military relations with Russia continue and border problems with China are an issue, the improvement in relations with the US is a remarkable turnaround from the years following American involvement in the brutal civil war that has scarred the country and the environment. The US embargo was one of the main obstacles to foreign investment, and there is little doubt that increased investment in Vietnam's cheap-labour industries will increase demands for energy production. The US$1 billion, 720 megawatt dam at Yali Falls, built with funding from Russia and the Ukraine (it drains into the Se San, which runs through Cambodia to the Mekong), has soured relations with Cambodia as downstream families have coped with ecological and socio-economic impacts (Fisheries Office, 2000).

Relations with China also occupy a great deal of importance for Hanoi. To some degree, these have normalized ever since the end of Vietnam's occupation of Cambodia and the fall of the Soviet Union (Ramses, 1997). However, there are several obstacles to long-term peace between the two, given the propensity of China to engage in regular shows of strength in the region. Contested sovereignty of the Spratly Islands in the South China Sea continues to brew diplomatic and military animosity (Chang, 1997). Reluctance to directly confront China pushes Vietnam into a stronger commitment to both ASEAN and potential US/Japanese investors.

Vietnam needs, above all, to maintain the extant dry season flow into the delta to sustain rice harvests and combat salinity (Bowder and Ortolano, 2000). Vietnamese agriculture boomed during the 1980s and 1990s: with a doubling of rice production, it became the world's third largest rice producer. The annual intrusion of saltwater into the delta from the South China Sea affords rice and shrimp culture, though concerns with salinity are a source of tension. Upriver, diversion of the Mekong, resulting from intensive damming in China or the Thai–Laos border, or from Thai plans to irrigate Isan, might threaten the saline-flushing effect of the river's annual flows.

Cambodia

Cambodia remains a severely underdeveloped state, struggling with the remnants of prolonged conflict, precarious government legitimacy and a tenuous relationship with other regional powers. The government has raised concerns about the impact of upstream development – in particular, Chinese activity – and there are incentives for China, which has supported Cambodia's governments, from the Sihanouk reign to the Khmer Rouge and the present, to avoid the excessive alienation of Cambodia. China cannot afford to let Thailand and Vietnam grow in importance to a point where they will directly confront the Chinese on every possible issue, especially considering recent ASEAN and Asian Free Trade Area (AFTA) expansion. A strong Cambodia on the side of the Chinese is a highly valuable commodity for Beijing, especially at a time when US–Cambodian relations appear strained (Hun Sen is disliked in Washington).

Cambodia needs to protect the hydrological integrity of the Tonle Sap by ensuring sufficient reverse wet season flows from the Mekong into the lake (Bowder and Ortolano, 2000). But it is also highly dependent on fuel-driven generators for power and would, in the long term, benefit from hydropower development itself. This is the lure of the proposed Sambor Dam, despite the ecological consequences.

Thailand

The new political leaders of Thailand want to transform the country into the 'doorway' to Indochina (Buszynski, 1994). Although Thailand has lived through turbulent political and financial times, it has maintained a stronger economic base than any other state in Indochina. However, political realities disrupt the type of investment and material commitment that Thailand would like to initiate with Laos, Cambodia, Vietnam and even China and Burma. Nonetheless, the Thais have initiated four-lane highway projects running from Bangkok to major centres in Laos, Vietnam and China, and from the west coast near Surat Thani across to the Isthmus of Kra to Krabi, with deep water ports as well as industrial and oil storage facilities at each terminus. In addition to this, the Thai–Burma Seaboard Development Zone proposal aims to develop additional land bridges from the Gulf of Thailand to proposed ports at Thavoy (Thawai) and Mergui (Marit) in Burma. These are designed to draw shipping out of the congested Straits of Melaka and to capture a large share of the freight transhipment trade from Singapore and Penang in Malaysia (Battersby, 1999).

Thailand has already exhausted most of its already limited potential for hydroelectric development. The Pak Mun Dam in the northeast, constructed from 1991 to 1994 under the auspices of the Electricity Generating Authority of Thailand, generates less than one third of the projected electricity and socio-ecological costs have been high: entire communities were relocated and 169 out of 235 fish species have disappeared from the Mun River above the dam wall. Despite this, there are several Thai/Japanese dam construction plans along Mekong tributaries in the works. Thailand already purchases power from Malaysia, Laos (since as early as 1971) and Burma (with further plans in the works, especially along the Salween River basin adjacent to the Thai border). In the long-term, however, it is clear that Thailand bases future industrial growth projections on imports of energy from Burma and China (and, perhaps, Vietnam as well). Indeed, Laos has recently agreed to allow the construction of a power line to facilitate electricity transmission from Burma and China into Thailand.

The relationship with China is vital in this regard. Thai–Vietnamese relations have always been tense; and Bangkok appreciated the military pressure that China applied to Vietnam when the latter occupied Cambodia. There are no Thai–Sino territorial disputes, no strong ethnic Chinese Diaspora issues in Thailand, and Thai investment in China is significant. This is the immediate foreign policy context in which we must view the investment agreement on jointly building the Jinghong hydro station in Yunnan.

Laos

The stretch of the Mekong under Laotian control represents a substantial portion of the river's hydropower potential, a consideration not lost on authorities in a country where per capita annual income is less than US$300. Naturally endowed with an abundance of tributaries, and with Thailand, the region's largest consumer of hydroelectric power, as an immediate neighbour and customer, Mekong development projects in Laos represent a substantial source of economic relief. Lacking any viable alternative sources of foreign exchange, the Lao government has proceeded with its own dam construction. The most recent project was the Theun Hinboun Dam, completed in 1998, whose operation has evinced criticism based on the reduction by up to 70 per cent of downstream fish catches, while villagers near the Theun Hinboun Dam have been forced to move because fish stocks have been depleted by as much as 90 per cent (Torode, 1998). Laos has been criticized for failing to ensure adequate compensation (promised by the ADB) for displaced individuals of the US$260 million, 210 megawatt dam. The military-run Mountainous Areas Development Corporation dominates logging in the area; most timber is exported to Thailand and Vietnam (Shoemaker, 1998).

The projected Nam Theun 2 Dam, if constructed, will involve flooding an area of 450 square kilometres and displacing approximately 5000 members of ethnic minorities living in villages in the area. The Nakai Nam Theun National Biodiversity Area will also be affected (Osborne, 2000a, pp241–243). This latest work faces much criticism based on the social and environmental impact of past projects; but the extreme poverty of Laos precludes, in the minds of the dam's proponents, its cancellation. One of the chief concerns about the dams in Laos is that the electricity being generated for Thai consumption is fulfilling an inflated energy demand. This will especially be the case in times of economic slowdown, but may become a more permanent condition if efforts to increase Thai efficiency continue. In 1992, Thailand represented the Lower Mekong region's greatest demand for electricity, a product of its rapid industrialization. Laos dams – Theun Hinboun, Nam Theun 2, the projected Nam Ngum 3 Dam, as well as Nam Ngum 2 and others – have all been proposed with an eye towards Thai consumption.

Criticism has arisen about the demand for electricity far exceeding Thailand's needs by as much as 40 to 60 per cent, as well as the manner in which the profits from their operation will be distributed. According to a commentary by Permpongsacharoen (1999), profits generated by Nam Theun 2 during its peak operating years will go primarily to its developers – Australian, French and Thai interests, with only a 25 per cent share owned by the Lao government. The project will only revert to Lao control after 25 years. By then its operational efficiency will be in serious decline, and the entire rationale for Laos's hydroelectric development projects – the alleviation of extreme poverty in the country – falls flat.

Beyond obvious concerns that China's Upper Mekong development could threaten the hydropower potential of the Laotian section of the river, Laos also needs to preserve dry season navigability if it is to be a shipping port of any consequence. In this sense the Chinese dams may, in fact, prove beneficial.

Burma

If the Cambodian government faces a legitimacy problem, the military junta ruling Myanmar takes this to international levels. Official relations with Thailand, on the strength of oscillating levels of cross-border trade and mutual hydropower exploration, vary. Thailand has a substantial population of Burmese–Karen refugees in its border regions, and an even larger population of Burmese illegal migrants working in the Thai construction, farming, fishing and sex trades. Unsustainable natural resource exploitation in the border areas is also significant. The state maintains a monopoly over all legal rights to natural resources and has shown its eagerness in exploiting them, especially hardwood lumber, as well as its willingness to provide foreign access to those resources (Lambrecht, 1999). According to one report:

> *The forests throughout the Mekong basin perform important flood regulation functions, absorbing the high floodwaters during the rainy season, to be slowly released in the dry season. Extensive deforestation increases the severity of flooding as rainfall on deforested areas washes quickly into river ways instead of being partially absorbed by forests. These 'quick-rising' big floods pose risks to riparian farmers who plant rice and vegetables on the banks of rivers in anticipation of beneficial silt-laden 'slow rising' floods. Rapid flooding often washes away crops, reducing rather than increasing riparian fertility and causing food security problems in the affected areas* (Miller, 2000).

This is relevant not only because of the damage caused by reckless forestry policies, but because they lend, at least, rhetorical support to China's chief claim of benevolence regarding its own upper Mekong projects: the possibility of enhanced downstream flood control. In general, Burma has approached the rank of a Sino satellite. Burma uses Yunnan Province for the export of logs, precious minerals such as jade and, increasingly, for the opium trade: there are less stringent controls and US leverage in Yunnan than in Laos or Thailand. But it is unclear who benefits most: the economic development of Yunnan demands raw materials, including timber, much of which will be sourced from Burma.

Relatively little of the Mekong's length falls within Burmese control, and Rangoon's heavy reliance on China suggests that there will be little in the way of complaint from Myanmar should aggressive alteration policies proceed to the north. The lack of citizen participation in Burma is glaring. Typically, the proposal to dam the Salween River in Shan State has been discussed with other regional powers, but in the absence of those very ethnic communities whom it would most disrupt (Barnes, 1999). Of course, this is hardly unique to Burma, but merely a continuation of old habits of steamrolling development programmes over any concerns other than state-building. In the meantime, Myanmar continues to benefit from what Battersby (1999, p487) refers to as the 'brutal logic underlying Thai and ASEAN policies toward Rangoon – namely, that the goals of regional economic cooperation and development are best served by a strong centralized state in Burma, however unsavoury this might be.'

Enter China

Finally, we enter our last state actor where the Mekong begins. The geography of the Upper Mekong region reinforces China's particular importance to the rest of the riparian states. Approximately half of its roughly 5000-kilometre length is under Chinese control. Chinese authorities, defending large-scale damming projects in Yunnan begun during the mid 1980s, have stated that a mere 16 to 20 per cent of water that flows in the Mekong comes from China. This, however, represents only a percentage of total volume. By the time the river flows from its source to the Laotian capital of Vientiane, the quantity of Mekong water having its origins in China reaches about 60 per cent. This represents a substantial natural monopoly, and a justifiable source of concern; as Osborne (2000a, p228) argues: 'as the experience of the Three Gorges project has shown, China has an almost infinite capacity to disregard external criticism ... that does not suit its interests'.

The political economy of market expansion makes China's long-term plans fairly clear: upper Mekong alteration will serve to power industrialization, expand Yunnan Province's access to global markets, and increase Beijing's regional diplomatic presence. Given the apparent aggression of Chinese authorities in dealing with the South China Seas disputes, particularly with regard to the drafting of a joint code of conduct for Southeast Asian states involved in that area, the Lower Mekong states risk being bracketed into a position of dependency on Chinese benevolence (Gonsalves, 2000).

The 1500 megawatt Manwan Dam in western Yunnan, begun in 1984 and completed in 1993, was the first major Mekong dam built by the Chinese. Intended to provide hydroelectric power to Kunming, the provincial capital, energy problems in the area have been solved at the expense of the approximately 25,000 displaced residents of 96 villages located in the subsequently flooded areas, about 24 square kilometres in extent. This is relatively light damage compared with what lies ahead. A dam downriver from the Manwan, at Dachaoshan, was begun in 1996, and two others will be underway by 2010 (see Table 11.1). One of these, at Xiaowan, located upstream from the Manwan, will have a waterhead 2.5 times the height of Manwan's 99 metres, producing a reservoir 169 kilometres in length. This cascade may include a further ten or so dams along the Mekong's Chinese route, built in a geophysical location known for frequent earthquakes.

Chinese authorities are only beginning to gauge possible downstream effects. Chapman and Daming (1996, p16) contend that, by the year 2010 and the completion of the Xiaowan Dam, 'the regulated dry season flow at the Yunnan–Laos border will commonly be up to 50 per cent greater than under natural conditions, and much greater again when Nuozhadu is completed. In the rainy season Mekong flows will be significantly less than under natural conditions'. Chapman and Daming stress the potential benefits of this change: greater hydropower generation for Laos, irrigation potential for north and northeast Thailand, including water diversion to Bangkok, and combating salt intrusion in the lower delta.

Even less work has been done in appraising the effects of deforestation and other industrial impacts along the upper Mekong in Tibet (Latiffe, 1996). Alteration of Mekong flows has already had serious repercussions in the Lower Mekong, particularly in terms of fish catches, and the 'evening out' of seasonal changes in river flow that the Chinese hope to achieve may present a serious problem for the natural functioning of Cambodia's Great Lake. The potential human cost is therefore significant, as a large proportion of the Cambodian population relies on fish catches from the Great Lake for its subsistence, and farming along its shores depends upon the rise and fall of the river.

Another proposed Chinese alteration of the Mekong would involve creating a passage from Yunnan to Vientiane, allowing for year-round movement of larger ships that are currently only able to navigate the waterway for a three-month period during which waters are at their highest levels. The proposal underscores the problems surrounding the use of the Mekong for transport. This alteration would involve large-scale blasting, with attendant impact on river species, and increased ship traffic would add further pollution problems.

Other infrastructure projects, including bridge, road and railway construction, have obvious benefits in terms of regional linkages. But the manner in which they have been pursued and implemented raises serious concerns about their necessity or value, especially in relation to the human costs of these programmes; a proposed 1000-kilometre railway linking Lhasa, Tibet, with the rest of China might be seen as a political expression rather than an economic necessity. The railway is part of an ambitious regional infrastructure programme that will include rail construction through mountainous passages into Central Asia, and another will parallel the Mekong, reaching from Kunming to the rest of the Mekong region.

Table 11.1 *Dams on the Upper Mekong River, Yunnan Province, China*

Location	Height (metres)	Generating capacity (megawatts)	Resettlement (persons)	Status	Completion (year)
Gonguoqiao	130	750	Unknown	Unknown	Unknown
Xiaowan	300	4200	32,737	Site preparation	2012–2013
Manwan	126	1500	3513	Completed	1996
Dachaoshan	110	1350	6054	Under construction	2003
Nuozhadu	254	5000	23,826	Feasibility study	2017
Jinghong	118	1500	2264	Feasibility study	2003–2010
Ganlanba	Unknown	150	Unknown	Unknown	Unknown
Mengsong	Unknown	600	Unknown	Unknown	Unknown

Source: Blake (2001)

China has not signed the UN 1997 Convention on the Law of Non-navigational Uses of International Water Courses, which would oblige it to seek downstream state approval of upstream projects. There are obvious pressures on Chinese authorities to utilize hydropower in its search for replacing a coal-based national infrastructure; but its apparent disregard for regional cooperation in the process will be a point of future tension.

China should be strongly encouraged by the major powers involved in the region to sign and ratify this convention, and to join the MRC.

Transnational actors

The foreign policy context outlined above is also home to a wide variety of non-state actors and organizations. In terms of financing, the trend today is away from centrally funded donor institutions and toward the so-called BOOT approach. This involves private capital investment, government-guaranteed profits (a 15 per cent rate of return is standard) and insurance offered by donor institutions, such as export credit agencies. A consortium of nine different firms, for example, will be instrumental in building the Nam Theun 2 in

Laos. After completion of the construction phase, the builder operates the dam for a specified number of years (usually 25 to 30 years), after which ownership reverts to the government, without compensation. This is seen as a private–public cooperation intended to generate start-up projects; however, many environmentalists dislike the involvement of private capital in projects with such serious social and ecological consequences, especially in the Laotian case – a state often accused of environmental neglect.

Several Australian NGOs play a prominent role in the region, as do regional NGOs, particularly those in Thailand. Regional NGOs include Towards Ecological Recovery and Regional Alliances (TERRA) and FOCUS on the Global South. Overseas-based NGOs include Community Aid Abroad, World Vision, Care International, Mennonite Central Committee, Oxfam (UK, Belgium and Hong Kong), Australian Catholic Relief, and others. Some of the transnational organizations involved have supported conservation efforts at the expense of supporting the right to state control of previously open areas, such as the International Union for the Conservation of Nature, also known as the World Conservation Union (WCU), and the US-based Wildlife Conservation Society (WCS), formerly known as the Bronx Zoological Society. Since 1994, WCS experts in wildlife and park management have been conducting wildlife surveys in the Nakai-Nam Theun watershed as part of the Nam Theun 2 project planning process. This is contentious, since aid for protected areas alongside dam construction is often viewed as an unacceptable subsidy to hydropower developers.

Finally, NGOs committed to wildlife conservation have found a *cause célèbre* in the endangered Irrawaddy dolphin, whose numbers are thought to have dwindled to under 100, and the Mekong giant catfish. They have fallen victim to habitat destruction as a result of the use of explosives, electric shock, poison and gillnets for fishing, growing pollution and dam construction. Other species threatened by large-scale river alteration include tiger, elephant, dhole, otter, crested kingfisher, lesser and grey-headed fish eagles, tawny fish-owl, white-winged magpie, green imperial-pigeon, Siamese fireback, red-collared woodpecker, pied falconer, brown hornbill, coral-billed ground-cuckoo and rhesus macaque.

It is obvious that non-governmental actors have varied interests in the region. Private capital is interested in guaranteed investments; local NGOs see environmental issues as both anti-developmental weights and a means toward greater citizen participation; foreign NGOs want to save endangered species and promote human rights. As for the MRC itself, there is no doubt that it is actively recruiting suitable environmental experts to gauge the impact of projects. However, it remains to be seen whether the commission's influence is even delta-wide, and it certainly does not include China. The MRC must work in tandem with the national Mekong committees, and there is little confidence in the latter. The relationship between the MRC and local NGOs has been acrimonious in the past, due to complaints about the MRC's lack of transparency and neo-liberal ideological fixation.

Conclusion: Toward human and environmental security

It is important to realize that there *are* alternatives to large-scale hydropower development, just as there are alternatives to fossil fuel-based industrial infrastructure. In fact, one might argue that states such as Cambodia and Burma are excellent places in which to begin experimentation based on small-scale energy production. Of course, political instability and international condemnation might preclude ambitious, nation-wide projects. But let us recall that this is a region with a long history of survival despite incredible adversity; that there is rich indigenous knowledge in the area; and that the tide of democracy, encouraged by support from abroad for civil society participation, will push against the insensitive displacement and ecological damage associated with drastic river ecosystem alteration, and affect the micro-politics of the region in the process (Hirsch, 2001). The pursuit of alternative energy sources, including biomass, solar, thermal, wind and – most promising, perhaps – small-scale hydro, is not without precedent in the region.

Thailand embarked on a fairly successful 'demand-side management' power-sector programme during the 1990s (preceding the financial crisis), increasing efficiency and reducing demand. Further efforts to promote efficiency in Thailand are being sponsored by the GEF, the World Bank, Australia and Japan. Yunnan Province has established a solar energy research centre. Even war-torn Vietnam has made some progress in the development of solar and wind energy (Tien Long, 2000). The final report of the World Commission on Dams (available at www.dams.org) stresses the need to at least consider alternative energy sources, recycling, increased industrial and irrigation efficiency and local water management (the industry-run International Commission on Large Dams has, predictably, questioned the report). Some have argued that, given the construction and maintenance efforts required, large dam construction does not lessen global warming (McCully, 1996). A recent World Bank study found that World Bank-financed hydropower projects, on average, incurred inflation-adjusted cost overruns of up to 30 per cent, three times higher than thermal power stations (Bacon et al, 1996). It would be folly not to investigate as many alternatives as possible, and for Western governments in the region to discourage this by refusing to abandon old infrastructural designs.

Southeast Asia retains many of the characteristics that have defined it for the better part of the past century. Borders lines are subject to contention. It is a diverse cultural and spiritually significant locale, but is ridden with the fragments of past warfare and the ravages of rapid industrialization and commercial agriculture. The Mekong, arguably the natural life source of the region, is the focus of not only potential cooperation, but ongoing conflict, and is under severe strain due to multiple demands. The demand to simply leave the river as it is would seem a far cry from possible at this stage; therefore, it is vital that organizations such as the Mekong River Commission do their utmost to prevent unsustainable use of the river and to protect the individuals whose environmental security is most heavily threatened in the process. However, the marked introduction of Chinese plans into the equation casts serious doubt on the commission's ability to take effective measures in this regard.

Flooding has always been a part of the life cycle in the Mekong Delta; it has been instrumental in rice cultivation in Cambodia and elsewhere (Fox and Ledgerwood, 1999). However, there are signs that heavy deforestation is increasing flood rates: in the autumn of 2000, the worst flooding in decades impacted the lives of millions (Crispin et al, 2000). However, the construction of upstream dams offers a poor promise of controlling such floods, since they will also obstruct fish migration and trap silt, and do nothing to reverse the deforestation process in Tibet, Laos and elsewhere.

From a foreign policy perspective, it is the lack of transparency attendant to Chinese Mekong policy, and China's willingness to pursue projects without consulting downstream states, that cause the greatest concern. The potential human costs are substantial, and the convenient alliance between Thailand and China may be short-lived in the event of further economic breakdown in the region. China's pursuit of regional hegemony remains the region's greatest threat. More broadly, however, all states must take into account the environmental and human consequences of collaborating in the grand design to 'modernize' the region by permanently altering its greatest source of life, the Mekong River.

Nearly half of the world's population lives in over 200 international river basins, and 13 of these are shared by more than 5 states (most famously, perhaps, the Nile, Ganges, Jordan, Tigris-Euphrates and Amazon). It is clear that international river management is of great importance for regional security; but it is equally clear that environmental security will be affected by management arrangements, which must not overlook the impact of globalization on the human rights of riparian peoples. Unfortunately, regional power relations, economic imperatives, and the natural advantage of upstream states continue to define the issue.

Chapter 12

Protecting the Marine Environment: International Assistance and the Vietnam Sea

Tran Duc Thanh, Tran Dinh Lan and Pham Van Luong

Introduction

The Vietnam Sea plays a very important role in the economic and social development of Vietnam, and it has a significant position in the ecology and environment of the peripheral seas of East Asia. During the last decade, Vietnam has been implementing a policy of opening up to the world. Economic and social development, population increases and human activities in catchments and coastal areas have negatively impacted upon the marine environment. Additionally, transboundary pollution and climate changes have affected the Vietnam Sea. Thus, Vietnam's marine environment has been experiencing degradation, with emerging problems such as increasing natural and technological risks, pollution, habitat loss and decreasing living resources. As noted in its Law on Environmental Protection, Vietnam has made efforts to protect the marine environment by establishing an organizational mechanism, building a legislative base, implementing environment projects and strengthening international cooperation. These efforts have brought results, to which international assistance has been recognized as a significant contribution.

As Vietnam enters into a new period of globalization, the demand for marine environmental protection is more urgent. This chapter illustrates this, demonstrating how environmental policies developed through international interactions have impacts at the national and sub-national levels. It examines

Vietnam's efforts to protect the marine environment, with particular focus on the role played by international assistance. Following a description of the Vietnam Sea and its environmental importance and vulnerabilities, this chapter looks at many of the domestic laws and institutions that have been dedicated to protecting this resource. It then examines the scope and content of related environmental programmes supported by assistance from governments and non-governmental organizations (NGOs). The upshot is that foreign aid has been instrumental in supporting environmental protection schemes at all levels. Having said this, we find some problems with aid, such as inadequate aid for local communities and some incapacity to fully exploit aid at some levels. However, the prospect that aid will continue to enhance environmentally sustainable development along the Vietnam Sea is good.

Vietnam's marine environment

Along Vietnam's shoreline, stretching over 3200 kilometres, there exist 114 river mouths, of which the largest is that of the Mekong River and the second largest the Red River. The Vietnam Sea is also situated in a strategically important trade route between the Indian and Pacific Oceans. The sea is about 1 million square kilometres in size, including 1600 square kilometres occupied by over 3000 islands. Every year, rivers discharge about 880 billion cubic metres of water and 200 million to 250 million tonnes of suspended sediments into the Vietnam Sea, which are concentrated in the estuaries of the Mekong and Red rivers. The Mekong River catchment includes parts of China, Burma, Laos, Thailand, Cambodia and Vietnam (see Chapter 11). The Red River catchment includes parts of China and Vietnam (Thanh et al, 2002, pp179–184). The Vietnam Sea is located in a tropical monsoon zone with an annual rainfall of 1000 to 2400 millimetres. From 1975 to 1995, the area was struck by an annual average of 2.5 typhoons, although the number has increased recently. The economic losses from typhoons are high (for example, US$600 million in 1997). What is more, sea-level rise has been recorded at some coastal sites (Thuy and Khuoc, 1994, pp16–23).

The Vietnam Sea is high in biodiversity and productivity of ecosystems such as estuaries, lagoons, mangrove forests, coral reefs and sea-grass beds. About 11,000 aquatic species and more than 1300 island species inhabit the sea and its coastal zone, including many rare and precious endemic species. Marine non-living resources are also abundant, especially oil and gas. Reserves have been estimated at about 5 billion tonnes, and current industrial reserves are 1.2 billion to 1.4 billion tonnes. There are also 100 nearby coastal locations with mineral deposits; coal mines in Quang Ninh have reserves of 3.59 billion tonnes, and iron ores in Ha Tinh are of a good quality and enough for supplying a plant with 5 million to 6 million tonnes of pig-iron capacity annually.

Human activities impacting upon the marine environment of Vietnam

The coast of Vietnam is a zone of active development. It has high population density and a high population growth rate. Of Vietnam's 80 million people, 24 per cent live in coastal districts and 54 per cent in coastal provinces. Along the coast, there are 12 cities and towns with populations of over 100,000 and up to 1.7 million; 37 ports and harbours and hundreds of other small fishing harbours; and some 3000 major factories. In 1992, Vietnam owned 124 fleets consisting of 800 ships totalling 1 million gross tonnes, as well as 54,000 fishing boats. Over 1 million tonnes of fish are caught in the Vietnam Sea each year, of which 80 per cent is taken in coastal waters. Fishery production has been over allowable catch numbers since 1996 (Ministry of Fisheries, 1996). Almost 200,000 hectares of brackish aquaculture ponds have replaced mangroves forests. Large parts of the tidal floodplain, including the mangrove marshes, have been reclaimed for agriculture. From 1958 to 1995, 24,000 hectares of the tidal floodplain in the Red River Delta were reclaimed.

Upstream forests have been destroyed by war, cultivation, logging and fire. Forest coverage decreased from 43 to 28 per cent during the period between 1943 and 1995 (Cuong, 1997, pp47–59). During the last 1000 years, a great system of dikes has been built to protect plains and their inhabitants from river and sea floods. In all of Vietnam, there are 5700 kilometres of river dikes and 2100 kilometres of sea dikes. The rivers have been dammed to create many reservoirs for irrigation and hydroelectric power. The dams and dikes system has greatly decreased the amount of water and sediments running into the Vietnam Sea.

Vietnam has a cultivated land area of over 7 million hectares, 60 per cent of which is paddy lands. A huge amount of river water is needed every year for irrigation. For example, in 1990, 47 billion cubic metres of water were used for irrigation. In 1993, 2.1 million tonnes of chemical fertilizers were used in the cultivated lands, including 1.2 million tonnes of urea, 793,000 tonnes of phosphate and 22,000 tonnes of potash. In 1988, 20,000 tonnes of pesticides were used, and their use had increased to 30,000 tonnes by 1994 (Sandoz, 1996, pp1–13). Annual domestic and industrial water demand is over 4 billion cubic metres. A great volume of wastewater, most of which is still untreated, is dumped into rivers and discharged into the sea.

About 41,000 tonnes of oil were dumped into the Vietnam Sea in 1995, 3 per cent of which came from oil drilling; 12.8 per cent was land based; 1.2 per cent came from oil spills; international shipping lines contributed 81.9 per cent; and domestic shipping and harbours produced 1.1 per cent (Minh, 1996, pp8–14). Coastal mining of coal, sand and gravel for construction and heavy minerals is an important activity that deforms the landscape, produces solid and liquid wastes, and increases coastal erosion. Coastal mining operations in Quang Ninh Province annually dump 10 million tonnes of solid waste and 7 million cubic metres of liquid waste into the coastal zone.

Emerging problems: Vietnam's marine environment and demands for its protection

Recently, dramatic changes in the Vietnam Sea environment and ecosystems have become obvious. Both natural processes and human activities have caused the changes. Changes due to human activities can be global, as in the case of sea-level rise and unusual typhoons and meteorological disturbances related to human-induced global warming, or regional in scale, as in the case of upstream deforestation and the construction of dams. They can also be localized in the coastal zone. Most coastal and marine risks in Vietnam appear to be related to climate change. Human activities have impacted upon Vietnam's coastal zones in many ways, such as through changes in supplies and distribution of water, sediments, nutrients and other materials to the sea; changes in the quality of coastal and marine environments by the increased loading and accumulation of pollutants; and marine and coastal habitat loss.

Increasing 'natural' risks

Coastal floods have increased in intensity and frequency. They are a consequence of the combined impact of upstream deforestation, heavy rains, sea-level rise and the blocking of lagoon inlets or river mouths by sedimentation. Coastal floods are especially severe and very dangerous when heavy rains and storm surges coincide during spring tides. Annual flooding in the Mekong River Delta, which lasts from two to six months, mainly between August and October, inundates an area of more than 1.7 million hectares and directly affects 9 million people. From 1926 to 2000, there were 24 heavy floods. Terrible floods in November 1999 along the central coast caused a great loss of life and destroyed much infrastructure.

Coastal erosion is of concern because it is increasing in scale and in the amount of resulting damage. Overall, 243 coastal sites, covering 469 kilometres of coastline, have eroded at a rate of 5 to 10 metres per year. In both the Mekong River Delta and the Red River Delta, which are known to be accreting, erosion has nevertheless occurred along one fourth of their coastlines. Sedimentation is also a major problem that is growing worse, with a particularly negative impact on the development of marine ports and harbours (Thanh, 1995, pp451–462). Hai Phong is a typical example. For more than a century, it was the biggest port in Vietnam; but recently big ships have not been able to reach it due to the heavy sedimentation. Along the central coast, long-shore sand drifts generated by wave action close lagoon inlets and river mouths, leading to coastal floods, the freshening of saltwater lagoons and the blocking of water on its way to the sea.

Because of tidal pressure, saltwater now penetrates 30 to 50 kilometres up the Red River and 60 to 70 kilometres up the Mekong River. More than 1.7 million hectares of land have been impacted by saltwater intrusion in the Mekong River Delta; this area is predicted to increase to 2.2 million hectares in the near future if suitable management practices are not implemented. Comparing the contour line of 4 parts per thousand salinity from 1978 to 1998, approximately 20 kilometres of landward movement was detected (Nguyen et al, 1999, pp212–217). During the dry season a combination of factors, such as the decrease in river-water discharge caused by dams, irrigation and sea-level rise, may have led to more saltwater intrusion. This is a serious problem not only for coastal agriculture but also for other sectors of the economy. Along the central coast, many provinces have been urgently lacking in freshwater for agriculture, domestic activities and industry because of saltwater intrusion in rivers during the dry season.

Environmental pollution

For the most part, the quality of Vietnam's coastal and marine environment is still rather good, although varying levels of pollution have been recorded at some sites due to contaminants produced by human activities in watersheds or in coastal areas. The most serious form of pollution is from oil. Oil pollution is growing worse, exacerbated by dumping from ships and oil and gas exploitation on the continental shelf. Oil spills are also a major sea-based form of pollution. Up to 1999, there were over 40 documented oil spills in the coastal sea and estuaries of Vietnam. In October 1994, 1865 tonnes of oil were spilled from a Singaporean ship at the Saigon Petroleum Harbour. In waters close to the coast, the oil content usually exceeds the accepted standards, and is even higher where there was oil exploitation and international shipping (Minh, 1996, pp8–14).

Although pollution from heavy metals is not yet widespread, concentrations of these pollutants may be increasing in coastal waters, sediments and wildlife. From 1996 to 1998, some heavy metal pollution was very serious (Dieu et al, 2000, pp125–134). Similarly, organic-matter pollution is distributed locally, but is heavy at some sites. In general, pesticide residues have been below standard limits, although evidence of their accumulation is widespread. Eutrophication is a problem in southern Vietnam, where nutrients such as phosphate, nitrogen and organic matter are produced as waste from domestic activities, agriculture and aquaculture. The widespread occurrence of brackish-water aquaculture diseases in the south may be related to eutrophication and red tides. In 1996, the brackish-water shrimp aquaculture industry in the Mekong River Delta lost large amounts of money due to eutrophication and red-tide blooms.

Loss of habitat and living resources

Recent natural and human-induced changes to the Vietnam Sea and coastal zones have led to the loss of tidal flats, mangrove marshes, beaches, sea grass beds and coral reefs. The mangroves have been heavily damaged by agriculture, aquaculture, logging and erosion (Hong and San, 1993, pp1–173). In 1943, there were 400,000 hectares of mangrove forests in Vietnam, including 250,000 hectares in the Mekong River Delta alone; but now only 200,000 hectares remain in the whole country. Beaches have been reduced by erosion and sand quarrying. Coral reefs and sea grass beds have been destroyed by turbidity, freshening of water, strong typhoons and pollution. During the El Niño of 1997 to 1998, the mean temperature of water in the Vietnam Sea increased 1.8 degrees Celsius (Dieu et al, 2000, pp125–134), contributing to widespread bleaching of coral reefs.

Degradation of coastal ecosystems, water freshening, turbidity, eutrophication or nutrient loss, pollution and loss of habitat lead to disruption of the ecological balance and to decreased biological productivity and biodiversity. These changes to the sea and coastal environments have threatened the survival of many marine species. The coastal zone contains breeding and spawning grounds essential to fish. Vietnam's marine fishery, which is mainly along the coast, has been faced with a decrease in living resources, while brackish water and marine aquaculture has begun to suffer from diseases caused by environmental changes and pollution.

The need for international assistance

Vietnam's economy has developed quickly during the last decade. Combined with population growth, this has increased pressure on the environment. Vietnam's marine environment has been facing degradation from the emerging problems noted above. The scale and the number of development projects by national and overseas investors will increase, and marine economic activities will be expanded during the next decade. The major development of industrial zones, construction of big dams for hydropower and irrigation, and the use chemical fertilizers and pesticides for agriculture will have an increasing impact upon the marine environment. Furthermore, risks to the marine environment could be increased by climate change.

By its nature, Vietnam's marine environment is very sensitive to impacts from human activities and the unusual natural changes experienced during recent years. Tropical marine ecosystems, such as coral reefs, mangroves and sea grass beds, are highly vulnerable. If marine environmental protection is not implemented effectively, Vietnam's social and economic development will not be sustainable, and people's quality of life will not be maintained. For these reasons, the protection of Vietnam's marine environment is an urgent issue.

Developing countries cannot successfully implement marine protection by themselves. Globalization affects all sectors of economic and social life, including environmental protection efforts. International assistance is needed. Vietnam is receiving more and more support from developed countries and international organizations for the development of its economy. According to Vietnam's law on environmental protection, investment projects are responsible for implementing environmental protection. Indeed, international assistance to help Vietnam protect its marine protection will have widespread benefits. Part of the Dong Sea (South China Sea) falls under the jurisdictions of many countries, and the Vietnam Sea plays some global and regional environmental roles. It serves as a sink for carbon dioxide, the major greenhouse gas, and it is an important transit area between the Pacific Ocean and the Indian Ocean. It has unique ecosystems and many endemic and rare species, and some very large areas along the coast serve as important sites for migrating waterfowl.

Vietnam's efforts to protect the marine environment

Vietnam's efforts in marine environmental protection have included establishing organizational mechanisms and a legislative base, building national capacity, formulating national plans and strategies, implementing environmental projects and strengthening Vietnam's international relations.

Agencies responsible for the environment

The existing organizational mechanism is fairly effective for environmental protection and management in Vietnam. The Ministry of Science, Technology and Environment (MOSTE) is the government institution responsible for – as its name suggests – state management of science, technology and environment. Under MOSTE, the National Environmental Agency (NEA) is responsible for making policies, strategies and regulations for environmental protection and sustainable development, focusing on the control of pollution and natural conservation. Environmental protection is also part of the work of some other ministries and government branches, such as the Ministry of Fisheries, the Ministry of Agriculture and Rural Development, the Ministry of Industry and the Ministry of Communication and Transportation (represented by the

National Maritime Bureau and its port authorities). Marine environmental protection is also carried out by local government organizations of coastal provinces. Every province has a department of science, technology and environment responsible for state management of the local environment. In addition, the National Maritime Bureau and its port authorities have responsibility for environmental management and protection related to maritime activities and harbour.

Environmental laws and regulations

The National Assembly, central government, MOSTE and other relevant ministries, and the people's committees of provinces make laws and regulations for environmental protection in Vietnam. The National Assembly declares laws and ordinances; the government issues decrees and directives; and MOSTE takes decisions and distributes circulars on environmental protection. Some decisions are taken by one relevant ministry or by inter-ministerial decisions between MOSTE and one or more other ministries. Each people's committee of Vietnam's 26 coastal provinces can issue regulations based on local conditions corresponding to environmental rulings of the National Assembly, government and MOSTE.

The most important legislative documents on environmental protection are the 1993 Law on Environmental Protection, declared by the National Assembly; the 1994 Decree No 175, which was issued by the government and addresses implementation of the Law on Environmental Protection; Decision No 1806 of 1994, issued by MOSTE and addressing the organization, operation and evaluation of environment impact assessments and the granting of environment licences; Circular No 1485 of 1994, issued by MOSTE and regarding environmental protection inspectors; and Circular No 2262, Guidelines for Oil Spill Resolution, issued by MOSTE in 1995. The National Assembly has also issued some other important laws concerning marine environmental protection and management, such as those on maritime activities (1990), petroleum (1993) and mining (1994). The legislative base for marine environmental protection in Vietnam is systematic and strict. However, effectiveness of these laws and regulations has been constrained by low public awareness.

Vietnam's environmental foreign policy

Vietnam's involvement in international environmental cooperation has been one of the most open aspects of its foreign policy over the last decade. The government has prioritized policies toward countries, international organizations, foreign non-governmental organizations (NGOs) and people training experts, conducting environmental research, applying clean technology, designing and implementing environmental improvement projects, controlling environmental risks, pollution and degradation, and carrying out projects on waste treatment in Vietnam. This is endorsed in Chapter 5, Article 46 on 'International Relationships in Environmental Protection' of the Law on Environmental Protection (Ministry of Science, Technology and Environment, 1999). The government has strengthened its efforts toward international environmental cooperation by joining many environmental agreements and protocols, including those pertaining to the marine environment (International Conventions on Environmental Protection, 1995). These include the Convention on Wetlands, the Convention Concerning the Protection of the World Cultural and Natural Heritage, the London Convention on Dumping at Sea, the Convention on Marine Pollution, the Basel Convention on Hazardous Wastes, the Convention on the Biological Diversity (CBD) and others. These agreements serve as the legislative base regarding Vietnam's international rights and responsibilities concerning environmental protection.

Implementing marine environmental protection

Establishing national strategies and plans has been a very important aspect of Vietnam's efforts to implement marine environmental protection. The National Plan for Environment and Sustainable Development (1991–2000) will be supplemented by the National Strategy on Environmental Protection Toward 2010 and the National Plan on Environmental Protection. Building national capacity, including facilities and human capacity, is considered a strategic solution for implementing effective protection of the marine environment. Support from the government, international organizations and developed countries has enabled the construction of new laboratories in research institutes and universities, and strengthened existing laboratories with modern equipment for analysing and monitoring environmental parameters. New tools have been applied to marine and coastal environmental management. There is also now more training of environmental experts at several universities, such as Hanoi National University and the Maritime University.

During the last decade, many marine environmental projects have been implemented under the National Plan for Environment and Sustainable Development. The state of the marine environment has been analysed by surveys and research projects, and reported annually to the National Assembly. Natural conservation is an important task for marine environmental protection. In addition to the internationally recognized protected areas, such as the World Heritage Site at Ha Long Bay, the Ramsar Convention site at Xuan Thuy and the Biosphere Reservation Area of Can Gio, a system of 16 marine protected areas have been recognized, including national marine parks, natural conservation areas and natural resource reservations (Hoi et al, 2000, pp317–339). Some environmental improvement and waste treatment projects have been carried out in the large coastal cities of Hai Phong and Ha Long.

Investment projects are subject to strict environmental impact assessments. However, the resulting reports have been of limited quality. MOSTE and the government have expanded a marine environmental monitoring system to all of Vietnam's coastal areas and marine waters. This will provide more information on annual changes in the quality of the marine environment. Inspection activities have also made an important contribution to marine environmental protection. Education and public awareness of marine environmental protection have been strengthened by public communication; but so far the effectiveness of these changes has been limited.

International assistance for marine environmental protection

As we have shown, over the last 15 years environmental matters have been given more attention in Vietnam. The environmental sector has also attracted international aid through official development assistance (ODA), and hence the pattern and nature of aid to Vietnam have changed dramatically. Environmental ODA to Vietnam – including for marine environment issues – has focused on building capacity for environmental and resource management and protection, establishing an environmental strategy, developing projects on natural conservation areas and initiating technical projects for local community assistance.

Conduits of assistance

There are three main conduits through which international aid is implemented in Vietnam: governments, international organizations and NGOs. During the decade between 1985 and 1995, two of these conduits – governments and international organizations (mainly the United Nations) – took on key roles and dominated the delivery of the international aid for Vietnam. The decade ended in a new phase in which multilateral agencies and loans took on an increasingly important role. Since 1995, governments, international organizations and NGOs have continued to participate in, and contribute to, environmental protection in Vietnam. Increasingly, they have paid greater attention to marine environmental protection as an important component of sustainable development.

Governments have been most active in providing international assistance for protecting the environment and the marine environment, in particular. So far, 15 governments have provided aid to Vietnam for environmental matters. By July 1999, among the 15 largest donors for ongoing environment projects, 9 were governments (UNDP, 1999, pp1–84). The government agencies that have provided aid for protection of the marine environment in Vietnam have included the Canadian International Development Agency (CIDA), the Danish

Agency for International Development (Danida), the Japan International Cooperation Agency (JICA) and the Swedish International Development Cooperation Agency (Sida) (UNDP, 1999, pp1–84). The main donor countries that have funded marine environmental protection are Australia, Belgium, Canada, Sweden, Japan, the Netherlands, Denmark and Norway. Development assistance has provided about one third of the cost of marine environmental protection in Vietnam.

Like the assistance from governments, aid from international organizations for environmental protection began after the matter emerged as a priority in Vietnam. Approximately one half of the 15 largest donors for ongoing environmental projects are international organizations – namely, the World Bank, the Asian Development Bank (ADB), the European Union (EU), the International Fund for Agricultural Development (IFAD) and the United Nations Development Programme (UNDP). Of these donors, the World Bank and the ADB are the largest, with a total budget of US$482.820 million and US$298.182 million, respectively, which has been provided in the form of grants and loans. The total budget for ongoing projects related to marine environmental protection provided by the EU, the World Bank, UNDP, the Global Environment Facility (GEF), the International Development Association (IDA) and the World Food Programme (WFP) recently totalled US$113.857 million. However, WFP is phasing out its programmes in Vietnam (UNDP, 1999, pp1–84).

NGOs have also made a significant contribution to environmental protection in Vietnam. Some of the NGOs that have been active include the World Conservation Union (IUCN), the World Wide Fund for Nature (WWF), Flora and Fauna International, BirdLife International, Oxfam, Helvetas and Save the Children. IUCN and WWF are two of the NGOs that participated in the early stages of marine environmental protection in Vietnam. They participated in compiling the Biodiversity Action Plan of Vietnam during 1993–1994 (Hoi, 1995, p221). IUCN is acting as the executing agency of a pilot project for a marine protected area at Hon Mun, Khanh Hoa Province, funded by the GEF and Denmark (Danida). Recently, NGOs have increased their assistance for coastal and marine environmental protection. However, most NGO projects are small, with budgets of less than US$20,000 each (Ministry of Planning and Investment and United Nations Development Programme, 1999, pp46–59).

Attributes of international assistance

The attributes of international assistance to the environmental sector have changed with time.

Capacity-building

Capacity-building for marine environmental protection and resources management was the earliest concern of the Vietnam government, and initial international assistance was directed at these issues. Most international aid to Vietnam's environmental sector during the 1990s was for building the capacity of government agencies and research institutions, and was concentrated in natural resource management. Aid for capacity-building has come mainly from bilateral cooperation between the Vietnam government and the governments of Australia, Belgium, Canada, Denmark, Sweden, Japan, Norway and the Netherlands. In addition, there has been multilateral assistance from the EU, IUCN, UNDP and World Bank. Up to 2000, total budget from overseas assistance for capacity building was valued at US$27.206 million (UNDP, 1999, pp1–84), amounting to 2 per cent of total commitments for the environmental sector. The greatest assistance came from Danida, which provided 25 per cent of the total budget.

ODA projects were targeted at human resources, facilities and technology, and institutional arrangements. Moreover, human resources have received support from other international programmes besides ODA projects. Many people working in the fields of research, management and planning related to the marine environment and natural resources were sent on training courses with support from international programmes. Through participation in regional or international programmes dealing with oceans, some research institutions have received support in both training and financing for implementing their own projects. For instance, the Hai Phong Institute of Oceanology participated in a programme on the application of spatial technology to natural resources and environmental management, which was supported by the National Space Development Agency of Japan. In the process, the institute has developed its human resources and basic equipment for applying spatial technology to coastal and marine environments, as well as for resource research and monitoring. Thus, while ODA for capacity-building in the area of marine environmental protection has been a relatively minor portion of total commitment to the environmental sector, it has made a considerable positive contribution to marine environmental protection in Vietnam.

Establishing an environmental strategy

International assistance for establishing an environmental strategy in Vietnam has often been integrated within projects for capacity-building. Since 1985, the three sources of international assistance – governments, international organizations and NGOs – have supported the development of a strategy for environmental protection and resource management. During the 1990s, IUCN, Sida, UNDP and UNEP supported the development of the National Environmental Strategy and the preparation of the National Plan for Environment and Sustainable Development (Ministry of Planning and Investment and United Nations Development Programme, 1999, pp123–124). Some environmental strategies, such as the National Environment Action Plan (NEAP) and the Biodiversity Action Plan (BAP), were also developed with overseas assistance. Since 1995, more ODA has gone to developing provincial marine environmental strategies and planning. Major donors in this period were CIDA, Danida, Sida, JICA, UNDP and the World Bank, as well as the governments of the Netherlands and Australia. An example is a project, supported by JICA, on environmental management in Ha Long Bay, which was focused on developing an environmental strategy for the People's Committee of Quang Ninh Province. The project – with a budget of US$3.545 million – ran from 1998 to 1999. Generally, ODA for developing environmental strategies at the national level is going down while increasing for those at the local level.

Projects on environmental management and natural conservation areas

After more than a decade of receiving environmental ODA for capacity-building and establishing environment strategies, Vietnam now needs ODA projects to be implemented in specific areas related to the environment and natural resource management. These kinds of ODA projects began during the 1990s, with the major target agency being the Ministry of Agriculture and Rural Development. Indeed, ODA projects for specific areas of the marine and coastal environments have really only started during the past five years. So far, there have been 16 ODA projects focusing on protection and management of the marine environment and natural resources coastal zones. Major donors are the government of the Netherlands, Sida, the ADB, the WFP, the EU, JICA, the World Bank, the GEF, Danida and UNDP (UNDP, 1999, pp1–84), with total commitment reaching US$190.096 million. The Hon Mun Marine Protected Area Pilot Project, mentioned earlier, is one of the most significant projects underway. It supports the conservation of critical marine biodiversity at Hon Mun Island and surrounding waters near Nha Trang City in Khanh Hoa Province, and develops methodologies for establishing and managing marine protected areas (Lan, 2000, pp220–224). The upshot is that environmental ODA for the development of marine environmental protection projects in Vietnam is very important. With this assistance, pilot projects such as the one at Hon Mun can be started, and the funds assist Vietnam in developing new programmes to protect the marine environment.

Technical assistance to local communities

Small environmental projects have received most of their funding from NGOs, which have also executed the projects. Some 300 NGOs are operating in the Green sector (but there is little concrete data on the small projects for marine environmental protection). Technical assistance to local communities has often been integrated within regional multipurpose programmes or larger projects for capacity-building or environmental management and conservation. For example, from 2000 to 2004, the Regional Programme for the Prevention and Management of Marine Pollution in the East Asian Seas, Phase II: Partnership in Environmental Management for the Seas of East Asia (supported by GEF and UNDP and executed by the International Maritime Organization) is promoting technical assistance to the coastal province of Da Nang for improvement of its marine environmental management system (Minh et al, 2001, pp19–20). Technical assistance for other projects could be a component or a sub-project. For example, part of a project on capacity-building in coastal management (supported by Sida from 1996 to 1999 with a commitment of US$250,000 and executed by IUCN Vietnam) involved technical assistance to six coastal communities for coastal protection and sustainable resource use (UNDP, 1999, pp1–84). There have also been medium and large projects to assist local communities for conservation and environmental protection. For example, the coastal provinces of Quang Ninh, Hai Phong, Thai Binh, Nam Dinh and Ninh Binh benefited from the rehabilitation and upgrading of sea dikes in a North Vietnam project, which was funded by the WFP in 1996–2000, with donor commitments of US$26.631 million (UNDP, 1999, pp1–84). Overall, technical assistance to local communities is in its early stages, with emphasis on developing case studies and demonstration sites.

General trends in international assistance

When considering international assistance to Vietnam for marine environmental protection, at least four factors can be considered: duration, location, beneficiary and size of the funding arrangement. Marine environmental projects average about five years in duration. The longest projects, such as those addressing coastal wetland protection and reforestation of coastal sandy soil areas, lasted eight years and were supported by the World Bank and Danida. Environmental ODA distribution is generally not equal among Vietnam's regions. From 1985 to 2000, the northeast region was the largest recipient of environment aid, receiving 28 per cent of total funds. It was followed by the six coastal provinces of Thanh Hoa, Nghe An, Ha Tinh, Quang Binh, Quang Tri and Thua Thien-Hue, which together received 19.7 per cent of environmental ODA. The other coastal regions received 24.6 per cent, while inland regions received 27.7 per cent (Ministry of Planning and Investment and United Nations Development Programme, 1999, pp57–58). In terms of the beneficiaries of marine and coastal environmental ODA, there are 17 major agencies and institutions at various levels (five ministerial agencies, six research institutes and universities, one NGO and several coastal provinces).

The size of marine and coastal environmental projects varies greatly. There are many small projects run by NGOs and generally undocumented. Meanwhile, there have been some large projects, with funding of tens of millions of dollars, such as the World Bank's 1999–2006 Coastal Wetlands Protection and Development Project (with donor commitments of US$65.2

million) and the 1996–2002 ADB Fisheries Infrastructure Improvement project (US$57 million). During the period from 1996 to 2001, total donor commitments for 31 coastal and marine environment ODA projects, ongoing and in the pipeline, including the categories of natural resource management and disaster management preparedness, amounted to US$216.773 million – about 10 per cent of the total ODA committed to the environmental sector in Vietnam. Approximately US$1.734 million per year, on average, went to the coastal and marine environments. For the category of natural resource management, including mangroves and wetland conservation and protection, as well as marine and coastal resources, ODA commitments were valued at 5 and 2 per cent, respectively (UNDP, 1999, pp1–84).

Evaluating marine environmental protection and international assistance

With one exception (Ministry of Planning and Investment and United Nations Development Programme, 1999), there have not been any official evaluations of international aid to the environmental sector in Vietnam. In the field of marine environment and natural resource management, such evaluation is rarely done systematically. Nevertheless, this section attempts to estimate the effectiveness and shortcomings of international aid to the marine environment and natural resource management, and outlines the prospects for future marine environmental ODA in Vietnam.

Effectiveness of international aid

At the macro level, the environment has been integrated within national policy and strategies, and several national action plans were developed with international assistance, notably BAP, NEAP and the National Plan for Environment and Sustainable Development (NPESD). Environmental awareness has been raised not only among government officials, but also within local communities in coastal areas. The capacity and capability of Vietnamese environmental institutions and agencies have been developed and improved, including with respect to institutions for marine research and management. The National Environment Agency and the Institute of Oceanology are good examples of this.

Although the qualitative evaluation of the immediate benefits and long-term advantages of ODA for marine environmental protection, as well as associated economic development, has not been conducted, benefits are clearly visible in some coastal and marine areas. The Ha Long Bay area in North

Vietnam is a good example. Through ODA and the Vietnam government's own efforts, the environment of the Ha Long Bay area has been much improved through the establishment of a unit for Ha Long Bay management. In general, ODA has made a significant contribution to the environmental sector. In fact, most major advances in the sector have been made with international support. The impact has been most visible in policy and institutional development. Furthermore, ODA has markedly enhanced awareness and skills in environmental management among government officials.

Shortcomings of international aid

In spite of the fact that international assistance has brought benefits to Vietnam's marine environment, there are shortcomings. Unequal regional distribution of ODA has created difficulties for marine environmental protection, which requires a cross-cutting and transborder administrative approach. In addition, there are still a few technical projects to assist local coastal communities. The factor of human resources is also a problem. Most international experts on ODA projects have little experience working in Vietnam. Additionally, the role of Vietnamese national project staff received inadequate attention, meaning that ODA projects give them less practical experience in tackling technical matters. Moreover, coordination between international experts and local specialists is sometimes not very close and smooth. Projects have been evaluated separately and there has been little sharing of documentation. It is difficult to relate ODA achievements to the maintenance of resource stocks or to environmental quality. While there are specific cases of improved resource management associated with international support, there are many cases where the long-term impact is difficult to assess.

Prospects for international aid

The prospects of ODA for the marine environment depend upon conditions in Vietnam, as well as international tendencies. An advantage for international donors is that the government of Vietnam has made environmental protection a national priority, particularly with regard to issues of the marine environment. The decentralization of ODA, which makes projects more effective for local coastal communities, is in progress. Regarding implementation of international aid and lessons learned from past ODA, donors and the Vietnam government are developing an improved understanding of each other, meaning that each increasingly meets the priorities of the other, thereby making environmental investments smoother and more effective. For example, Vietnam can now take full advantage of GEF assistance made available to developing countries for the protection of international waters and the conservation of biodiversity. It is likely that Vietnam's marine environment will continue to benefit from increasing international assistance as the donors and recipients become more diversified.

Conclusion

The Vietnam Sea and its coastal zone have become an area of active economic development, and its islands and coasts are high in population density. Human activities in the Vietnam Sea and in river watersheds have strongly influenced the marine environment. The sea has also been affected by transboundary factors and climate change. These factors have resulted in emerging problems for Vietnam's marine environment, including increasing risks of floods, erosion, sedimentation and saltwater intrusion; environmental pollution from, for example, oil, organic matter, pesticide residues and, to varying degrees, heavy metals; and the loss of habitats and decreases in the quality and quantity of living resources. These impacts will increase under the pressures of demographic changes and economic development. For these reasons, marine environmental protection has become an urgent requirement.

Vietnam has made great efforts to protect its marine environment. An effective system of central and local management agencies has been established; a strict legislative base, including laws and regulations, has been built; a national strategy and plans for environmental protection have been adopted; and many environmental projects, resolutions and actions, including monitoring, inspection and environmental impact assessment, have been implemented. Protecting the environment, particularly the marine environment, derives much of its strength in Vietnam from international relationships endorsed in the Law on Environmental Protection. Many international agreements and protocols related to the environment, including the marine environment, have been signed and ratified. Indeed, Vietnam's international relations in the area of environmental protection have been among its most open policies over the last decade. Combined with international assistance, this has helped to bolster marine environmental protection initiatives in Vietnam. Over 15 years, international assistance has primarily addressed capacity-building among central and local agencies and institutions working in relevant areas. A minor portion of this assistance has gone to local coastal communities.

International assistance administered both bilaterally (government to government) and multilaterally (from international organizations) has, despite many limitations, brought benefits. NGOs have shown their ability in running small-scale projects. The impact of international support is visible in policy and institutional development, although it has not been sufficiently transparent to allow complete assessment of the effectiveness of international aid for the maintenance of coastal and marine resources and the protection of marine environmental quality. The unequal distribution of environmental ODA grants and loans, in issue areas and geographic locations, has limited its effectiveness. Although the systematic evaluation of the international aid to the environment sector in Vietnam, generally, and marine environmental protection, particularly, needs more time and effort, it is clear that most of the major advances in marine environmental protection have been made with international support. With the new open policies of Vietnam and other improvements made during the past 15 years, international investment in marine environmental protection is increasing.

Chapter 13

Sustainable Development in Canada and Taiwan: Comparative and International Perspectives

Tse-Kang Leng

Introduction

Sustainable development is a vital issue for humankind. In the developing countries, economic growth is achieved at the price of environmental deterioration and social injustice. In Taiwan, like many newly industrialized economies, the public has a vague understanding of sustainable development. The synthetic content of sustainable development is always confused with the single-facet concept of environmental protection. In reality, sustainable development is not just a scientific consideration. It is a political, economic and environmental concern (Schnurr and Holtz, 1998). A long-term vision, focusing on the appropriate role of the state in balancing competing social, economic and environmental needs, is required for a grand strategy to maintain a sustainable future.

The purpose of this chapter is to analyse domestic and international approaches to sustainable development, juxtaposing the experience of Canada to that of Taiwan to learn lessons for East Asia. These countries represent different stages in the trajectory of sustainable development. A comparative analysis of these two countries sheds light on general principles of sustainable development in changing political and economic environments. This chapter argues that in order to ensure sustainable development that meets the needs of the present without compromising the ability of future generations, an appropriate role for the state is needed. The state must develop a mechanism of collaborative governance with the business community and civil society. International participation facilitates market benefits and the compliance of the business community.

The chapter first discusses the Taiwanese and Canadian concepts of sustainable development. Given the fact that sustainable development could not be achieved by direct state action alone, this chapter examines the interaction between the state, business community and political forces in the process of balancing competing goals of sustainable development. Given that bottom-up inputs to governmental policies are increasing, it points out various forms of public participation and analyses the role of non-governmental organizations (NGOs) in sustainable development. Finally, the last section analyses the advantages and limitations of Taiwanese and Canadian approaches to international participation for sustainable development. By doing this, we can learn more about how these concepts fit notions of national interest that feed into – and are affected by – the processes of environmental foreign policy, particularly at the level of implementation.

Conceptualizing and institutionalizing sustainable development

The Canadian concept of sustainable development

Bell and his colleagues elaborate upon the content of sustainable development from the Canadian perspective (Bell et al, 1999, pp3–5). Bell argues that sustainability requires feedback systems that allow its three core elements – environment, economy and society/community – to be tracked simultaneously. Governments can find numerous opportunities for win–win policies that are economically sound, environmentally friendly and socially responsible. In effect, sustainable development proposes a new paradigm of decision-making for all sectors of society. It entails a new perspective on present-day issues and challenges, and requires a better appreciation of the complex interconnections between the economic, social and environmental aspects of current challenges. In order to effect sustainable development, environmental policies need to be socially and economically feasible; social policies need to be environmentally and economically feasible; and economic policies need to be socially and environmental feasible.[1]

Canada has been dedicated to a comprehensive goal of balancing economic development, social justice and environmental protection. In addition to environmental regulations and infrastructure-building, market incentives have been one major tool for Canada to achieve sustainable development. As former Canadian Minister of Environment Christine Steward indicated, Canada challenges the proposition that environmental protection will disrupt economic development. Working towards a cleaner environment benefits the economy through creating new job opportunities (Steward, 1999). The Canadian concept of sustainable development is much broader than environmental protection. Sustainable development emphasizes co-existence and co-prosperity between the state and society, and between current and future generations (Kirkpatrick and Lee, 1997). Multiple actors – including the central government, local governments, business communities, industries and NGOs – are involved in the sustainable future of the nation. Even though the promotion of sustainable development requires coordinating top-down and bottom-up endeavours, the state still plays a determining role. Through the exercise of political power and policy tools, it serves as a catalyst to educate the general public and to integrate interests of various stakeholders for the goal of sustainable development.

Taiwanese concepts of sustainable development

Taiwan's political system during the 1970s and early 1980s remained one of authoritarian control. Voices from civil society were rarely heard. Public policy-making was top-down rather than interactive (Gold, 1986). Furthermore, economic development was achieved at the expense of the environment. Development was not environmentally sustainable, resulting in catastrophic environmental problems. Cars, trucks and motorcycles contribute to serious air-pollution problems. Loss of ground cover, deforestation, poor water distribution systems and low sewage coverage are the main reasons for problems related to water quality (Yao, 1997). Most urban areas in Taiwan lack green and open spaces.

The rise of a sustainable development consciousness emerged with Taiwan's democratization process. Beginning from the mid 1980s, public resistance to poor environmental management became a spur for political democratization. In other words, Taiwan's bottom-up new environmental movement has played a dual role of pushing political democratization and sustainable development. However, the term 'sustainable development' was new to Taiwan, even during the 1990s. To cope with the new challenges of sustainable development, the Taiwanese government has adopted various instruments to achieve balanced goals of environmental protection and economic development. In addition to traditional command-and-control methods of environmental management, environmental impact assessment (EIA) has become a prerequisite for major development projects (Tang, 2000, pp17–35). In practice, EIAs have gradually become a starting point for state–society interaction. Local governments and environmental non-governmental organizations (ENGOs) also get involved in the interactive process of achieving sustainable development.

Today, Taiwan is in a transitional period of forming consensus on sustainable development for the whole society. The state is adjusting its role in promoting balanced goals for national development. At the same time, the business community and civil society are strengthening their capacities to channel their demands. In 2001, the Taiwanese government released its plan of building a Green Silicon Island (GSI). Similar to the Canadian concept of sustainable development, the GSI plan makes environmental protection a major policy goal and emphasizes the harmony of economic development, social justice and ecological sustainability. In contrast to the path of economic development during the 1970s and 1980s, the GSI plan indicates that environmental protection and economic development are not incompatible; on the contrary, environmental protection is a precondition of economic development. The ultimate goal is to rebuild confidence between the state and society, and to promote initiatives of joint implementation in sustainable development. Seven major approaches are included in the action plan of GSI: knowledge-driven economy; priority in environmental protection; efficient usage of natural resources; social justice; regional equality; cooperative mechanisms; and international connections (Council for Economic Planning and Development [CEPD], 2001).

The Canadian and recent Taiwanese conceptualizations of sustainable development indicate that the process of consensus formation may sometimes be a painstaking one and may require careful calculation by all parties involved. Sound management of the environment cannot be achieved through one-time deals or decisions, but is rather a continuous challenge requiring diverse groups to work together despite different views and values. Since the goals of sustainable development may involve conflicting interests within the state and society, the consensus process is deliberately directed at devising 'do-able' actions and clearly identifying how agreements are to be fulfilled. The flexibility of consensus processes allows parties to fine-tune solutions as needed. By including everyone who has a stake in making the agreement work, especially those who will be needed for implementation, practical and detailed plans can be spelled out (Cormick at al, 1996, pp105–106).

Institutions implementing sustainable development

The National Council of Sustainable Development (NCSD) is the Taiwanese institution for promoting bureaucratic coordination and consensus-building at the central government level. In June 1989 and August 1991, the Ministry of Economic Affairs (MOEA) and the Environmental Protection Administration (EPA), respectively, formed committees to respond to the Montreal Protocol on ozone protection. In May 1992, the Executive Yuan formed the Global Change Working Group (GCWG), chaired by the EPA's deputy administrator, to coordinate global environment-related activities in all government branches. In December 1996, the Executive Yuan elevated the position of the GCWC and reorganized its mission under the name of the National Council of Sustainable Development (Energy and Resources Laboratories, 1997, pp1–2). Major functions and working groups of the NCSD are illustrated in Figure 13.1.

Figure 13.1 *The National Council for Sustainable Development*

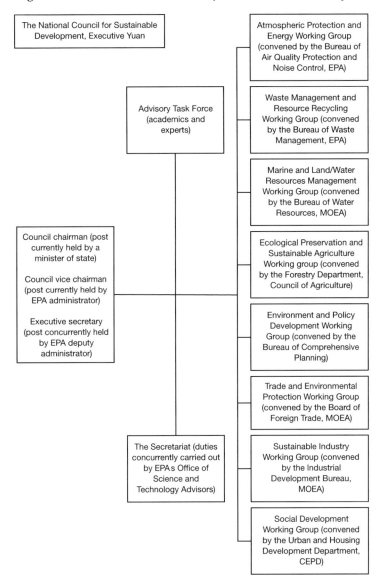

Source: Environmental Protection Administration, Taiwan (1999, p30)

In Taiwan, the government recognizes that the co-existence of economic development and environmental protection can be realized through innovation of environmental technologies; yet it lacks the momentum to take an active part in pushing these steps forward (Environmental Protection Administration, 2000, 2001). In 1999, total funding for governmental research and development on environmental innovation reached only US$24 million. Moreover, Taiwan still lacks an institutional mechanism to coordinate cross-sectional research on sustainable development. The EPA is still not a governmental department at the ministry level. In most cases, production ministries such as the Ministry of Economic Affairs have first priority in governmental budgeting. In other words, environmental innovation based on market incentives is still underdeveloped in Taiwan.

As indicated above, one salient characteristic of the Canadian approach towards sustainable development is the process of consensus-building. This consensus-building process includes bureaucratic coordination and state–society interaction. Among various mechanisms to promote consensus-building, the National Round Table on the Environment and Economy (NRTEE) plays a key role. The major difference between the NRTEE and NCSD is that, while the Canadian model focuses more on a multi-stakeholder approach, the Taiwanese model emphasizes a bureaucratic-coordination and elite-oriented approach to achieving sustainable development.[2] Instead of following the more traditional institutional model of bringing together individuals or businesses who have common interests or goals, NRTEE is multipartite and reflects different backgrounds and experiences, different perspectives and insights, and different values and beliefs. Four broad categories for membership are included in the NRTEE: government, business, strategic public policy and environmentalists. In a sense, the NRTEE is a microcosm of society (Dale, 1995) – quite unlike Taiwan's NCSD.

Accommodating competing economic and political goals

The previous section explains the conceptualization and institution-building for sustainable development in Taiwan and Canada. In the process of carrying out strategies for sustainable development, accommodating the competing goals of economic development and environmental protection is the key for success (Adkin, 1998). Voluntary compliance from the business community, based on market incentives, provides a pathway towards sustainable development.

Business interests and sustainable development in Canada

The goal of sustainable development to balance economic development, social justice and environmental protection is not easy. The first and direct challenge to this goal is the argument that environmental protection will harm economic development (Schramm and Warford, 1989). Economic depression means less funding for technological innovation and government intervention to protect the environment, and thus creates a vicious circle, leading to deterioration of social justice and environmental quality. In Canada, however, the government and industry have gradually created a market-based formula to achieve the goal of sustainable development. Market incentives provide a new tool to change perceptions and policies of local governments, which are the main actors for implementing sustainable development goals. The policy shift of the Alberta provincial government provides a good example.

As a major mining and oil-producing province of Canada, Alberta had long opposed greenhouse gas (GHG) control regulations set up by the federal government. The Alberta government of Ralph Klein bitterly denounced the federal government's agreement to binding targets in the Kyoto Protocol. Former Environment Minister Ty Lund threatened to resist federal regulations introduced to meet the target, while Klein warned that Alberta's growing energy industry could face ruin. At the end of 1999, however, the Klein government announced new policies to introduce measures that would put Alberta at the forefront of provincial efforts to reduce GHG emissions. Alberta planned to adopt an action plan to highlight what is possible by applying voluntary, technology-driven solutions to the problem of rising emissions levels. Klein's Conservative government and Alberta's industry would commit Cdn$20 million to $30 million to short- and long-term plans. These plans include lowering speed limits; offering financial incentives for the purchase of fuel-efficient vehicles; developing eco-efficient industrial parks; introducing an annual target for the government's purchase of electrical power produced from Green sources; developing a sequestration programme for carbon dioxide (CO_2) that would inject it into depleted oil deposits; and adopting National Energy Code standards for Alberta's governmental facilities in order to improve energy efficiency.

At the core of Alberta's 180-degree turn was the realization that an energy revolution was taking place. Alberta firms have developed considerable expertise in energy-efficient oil and gas extraction, technology that could become a valuable export commodity as the world moves to control such heat-trapping gases as CO_2. The province also has huge reserves of natural gas. Since natural gas burns cleaner than coal or oil, it is expected to become a valuable part of the answer to GHG-emission levels. Given these new technology innovation and market values, the Alberta Economic Development Authority, a business group that offers the government strategic advice, finally pushed the Alberta government to take new action. Furthermore, pressure from progressive companies played a significant role in the province's new approach. Executives from such firms convinced Klein and the majority of his cabinet that moving toward an energy-efficient economy has its rewards (*Ottawa Citizen*, 1999).

No easy choice: The case of Taiwan's fourth nuclear power plant

In Taiwan, the case of the fourth nuclear power plant demonstrates – as in Alberta, Canada – that policies of sustainable development involve balancing competing social interests and economic benefits. The 2000 presidential election made Chen Shui-bian the first Taiwanese president from the opposition. It was Chen's campaign promise, and his party's major platform, to scrap the fourth nuclear power plant in northern Taiwan. In October 2000, the new premier reversed a decision made by the former government, ordering a halt to construction of the plant. However, due to the fact that the ruling Democratic Progressive Party (DPP) only occupied a minority of seats in the Legislative Yuan (parliament), the decision to halt the project was under severe attacks from the now-opposition Nationalist Party (KMT) and the business community. The nuclear plant controversy later escalated into political turmoil, causing a possible recall of the president. Consequently, in February 2001 the premier yielded to opposition pressure to revive the project in order to save the Cabinet and Chen's presidency.

While announcing his decision to halt the construction of the nuclear power plant in 2000, the premier indicated six major points for consideration:

1   Taiwan will not experience power shortage after halting the project.
2   Alternative options to nuclear power plants are available.
3   Nuclear waste will cause permanent damage to the environment.
4   Managing a nuclear disaster caused by a malfunction is beyond current capacity.
5   The cost of halting the ongoing construction contract will be lower than continuing investment.
6   The ultimate goal is to build a non-nuclear Taiwan (*Lien Ho Pao* [*United Daily News*], 2000b, p8).

However, the government failed to persuade the business community, especially the high-tech sectors, that alternative options to the nuclear power plant would guarantee a stable supply of power. The businesses raised the issue that the government should not reverse the ongoing project, which had been approved and carried out for a period of time. By doing that, the business community might lose confidence in the government and choose to move out of Taiwan. Leaders of major unions in Taiwan also indicated that the halt of the nuclear project might increase the cost of power. Alternative options such as private power plants might create more problems, such as resistance from local communities and environmental pollution.

However, as the Canadian case indicates, a shift to the policies of sustainable development is also a process of redistributing interests within society. Formosa Plastics, one of the biggest business groups in Taiwan, supports a fossil-fuel power plant as an alternative to the nuclear power plant. Wang Yong-ching, president of the Formosa Group, argued that power plants that burn coal should be the major source of power in Taiwan. Wang Yong-ching indicated that his current and future power plant projects could supply stable power to meet the needs of economic development. He emphasized that Taiwan should not abandon fossil fuel as the major power source before figuring out other ways of solving the problem of global warming. In other words, the decision to halt the nuclear power plant may create potential business opportunities for those who build fossil fuel-based power plants around Taiwan. However, environmental pollution caused by fossil fuel created other problems for sustainable development.

Sustainable development has been utilized as a useful vehicle in the power-plant struggle. The opposition raised the issue of sustainable development to attack the plan of halting the nuclear power plant. They argued that nuclear energy is 'clean'. Advanced industrialized nations have the capacities and have expressed their intentions to help Taiwan manage nuclear waste. If Taiwan substitutes the nuclear power plant with fossil fuel-based power plants, the opposition camp argued, the amount of CO_2 emissions from Taiwan would increase by 16.9 million tonnes annually. If Taiwan does not take substantial actions to cut CO_2 emissions, the total emission amounts will reach 501 million tonnes, which equates to 19.6 tonnes per capita, in 2020 – higher than the Organisation for Economic Co-operation and Development (OECD) level of 12.14 tonnes per capita in 1990. This high amount is arguably not acceptable to international society (Tsai, 2001, pp3–5).

The reversal of the nuclear power plant decision reflects the current political and economic structure in Taiwan. The opposition parties formed strategic alliances with the business community to press the ruling party to honour decisions made by the former KMT government. The opposition parties supported the 'sunset clause' to abolish nuclear power plants in 30 years, but asserted that in order to guarantee continuous economic development and CO_2 emissions reductions, the nuclear power plant is the best solution for Taiwan at present. On the other hand, the DPP's long history of anti-nuclear plant ideology restricts its capacity to negotiate interim options with the opposition parties and the business community. The major weakness of the DPP in the nuclear power plant controversy is its failure to form alliances with the business community, except with those who have the interests in investing in private power plants by burning coal.

As the case of Canada's Alberta province demonstrates, energy-efficient technologies provide a promising solution to solve the dilemma of economic development and environmental protection. Introducing advanced energy technologies from abroad and investing in alternative energy options, such as domestic natural gas supplies, may promote market incentives for the business community. Unfortunately, the ruling party in Taiwan emphasized the moral aspects of abolishing nuclear power, but failed to indicate that alternative options may increase business benefits in the long run. The loss of business confidence pushed the ruling DPP into the trap of an ideological crusade, and thus increased the power of the opposition camp to utilize the interim 'nuclear sunset clause' as a balancing act for achieving sustainable development.

The Taiwanese and Canadian cases demonstrate that various goals of national development are not necessarily contradictory. In the policy-making process of achieving sustainable development, a win–win situation of continuous economic growth and environmental improvement is possible with appropriate state intervention. State actions involve various forms of alliances with key actors in civil society, especially the business community, and opposition parties. Local interests, business benefits and environmental concerns can be linked together through market incentives and technological innovation.

Grassroots dynamics: The public, NGOs and sustainable development

The real momentum to push forward sustainable development depends upon the consciousness of the general public. Interaction between the state and civil society on sustainable development is not a zero-sum game. NGOs educate the general public and channel rising demands from the grassroots level. In industrialized countries, the evolution of a public environmental interest has been characterized by a transition from preoccupation with ad hoc, reactive and transitory forms of citizen input to better-organized, longer-term and increasingly proactive activities (Hess and Howlet, 1997, p116). Environmental organizations have become a significant force in political lobbying, demanding increased public involvement in resource and environmental decision-making in the domestic and international arenas (Van Rooy, 1997, pp93–114).

Environmental activism and NGOs in Canada

The Canadian environmental movement comprises at least 1800 groups that vary in size from small local ones to large national groups such as Greenpeace (over 300,000 members) and the Canadian Wildlife Federation (which claims 620,000 members, supports and affiliates). In between these poles we find major national groups such as the Canadian Nature Federation (36,000 members) and Friends of the Earth (25,000 members), along with large provincial and regional organizations such as the Western Canada Wilderness Committee (over 25,000 members) and Pollution Probe (20,000 members). It seems safe to conjecture that over 1 million Canadians belong to at least one group (Wilson, 1992, pp110–111).

The activities of Friends of the Earth (FOE), Canada, are indicative of ENGO activities. In addition to the traditional tactics of ENGOs, FOE adopts more cooperative strategies with industries in order to improve the environment. The main purposes of FOE's cooperation with industries are to introduce more business opportunities in environmental protection and to achieve the goal of sustainable development at the same time. Staff at FOE keep regular contact with business leaders, debate and discuss various environmental issues with them and help to promote the 'community consciousness' of firms. According to Beatrice Olivastri, chief executive officer of Friends of the Earth, FOE actually tries to promote the 'transparency' of the industry process and to expose the process to public accountability.[3]

A unique body for coordinating various environmental ENGO activities is the Canadian Environmental Network (CEN). The CEN began operations in 1977 when ENGOs formed a national steering committee to help facilitate meetings between environmentalists and Environment Canada. A national steering committee consisting of representation from the various regions governs the CEN. The CEN is a network of hundreds of ENGOs, each of which retains the power to speak on its own behalf. This decentralized form of organization allows member groups to retain their autonomy and secures an objective role for the CEN itself. Hence, the CEN provides a cooperative forum for groups to share knowledge and expertise, and to involve public interest groups concerned with the environment in consultations on environmental legislation, policies and programmes. The CEN serves the function of a 'liaison institution' between the government and ENGOs. Indeed, a majority of the funding of the CEN is derived from the federal government of Canada through the annual contribution agreement with Environment Canada.[4] In addition, CEN promotes international connections between Canadian and international environmental groups. Designed to assist both Canadian ENGOs and their overseas partners, CEN's International Capacity-Building Project (ICPB) creates links through international networking, provides training in project management and furnishes information on such crucial environmental topics as climate change. Core funding for the project comes from the Canadian International Development Agency's Environment and Sustainable Development Programme (Canadian Environmental Network, 1998, p2).

The influence of Canadian ENGOs in the policy-making process should not, however, be overestimated. Hess and Howlett (1997) argue that in spite of considerable publicity, Canadian public interest groups remain underrepresented in regulatory and policy proceedings when compared with producer groups. The establishment of various ad hoc commissions may serve to postpone or divert public attention from the issue. The discretionary character of contemporary practices of public involvement may be inadequate to ensure the inclusion of all interests. There is not yet a mechanism for ensuring that a range of environmental perspectives is represented or that their relative importance to, or impact upon, the environment are assessed. An environmental 'tokenism' may result in the selection or appointment of a limited number of environmental representatives. Hence, the rhetoric of public participation is primarily geared towards discretionary forms of public consultation rather than mandatory and adequately supported inclusion on formal agenda-setting bodies (Hess and Howlet, 1997, pp123–133).

Public consciousness and sustainable development in Taiwan

In contrast to the Canadian model of interactive decision-making between the state and ENGOs, the major instrument of environment management in Taiwan is top-down command-and-control methods. In the process of environmental management, the legal basis for public participation is weak. Moreover, public attention to environmental issues focuses more on the *ex post* treatment of environmental impacts rather than preventive actions to protect the environment. This tendency is linked with the lack of public participation in the policy-making process. The general public has no voice until some disastrous outcomes emerge. Thus *ex post* action from the grassroots level always causes confrontation between the state and environmentalists.

As Taiwan made the transition to a plural democratic system, civil society gradually regained momentum for taking part in social issues related to sustainable development. Surveys show that the environmental consciousness of the Taiwanese people has increased since the 1980s. According to an opinion poll conducted by Academia Sinica, 90 per cent of the Taiwanese people acknowledge the controversies surrounding the impact of nuclear power plants on the environment (compared to 70 per cent 13 years ago); more than 70 per cent of the people agree that the establishment of highly polluting industries must be approved by referendum; 23 per cent of the people disagree that technology can solve every environmental issue (compared to 8 per cent 13 years ago); more than 70 per cent of the people agree that the current legal framework is not sufficient to protect Taiwan's environment; and about half of the respondents agree that the government must be responsible for the worsening environment (*Lien Ho Pao* [*United Daily News*], 2000a, p14). The poll results show that the Taiwanese public has gradually developed a more balanced concept of achieving sustainable development. At the same time, discontent towards governmental environmental protection policies remains high.

The traditional way for Taiwanese ENGOs to make their voices heard is to launch public demonstrations and grassroots resistance. The environmental movement is also closely connected with Taiwan's former opposition forces that challenged KMT rule during Taiwan's authoritarian era. However, as the opposition force became the ruling party in Taiwan after the 2000 presidential election, the grassroots ENGOs faced new pressures to institutionalize the environmental movement. In some senses the Taiwanese ENGOs supported by the former opposition parties lost their target of struggle after the political triumph of the opposition in 2000. For example, former environmental minister of the first DPP Cabinet, Lin Chun-I, the so-called 'Father of the Anti-Nuke Movement', declared that 'since there is no authoritarianism now, there is no need to oppose the nuclear power plant' (*Lien Ho Pao* [*United Daily News*], 2000d, p4).

Adopting institutionalized strategies other than public demonstrations, in the same way as the Sierra Club and FOE have been doing in Canada, has become the most urgent topic for Taiwanese ENGOs. Recently, new ENGOs focusing on sustainable development issues, such as high-tech pollution and collaboration with local governments, have emerged in Taiwan. The Taiwan Environmental Action Network (TEAN), a new ENGO focusing on forest protection, high-tech pollution and aboriginal people, has adopted new strategies of promoting sustainable development. Initiated by Taiwanese students in the US, TEAN uses the internet as a vehicle to join with domestic and international ENGOs to raise important issues of sustainable development in Taiwan. For example, TEAN and the Silicon Valley Toxic Coalition (SVTC) organized a joint taskforce to push forward sustainable high-tech development in Silicon Valley and Taiwan's Hsin-Chu Science-Based Industrial Park. TEAN also participated in international environmental conferences to put Taiwan's environmental issues in the international context.[5]

A successful case of collaborative governance between the local government and ENGOs is Taipei City's decision to undertake demand-side management of garbage treatment. Due to environmental and health concerns, Taiwanese ENGOs have led public resistance to building more waste incinerators. After years of negotiation and public hearings, the city government of Taipei finally launched a new policy of collecting waste. Instead of building more incinerators, it decided to utilize financial instruments to reduce household waste. According to new policies, all household waste must be put in special bags sold at price. Environmental NGOs have helped the city propagate the new concept of 'users pay' and thus achieved success in the first stage. From 1 July 2000 to 1 August 2000, Taipei reduced household garbage by 38 per cent and increased recyclables 400 per cent (*Lien Ho Pao* [*United Daily News*], 2000c, p15).

International participation and sustainable development

Canadian participation in international sustainable development

In Agenda 2000, the Canadian government declared four major sustainable development goals: economic growth and prosperity; building peace and security; Canadian values and culture; and greening operations. During past decades, Canada has demonstrated its leadership in encouraging international actions on environmental issues such as protecting the ozone layer, reducing GHG emissions and conserving biodiversity. Moreover, Canada plays a key role of 'knowledge broker' to promote ideas and actions on sustainable development. Canada worked actively in the Asia-Pacific Economic Cooperation (APEC) Environment Ministerial Meeting on Sustainable Development, which declared a joint statement on sustainable cities, sustainability of the marine environment, cleaner production and sustainable growth. Through international participation, Canadian values on sustainable development could be delivered and spread to less-developed countries. Environmental diplomacy is also the realization of moral obligations of Canada in international affairs.

In addition, Canadian initiatives in international environmental affairs provide business opportunities for environmental industries in Canada. The real momentum for the industry to promote environment-friendly ways of production comes from the market potential to adopt clean technologies. The case of Canada shows that one major approach to promoting market-oriented clean technologies is to develop international markets for Canadian environmental industries. Among Canada's various international endeavours to combine sustainable development with market benefits, the Sustainable City Initiative (SCI) is a recent undertaking. The SCI attempts to expand urban markets; increase opportunities for Canadian participation of public–private infrastructure in developing countries; help Canada attain its climate change commitments; assist developing countries in addressing their air quality and broader health concerns; and make Canadian development programmes more effective (National Round Table on the Environment and the Economy, 1999, p13).

Taiwan's participation in international sustainable development: Challenges and opportunities

In contrast to the active participation in international environmental affairs of Canada, Taiwan's international participation is constrained by political obstacles. During past decades, Taiwan's participation in major international environmental organization was handicapped by the fact that Taiwan is not a member of the UN. Thus, Taiwan has not been able to send official representatives to participate in any UN-related environmental conferences since 1971. For example, Taiwan could participate in the UN Framework Convention on Climate Change (FCCC) Conferences of the Parties (COPs) only as an NGO. Taiwan's international isolation thus distorts its rights and obligations in international environmental affairs. Taiwan also lacks institutionalized channels to report its progress in multilateral environmental institutions (Young, 1999, p2). Taiwan's absence in international environmental conferences also prevents it from promoting regional and global sustainable development.

Under this unfavourable situation, Taiwan's priority of international participation begins with bilateral environmental relationships with industrialized countries that have no diplomatic relationship with Taiwan but maintain close economic interaction with it (Environmental Protection Administration, 2000, 2001, p406). During the past decade, Taiwan signed various agreements on environmental cooperation with the US, Canada, Norway, France, Japan and other industrialized countries. For instance, Taiwan's Memorandum of Understanding on Environmental Cooperation with Canada includes exchange of information, visits and training of personnel, development and implementation of joint projects, and promotion of cooperation in trade, industries, science and technologies for achieving a sound environment. The scope of cooperation includes a variety of issues, such as environmental planning, pollution prevention, eco-labelling, environmental standards, waste water treatment, and solid and hazardous waste management.

The only major international organization in which Taiwan can participate under the title of Chinese Taipei is APEC. From 1998 to 2001, Taiwan played the role as a leader in the APEC Marine Resource Conservation Working Group (MRCWG). Under the APEC framework, Taiwan has the opportunity to report its own status of sustainable development and exchange information with other Asian-Pacific countries. In a similar fashion to the Canadian initiatives on sustainable cities, which put economic benefits and private–public cooperation at the core, Taiwan's participation in MRCWG also emphasized the role of private sectors in marine sustainable development.

Due to Taiwan's special status in international society and the need to enhance market forces, Taiwan's strategy of promoting private participation in the APEC framework is a reasonable choice. For example, Taiwan has indicated that the private sector could and should play a part in developing ocean and coastal management strategies. With land-based sources of pollution being a major contributor to coastal environmental degradation, the business community is important, extending beyond those enterprises that derive a direct benefit or have a direct impact. The APEC MRCWG also provides a unique opportunity for both sides of the Taiwan Straits to work together and enhance mutual understanding.

Like Canada, one of the major drives for Taiwan to expand its international outreach is the huge market benefit of environmental protection industries, especially the market in mainland China. From the political and military perspectives, the relationship between China and Taiwan is constantly intense (Leng, 1998, pp404–509; 2002, pp230–250). Cooperation on sustainable development between Taiwan and China may promote confidence-building on issues connected to people's welfare on both sides of the Taiwan Straits. Similar to the Sustainable City Initiative in Canada, economic benefits and private momentum may become the major boosters for further cooperation in environmental protection.

According to various surveys, China will spend more than US$100 billion on environmental infrastructure construction (Economy, 1999, p16). In order to host the 2008 Olympic Games in Beijing, China will pour additional funding into improving its highly polluted environment. Although Taiwan is not the global leader in environmental technologies, its practical experiences in solving problems for small- and medium-sized enterprises help to maintain competitiveness in the China market. A recent report demonstrates that about 49 per cent of Taiwanese companies choose China as their first priority for projects under the FCCC's Clean Development Mechanism (CDM). Because Taiwan is not a UN member, hosting CDM projects under the FCCC framework may involve political considerations, especially opposition from China. However, according to polls of industry, only 3 per cent of the respondents answer that the Taiwan should withdraw from the CDM if China raises political issues to question Taiwan's sovereignty (Li, 2000, p6). In other words, the economic benefit has become the major concern for the private sector on the issue of environmental cooperation across the Taiwan Straits.

Geographic vicinity and cultural similarity give Taiwan a unique role to serve as a liaison between multinational corporations and environmental markets in mainland China. Taiwan and advanced industrial countries have established stable, cooperative relationships in environmental cooperation. This cooperative relationship could be extended to develop the market for the mainland. For instance, Canada has signed agreements on environmental protection with governments on both sides of the Taiwan Straits. Taiwanese businesses could invest in Canadian projects, hosting the CDM with China, thereby avoiding sensitive political controversies. These strategic alliances, based on mutual economic benefits, could realize domestic sustainable development and improve environmental protection for developing countries at the same time. In other words, both Taiwanese and Canadian experiences indicate that increasing international participation will facilitate a win–win situation of simultaneous economic development and sustainable development.

Conclusion

The Taiwanese and Canadian experiences indicate that in order to achieve sustainable development, special emphasis must be put upon integrating:

- different national goals;
- an open process for public participation;
- accountability through multi-stakeholder supervision; and
- market-based incentives for international participation.

The top-down, command-and-control methods are not sufficient to address and tackle major issues of sustainable development. In order to persuade the business community to voluntarily follow policy adjustments for sustainable development, creating market incentives is the key. Multiple channels of communication between the state and society are established to avoid direct confrontation. Public consciousness and constant interaction between the state and society help to lay a solid foundation for continuous improvement of sustainable development.

During the 1980s and 1990s, many developing countries experienced bottom-up democratization (Huntington, 1991; Haggard and Kaufman, 1995). Democratization changes the balance of power between state and society. However, for many developing countries, demands from civil society need to be channelled into, and represented in, national and local politics. Otherwise, environmental and sustainable development issues could spark serious confrontation between the state and society. Environmental NGOs play the roles of agents who bridge the interests of state and society (Chasek, 2000, p28). Strengthening ENGOs could help to spread knowledge of sustainable development, supervise business activities and represent grassroots interests for sustainable development in developing countries. The state alone cannot carry out responsibilities for sustainable development. Collaborative governance between state and society is the pathway towards a sustainable future for development countries.

One major concern for developing countries in promoting sustainable development is that environmental protection strategies may deter economic development. However, experiences in Taiwan and Canada demonstrate that economic development and sustainable development are not necessarily in conflict. In order to obtain voluntary compliance from the business community, introducing 'marketable' environmental technologies, such as high-efficiency clean technologies, is important to create a win–win situation for the state and the business community. Given the fact that most developing countries are facing financial constraints on technological innovation, privatization of environmental industries and attracting foreign investment in environmental infrastructure construction are potential solutions. For newly industrialized countries, governments can increase investment in international markets for environmental industries and can promote international strategic alliances in environmental products. All in all, a win–win situation is possible after careful calculation of market potential for sustainable development technologies in developing countries.

Taiwan's achievement in economic development during the past few decades has been recognized by the international society as a 'miracle' (Gold, 1986; Haggard, 1990). However, behind the rapid economic growth is the deterioration of natural resources and degradation of the environment. It is time for Taiwan to develop strategies to sustain economic growth and protect the environment for future generations. Raising public consciousness and strengthening channels of interaction between the state and society are two key tasks for the government to undertake immediately. Taiwan also needs to develop energy-efficient ways of production and to promote technology innovation. These policies could provide market incentives for the business community to improve the environment. International participation in international environmental affairs may also boost technological innovation and increase business opportunities for environmental industries. A new Taiwan endeavouring to achieve sustainable development will benefit future generations, both in Taiwan and the rest of the world.

Chapter 14

Community-based Conflict Management and Environmental Change: A Case Study from Papua New Guinea

Philip Scott Jones[1]

Introduction

International responses to environmental degradation increasingly involve partnerships among key stakeholders. In pursuit of these partnerships, the policies of international development actors often include capacity-building measures for some form of social analysis. These may include poverty assessments and analyses of stakeholders, gender and community strengths and needs. In this way they seek to identify groups who, because of their vulnerability or power, stand to gain, lose or otherwise influence programme success. Although analytical tools may support policy, operational problems remain on how to implement an effective environmental foreign policy dialogue between, for example, villages and government, or local non-governmental organizations (NGOs) and international agencies.

This chapter reflects on the need for the makers of environmental foreign policy to consider and address what follows their efforts – namely, implementation issues on the ground; it is about the importance of how environmental foreign policy is implemented in affected states. Environmental foreign policy, international environmental agreements and funding decisions by international financial institutions need to address community conflicts and priorities.

Conflict management (CM) principles, applied at community level within a sustainable livelihoods (SL) framework, can identify these and inform the development of foreign policy in environmental conservation that is consistent with economic development. The chapter examines the effectiveness of combining SL approaches with conflict management principles in order to protect natural resources (NR) while developing local and national economies. It takes as its case study the Lakekamu Basin in Papua New Guinea's (PNG's) southern peninsula. This is a 2500 square kilometre lowland rain forest facing significant environmental change through conversion to oil palm or smaller-scale extraction initiatives (for instance forestry and mining). Here, international agencies and their local NGO counterparts have been exploring an alternative: protection of the basin as a wildlife management area (WMA). Major actors involved include local peoples, local and international NGOs, provincial and national departments of the PNG government, local and international agribusiness and forestry companies, bilateral donors and the World Bank.

Tyler (1999) discusses elements of a policy framework for managing natural resource conflicts, including stakeholder analysis, developing processes for interaction, information-sharing and communications among stakeholders, and developing effective roles for intermediaries. Filer and Sekhran (1998, pp381–398) echo some of these ideas for forest policy in Papua New Guinea, emphasizing iterative policy-making processes with a 'progressive integration of negotiations' among different stakeholders and a 'fundamentally flexible method of working in the interface between the village and the state'. They advocate policies that actively encourage engagement with stakeholders at all levels, especially at the grassroots. They note that there is 'no shortage of new institutional structures' in PNG; what is missing is 'the "route map" and the managerial capacity at lower levels of the state' (Filer and Sekhran, 1998, pxviii). Like Tyler, they point out that transforming relationships takes time.

In many countries, including PNG, building effective linkages among stakeholders is, in practice, left to NGOs that work in the gaps between local institutions and government or international agencies. Where these NGOs have appropriate capacities to operate within a broad range of democratic processes, vertical linkages may successfully provide conduits to enable synergies between policy and practice. In other circumstances, there may be constraints to creating horizontal linkages. In PNG, these include a weak state, a fragile NGO sector, geographical barriers, strategic and political alliances that rely heavily upon patronage, and distant stakeholders with little understanding of each other's needs. All of these factors have implications for how PNG and other developing countries in Southeast Asia confront environmental change and how actors from within and beyond the region formulate their individual and collective environmental foreign policies.

International and foreign policy contexts

PNG's mineral wealth, extensive forests and strategic location in World War II have assured it the attention of foreign governments and companies. PNG's resource management policies have owed much to Australia (the colonial administrator until independence in 1975) (Whimp, 1997). Recent global and regional environmental agendas have challenged extractive forestry and mining practices, associating questions of governance, peoples' rights and environmental laws with broader issues concerning sustainable development and political and social stability. Some donors, notably the Australian Agency for International Development and the World Bank, have been heavily engaged with PNG's policy process in these areas (Filer and Sekhran, 1998). The policies and programmes of these two agencies form a major part of the international environmental policy context in PNG, together with regional and global conventions and agreements to which PNG is a signatory. Environment-focused international NGO policies and activities, especially in biodiversity conservation and forest-sector issues, are also relevant. It is particularly important to note the forestry and environmental implications of the World Bank's Structural Adjustment Programme and the March 2000 International Monetary Fund (IMF)/World Bank austerity package. These have been a subject of prolonged debate within PNG and between donors, NGOs and some communities (Filer and Sekhran 1998; Forests.org, 2001; Government of Australia, 2002).

What has been largely absent in environmental foreign policy is a dialogue with local peoples who stand to gain or lose in PNG's present context of balancing environmental protection and biodiversity conservation with the need for economic development. Sustainable livelihoods approaches and the tools of conflict management are useful in addressing this weakness by providing practical ways forward for locally relevant policy implementation and providing a vehicle for environmental foreign policy-relevant information to reach policy-makers.

Sustainable livelihoods (SL)

Agencies adopting SL approaches use different definitions, most referring to the work of Chambers and Conway (1992). The UK's Department for International Development (DFID) uses the following definition:

A livelihood comprises the capabilities, assets (including both material and social resources) and activities required for a means of living. A livelihood is sustainable when it can cope with and recover from stresses and shocks and maintain or enhance its capabilities and assets both now and in the future, while not undermining the natural resource base (DFID, 1999, p1).

People's 'livelihood strategies' are based on five capital 'assets': human, social, natural, financial and physical. These may be thought of as resources offering opportunities to achieve certain 'livelihood outcomes', such as increased income and well-being, or reduced vulnerability to shocks, trends and seasonal events.

Forest-dwelling people in PNG draw on high levels of natural capital (forests, soils, rivers) and have appropriate human capital (skills, knowledge) to use their natural environment sustainably. Their social capital (rules, networks, trust, confidence) is intimately linked with subsistence forest life. Financial and physical capital assets are low and people are vulnerable to environmental change, especially in their forests. A livelihoods approach allows holistic exploration of the nature and interaction of the five capital assets and forest dwellers' livelihood context and vulnerability.

Conflict analysis and conflict management (CM)

Links between CM and SL have been made explicit in recent World Bank publications on urban violence. In one of these (World Bank, 2000) a framework of political, economic and social violence is presented with causality related to individual, interpersonal, institutional and structural contexts that have impacts on physical, human, social, natural and financial capital. Policy and practice implications likewise are presented within a livelihoods framework. Building on this work, Moser and McIlwaine (2000) reported on 'participatory appraisal' techniques for analysing urban conflict, using tools developed in the rural natural resources (NR) sector.

It is important to note that the CM approaches of many NR agencies tend to focus on conflicts within communities, or between communities and outside agencies, which could threaten project viability, in order to inform strategies for managing risks from conflict.

A project in environment and community-based conflict management

Several case studies were developed from a DFID-funded CM project in the Lakekamu Basin. This two-year project took place within and alongside a long-term Integrated Conservation and Development (ICAD) project. The local NGO working with both projects was the Foundation for People and Community Development (FPCD). The case study that follows examined a land dispute between two communities.[2] It addresses conflict over land use in the Lakekamu Basin within and among communities, companies from outside the area, and government and non-government agencies.

The Lakekamu Basin contains the largest intact humid forest in southern peninsular PNG. There are no roads or telephones and only a handful of generators. Tekadu, in the north, is a three-day walk over mountains along narrow forest trails from Wau, the nearest small town. Weather permitting, two flights a week connect Wau to grass airstrips in Tekadu and Kakoro, towards the south. Lakekamu is a global priority for biodiversity conservation because of the number of species (many endemic to Lakekamu) and the size and quality of the lowland forest habitat. There has been minimal forest impact from a subsistence population whose density is about 0.5 people per square kilometre and whose agriculture is largely confined to riverbanks. Until regular aircraft service about 20 years ago, the biggest impact in the basin occurred during World War II. In response to invasion threats, Australians and allies built the Bulldog Trail through the basin. Forest clearance, money from employment, tensions with refugees, and a large foreign and mechanized army all left their mark. The overgrown trail is now a potential tourist attraction the existence of which plays a role in contemporary land-use conflicts.

Only two options for significant changes in customary land use have been seriously proposed: conversion of large areas to oil palm plantations and/or the creation of a protected WMA. These developments present opportunities and threats with which the CM project was concerned. The diversity of social, cultural, legal and administrative systems echoes the biological diversity that brought the basin international recognition. Even local people admit that there are many changing perspectives on local issues. For outsiders such as the FPCD, CM required mapping these multiple conflicting perspectives.

Local people, land ownership and resource rights

Land ownership and resource rights are subject to competing claims by four landowner groups, each with a different language: the Biaru, Kamea, Kurija and Kovio. Villages have developed around two airstrips, with small stores, limited schooling and very limited access to markets and government services. Part of ongoing CM work consists of building consensus through interpretations of each group's history relevant to land ownership and resource rights. The FPCD's initial CM work identified several local conflicts and started building local capacity to manage them. Local people identified the big issues as 'the future' and 'change' (see Figure 14.1). The women, men and youth of each village sought explanations and answers through their customs, history, sense of identity and ancestry. Potential solutions also lay with local and provincial governments, NGOs and outside businesses. The FPCD needed to build effective relationships horizontally within villages and vertically between villages and these external agencies.

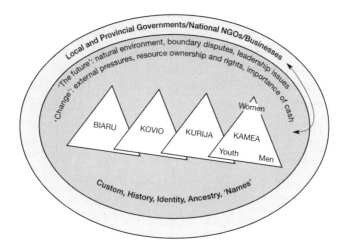

Figure 14.1 *Big Issues for Local People in Lakekamu Basin:*
'the Future' and 'Change'

Each of the four groups is subdivided into tribes and clans. For example, Tekadu's 400 people form one language group, the Kamea, in six villages, four with Lutheran allegiances and two with Baptist and Catholic adherents. In these villages are 5 tribes divided into 18 clans. Marriage among language groups is possible. This means that people from one family, clan, tribe, language group and location may move elsewhere within the basin. These moves create further layers of complexity but offer opportunities for alliances and conflict resolution, as well as dissension. To this complexity may be added the administrative, legal and governance issues of the basin, which straddles the Gulf, Morobe and Central provinces.

Establishing claims and rights

In the PNG highlands, ancestry features strongly in determining customary rights. Land ownership is customarily determined by each generation according to a review of ancestry, which itself is not a fixed element of social reality. Each generation has the right to re-formulate ancestry, referring to a genealogy that is always shifting and open to debate. For example, a son may claim rights to land after his father's death. But others may also make a claim if they have the same name as the father; the name itself carries rights. If a claimant calls for names, rights are immediately given to living people who have names associated with the land, stretch of river or tree in question. Multiple claims may exist, presenting options for resolving 'rights'. For example, claimants may share the land or one claimant may cede rights to another. Where claimants do not agree, difficulties, even fighting, may ensue. These issues must be considered with respect to land rights and legal registration. For some people, registration may not set a recognized precedent. What happens in the next generation may remain an open question, with the fact of registration just another truth to be considered. This is especially relevant when two or more administrative boundaries cross the land in question, as described in the case study.

Arrival of conservation initiatives

Conservation initiatives began in 1996 in response to the mission, policies and strategies of Conservation International (a US-based biodiversity conservation NGO) and the Biodiversity Conservation Network's Support Programme (a US-based consortium of the World Wide Fund for Nature, US, the Nature Conservancy and the World Resources Institute, which were funded by the US Agency for International Development). Activities began with the arrival of a Western research team and the construction of a research station at Ivimka. By then Lakekamu was a conservation priority, following the 1993 Lakekamu Basin Conservation Initiative. An ICAD project followed, with significant grant money arriving but without a relevant plan. It is fair to say that the ICAD project began amidst enthusiasm and with honourable goals, albeit insufficiently supported by analysis and planning. Meaningful, early discussion with local people seems to have been absent. Until the arrival of the CM project, there were no appropriate written plans for identifying and achieving goals. Inventory of the basin's biodiversity began with a rapid survey, subsequently extended.

The social, cultural, political and historical context of its peoples, in contrast, appears to have had only one review (Kirsch, 1998), by which time significant infrastructure had been built. In the words of John Sengo, an FPCD worker:

> *We ended up raising ... expectations way too high. We should have gone in and done realistic planning and held discussions with people before getting the ... funds. As it is, the people were not involved in the project. They still don't understand what the project is or what it is supposed to do* (Salafsky and Paka, 1999, p166).

In short, the ICAD was in a precarious state in 1998, and the situation of FPCD staff bordered on dangerous.

Today's situation

The opportunities created by communications, commerce, computing and knowledge generation are almost inaccessible to most people in Lakekamu. Changes in social and human capital have led to vulnerability and the possibility of significant environmental change, with realigned power relations and uncertainties over how to protect or manage natural capital. The people are very poor, isolated from many positive benefits of change and vulnerable to many of its negative effects. Most people in Lakekamu have difficulty in knowing about or interpreting events outside the basin. There is a large gulf between what people know and what they need to know in order to take decisions on how to manage change effectively. Without external support, they are unable either to relate directly to environmental foreign policy that affects them, or to contribute to its development.

Social, human and natural capital form a dominant triangle in Lakekamu. Financial capital is absent for most, miniscule for nearly everyone else. Most physical capital (mainly houses) was built locally from forest products. Lakekamu has seen considerable erosion or reorientation of social capital over the past 20 years. Informants described new precedents being set by some individuals who gave primacy to their nuclear family, rather than village, language group or community, in seeking financial benefits from development. These new precedents have eroded cognitive forms of social capital, such as trust, confidence and a belief that others would reciprocate 'for the greater good'. This, in turn, has led to the loss of customary forms of structural social capital, such as rules, roles and networks.

In Lakekamu, I spoke with people who mourned the loss of 'the traditional ways' and were uncertain how to proceed with a new system described as 'selfish', 'people going their own way', or 'people going outside the community'. This is the reverse of what many writers see as desirable ways of building social capital, where the creation of ties that cut across groups is important. For example, building associations involves a transition 'from loyalty to primary social groups [towards] networks of secondary associations whose most important characteristic is that they bring together people who, in some ways, are different from the self' (Narayan, 1999, p12). In PNG, such cross-cutting ties might consist of networks, resource mobilization and benefit distribution among, rather than within, language groups or villages. Implementing environmental foreign policy depends on partnerships with local peoples. But this cannot be achieved when trust, confidence and other aspects of social capital have become eroded and people have limited financial and physical assets. One way forward was to build capacity in a local NGO that might be able to bridge gaps between policy and practice.

Building NGO capacity for managing conflict

The FPCD is a Port Moresby-based NGO focusing on community development and environment. It was a neutral outsider in some conflicts that were not relevant to overall ICAD project goals, which aimed to establish a protected area in Lakekamu. The FPCD welcomed the opportunity for CM training, since the ICAD became mired in a range of conflicts that almost led to the withdrawal of FPCD staff. The initial idea behind CM training for FPCD staff was to help them analyse and respond to conflicts within Lakekamu, and, in the process, to train local people in CM so that they could solve their problems themselves and negotiate collectively on Lakekamu's future. One of the consequences of this was to increase the ability of local people to debate implementation issues that emerged from an understanding of environmental foreign policies and strategies that affected them. After initial workshop-based CM training, the FPCD coordinator conducted several CM training events in Lakekamu, sometimes alongside staff from another NGO, the PEACE Foundation. Training examined attitudes, including assertive, aggressive and submissive behaviour, as well as the themes of leaders and power, and gender. It also focused on developing interpersonal, communication and teamwork skills. A major emphasis was placed on developing skills in facilitation, negotiation and mediation.

Just as the village context needed to be understood by FPCD and the international agencies whose environmental policies they were working with, the reverse was true. This is an important point to keep in mind with regard to policy development or transferring learning from this project to other cultural and political contexts where different intermediaries may operate. As local people take major decisions about their livelihoods, it will become even more important for them to clarify the level and boundaries of FPCD's capacity and any circumstances under which FPCD's role may alter. These issues apply to most projects and have policy implications for FPCD's donors and international NGO counterparts.

Case study in environmental conflict management

This case study concerns a conflict about land ownership between the Tekadu and Kakoro communities. The question of 'who owns what' embraced deeper questions, such as 'who are we', 'where did we come from' and 'how do we approach decisions about change?' To answer these questions, new CM processes and structures had to be developed from or alongside customary CM approaches. Importantly, the demands of today (brought about largely by new monetary values on resources and property rights) required a level of certainty and permanence to the answers that was not previously needed. These issues and the international environmental policy context within which they operate are barely familiar to local people, many of whom were fearful of the future and openly confused regarding potential environmental change. Local leaders, with limited experience of the world outside Lakekamu, felt a particular burden. Anger and possibly violence are not uncommon responses to uncertainty and fear. Under these circumstances, villagers and CM teams faced challenges that were particularly demanding in PNG because of the scale and speed of change, the social and cultural complexity, and the disparity between the 'old' and the 'new'.

A pre-existing land dispute in the Ivimka station area arose between the Biaru and Tekadu communities when a company received a gold prospecting licence. In 1992, a Land Court judgement in Wau was made in favour of the

Tekadu, stating that they had won their right to the land through war. The situation is made more complex because land around the research station is in two provinces. Tekadu is in Morobe Province while Kakoro (where the Biaru live) is in Gulf Province. Community-based conflict analysis revealed that the situation, although twice resolved legally, was not satisfactory to the Biaru. When mining options ended, the potential to earn money from the research station led them to consider the potential bias that a court in Morobe might have toward the Tekadu. Conflict analysis also clarified other groups' involvement. The Tekadu had support within Kakoro from the Kurija who originated from Central Province, while some Kamea migrants (who settled in Kakoro) remained neutral, despite ties with Tekadu. The situation was an example of complex issues that are not amenable to legal definition and adjudication where definitions 'in terms of narrow "rights" through formal legislation are both clumsy and inflexible' (Tyler, 1999, p275).

Seeking workable alternatives, the CM team visited lawyers in Morobe to search relevant court cases. The project coordinator also conducted CM training at Ivimka, and held meetings with elders concerning the dispute. These were followed by two community-mapping events in each disputant's area, which were of great significance. The maps generated were of proposed conservation-research land boundaries and of sites for possible new conservation or oil-palm areas, and potential related environmental impacts. In both cases mapping was done by villagers according to traditional identifications of land rights. This required careful facilitation from the CM coordinator and the development of consensual negotiation skills among the groups involved because force, withdrawal or continual accommodation of one side's views failed to solve the problem. Training village 'negotiators' in CM principles and skills relied on local knowledge and the ability to marry customary approaches with the new approaches offered by the CM team.

The mapping exercise was a pivotal moment for everyone. Local people saw an opportunity for progress but felt unsure of the process for reaching consensus. The history of Lakekamu is one where stability and previously sustainable livelihoods grew from complex tensions between a state of peace and a state of war (Dinnen and Ley, 2000). In a changing world the people have met forces that make them vulnerable to exploitation, to the influence of money and to social disruption. All of these issues affected people's responses to environmental change. The social capital built up over generations had become disturbed and was being rebuilt in different ways. Previous forms of social capital were under threat as old institutions, customs and relationships revealed their weak ability to interpret and manage outside pressures for environmental change, increasing non-conformity by some to long-established social rules, and the restructuring of alliances and relationships as opportunities emerged to obtain money. Added to these things was a fear of the unknown and of losing possible opportunities – a feeling that the changing world, with all that it offers, may pass them by.

The willingness of local people to construct maps required trust and confidence (cognitive social capital). It also required careful facilitation within a structure that had rules and roles that everyone could understand (structural social capital). These horizontal forms of social capital were developed through a CM training process that enabled people to work collaboratively on issues of mutual importance. Importantly, the process was public, open to most relevant stakeholders and undertaken at a pace that all could manage. Local people were well aware that these maps could be used in negotiations with powerful outsiders. The process of building horizontal social capital would subsequently need to be applied vertically between peoples of the basin, as a whole, and the government, law courts, NGOs and company stakeholders outside of the basin (see Figure 14.1). Therefore, local people needed to be sure that FPCD could understand the outside world well enough to facilitate this where necessary. They also relied on FPCD's access to these agencies and its ability to help communities interpret complex issues.

Provisional maps were referred to for within-village agreement before a workshop was established with all four ethnic groups, facilitated by FPCD. Negotiations between FPCD and communities were held to verify views regarding research and conservation area boundaries, and negotiations with outside agencies. Other actions were to include supporting local examination of land rights, understanding the protected area registration process and poverty-alleviation strategies, linking with international, national and local environmental policy on ICAD strategy, and establishing dialogue with international stakeholders.

As these issues became clear, local people were in a position to discuss whether areas in the basin should be protected or used for growing oil palm. The question of neutrality became important because FPCD staff functioned as brokers (Jones, 1998, p11). They were not neutral with respect to the outcome, as they had been with the land dispute. In fact, FPCD had a vested interest in developing a protected area as part the ICAD project.

Villagers realized that they did not have the capacity to effectively negotiate over the oil palm plan. As a result, initial CM work focused on capacity-building to manage micro-level conflicts, focusing mainly on generating information and building horizontal social capital. These efforts were important in enabling local people to develop consensus about protected area management issues that would involve partnerships among them. Further CM work involved helping local people to develop mechanisms for establishing vertical connections with NGOs, government agencies and legal authorities. The establishment of a legally protected area (WMA) would require negotiations with these outsiders. Individuals who had shown leadership and ability in negotiations and mediation during the research station conflict (and others) emerged as potential representatives to take negotiations forward. To prepare them, further training activities were developed, drawing on skills and experiences gained during earlier conflict management activities.

In time, the FPCD was asked to help set up a WMA and establish community organizations in four areas to consider land zoning in hunting areas, and gardens and protection areas, based on local needs and scientific surveys. The FPCD was also asked to form a WMA management committee and to establish community-based organizations (CBOs) to address small-scale development. With these things in mind, the team developed plans to build CM capacity among external stakeholders and to establish effective communications and confidence between local peoples and outsiders.

Lessons from Lakekamu

Benefits of the CM approach

The CM activities described here helped to remove and mitigate conflict as an obstacle to sustainable livelihoods in the Lakekamu Basin. This provided:

- a basis for stronger representation to authorities outside the community;
- confidence to approach and interact with these authorities;
- examples for analysing and managing future community conflict;
- a more stable context within which to implement development programmes; and
- a basis for developing trust and confidence, horizontally and vertically, for those involved in development programmes.

The role of training and CM processes in analysing and building capital assets was perhaps the most important project outcome. Villagers felt that CM training had broadened their perspective to consider a range of assets, not just money, buildings or environment; to consider their vulnerability to environmental change and asset loss, degradation or change; and to consider opportunities from protecting or building natural and other capital assets. Relationships among capital assets can be complex. However, in this project CM processes and SL principles coincided so that capital assets could be explored holistically.

The most useful tools related to conflict analysis. They proved helpful in framing ideas and suggesting alternative approaches. Sectoral expertise (for example, the special area covered by agriculture, forestry or environmental conservation) became important following broad CM analyses that took an SL approach. This prioritized broad, non-sector specific questions whose answers provided information about people's livelihood strategies and vulnerability, and typically suggested complementarity and overlap among sectors. This suggests that the CM approach can transcend strong sector bias, without compromising the overall objectives of an existing NR project (such as biodiversity conservation). The people-centred approach provided an effective entry point into an SL framework in a project where a very strong NR emphasis had failed to take account of poverty, vulnerability in areas outside the sector and important cross-sector links.

The CM analysis helped NGO staff to refocus strategically on the 'big picture'. Following CM analysis, the question 'why are we doing this project' was answered as: 'to develop processes for biodiversity conservation *in the context of* people's need to overcome poverty'. Trying to implement policy on the ground required a far more holistic approach than existing environmental foreign policy and international NGO strategies allowed. Subsequent questions about how to implement international environmental and foreign policy concerned what poverty meant and how it might be overcome (see Figure 14.2).

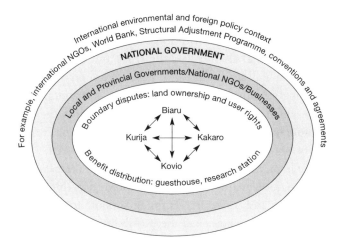

Figure 14.2 *International Environmental and Foreign Policy Context*

What this meant, in practice, was searching beyond the environmental foreign policy context and seeking ways of integrating that context with policies on economic and community development. In order to implement policy on environmental protection, pragmatic links with policies in a broad rural development context were required. These were highlighted through the SL approach. Many agencies that adopt a livelihoods approach to development emphasize the importance of macro–micro links in the development of horizontal associations, with policy processes taking a lead in supporting development at the micro level through addressing structural changes that are predisposed to conflict (Carney, 1999). However, our evidence indicates that capital assets at the village level can be built, protected and enhanced through locally appropriate CM activities. Social capital can be developed horizontally in the absence of strong macro–micro links (Warner, 2000). Principled CM processes, skilfully deployed, can play a key role in building social capital horizontally, from which critical vertical associations may develop.

How does this work? Tyler (1999) notes the importance of relevant, accessible information as a prerequisite to consensus-based planning, pointing out that participatory research processes give control and initiative to those involved. In providing transparency of information and analysis, participatory research methods enable 'politically weaker stakeholders to elucidate their needs and validate assumptions', important issues in 'building and maintaining trust' (Tyler, 1999, p269). The CM process in Lakekamu could be called participatory research. Indeed, it would be better to refer to the training and analysis as participatory, facilitated learning, where the perspectives of many stakeholders inform the search for solutions and consensus-building.

Although environmental foreign policy needs to explicitly embrace a broad livelihoods perspective, it may not be necessary to focus policy frameworks and capacity-building mainly on developing *structural* social capital. The rules, roles, networks and institutional structures may be well established. What was missing in Lakekamu was the trust and confidence to use them, either because these had been eroded, or because nobody had tried to develop vertical links using structures that performed well horizontally within groups. A major achievement in the Lakekamu CM process was the restoration and rebuilding of horizontal, cognitive social capital. The actual resolution of conflicts occurred when participatory analysis was far advanced, mutual trust and confidence were high, access to significant social capital assets was strong, and local people felt empowered to move things forward within existing or newly developed structures and processes. Training support for the agency that was facilitating these things strengthened the possibility for successful implementation of environmental foreign policy and related international NGO strategies.

Conflict management and sustainable livelihoods

Impacts on physical capital

CM processes are important in analysing, protecting and developing physical capital. For example, a guesthouse was an opportunity to build financial assets from eco-tourism. However, conflict analysis showed that this represented an opportunity only for a few, and was constructed and managed against local norms of mutually beneficial collective action (Krishna and Uphoff, 1999). One group wanted to burn down the guesthouse. Conflict analysis examined alternatives, based on specific and common needs and a restored sense of community goals, focusing on the advantages (individual and collective) of having the building and the disadvantages of burning it down (poor community reputation, negative visitor perceptions, social disharmony and conflict escalation). The protection of this asset signalled other forms of asset-building, including rebuilding social capital.

Impacts on financial capital

Cash income was one issue with which CM project staff were involved. Key questions related to what money was needed for. Other (unexplored) questions concerned the social and cultural meanings that people ascribe to money. Money involves exchanges to which social meanings are attached beyond the simple transfer of cash. Importantly, the CM process revealed needs for further analysis on policies that address local requirements to manage cash stocks and flows. The amount of money in Lakekamu is small but locally significant, profoundly affecting local interest in managing natural resources. Local meanings of money are also significant; reciprocity and generosity are important aspects of social capital. Small money ('wok money') has a crucial role as a source of power, or perceived power, and as part of social identity connected with 'sharing'. Thus, conflict analysis applied within an SL framework revealed needs for capacity-building of NGOs, as well as communities dealing with book-keeping, accounting, savings and cash flow. The special relationship between the meanings of cash and the development of social capital is significant for environmental policy (for example, eco-tourism), where people are moving from a cash-scarce society to one where money is an important medium of exchange.

Impacts on natural capital

The CM work had positive effects on protecting natural capital, bringing people together to analyse their needs and focusing attention away from short-term possibilities to earn small cash, towards long-term environmental sustainability and security issues. Local people said that the CM process helped them to clarify the nature of environmental and livelihood changes at issue. To register a WMA and enhance income in the absence of oil palm, they sought further training in CM so that they could work with outside agencies. Other links will include provincial and national government actions in legal processes to protect a globally significant rain forest, and to step up development initiatives to reduce poverty and vulnerability and enhance local development prospects. These objectives are part of a growing national and international foreign policy discourse on the environment (see Figure 14.2).

Impacts on human capital

The CM project provided significant direct support and some indirect support to building human capital through participatory approaches to specialist training and knowledge generation, facilitated by the CM teams who prioritized building on existing local knowledge. The knowledge gained was useful in helping people to make decisions about outside problems and opportunities. Lakekamu's people need to speak with one voice to negotiate with outsiders, an aspect of their learning not lost on community leaders. Given the cultural, social and administrative complexity in the basin, national government is unlikely to be able to recognize the legitimacy of such a large array of stake-holders (Tyler, 1999). The knowledge that this was the case came through the CM process and acted as an impetus for consensus-building within the basin.

Impacts on social capital

Research on relationships between CM activities and building social capital is of concern to international donors, who place a strong emphasis on macro–micro links in social capital development (DFID, 1999, 2000), and to the World Bank, which has specific questions about whether social capital could be purposefully increased. Understanding changes in social capital in Lakekamu involves considering the meanings that people ascribe to *wantok*, a pidgin term where *wan* means 'the same or similar, and often implies solidarity ... a shared interest', and *tok*, or talk, implies that these meanings reside within a language group (Guy, 1997, piii). The *wantok* system is a form of horizontal social capital, itself undergoing change. Vulnerable people rely heavily on the *wantok* system where state services are weak. Local descriptions about new precedents giving 'family' primacy over the 'community' relate to people's exploration of a world where choice is now an option and it is acceptable to ask questions about *wantok* obligations. This has brought serious concerns for people, not least because there is no longer certainty about obligations of reciprocity, or even about trust within *wantoks*.

Changes in the *wantok* system echo many changes within other 'in-groups', whether based on language, religion, age, seniority or anything else. For example, savings and credit projects often lack support to help people manage changes in the nature of social capital that typically accompanies the arrival of cash in poor communities. Forming a micro savings and credit group creates an in-group that needs to develop other relationships. Moreover, changes are set in motion within and among other pre-existing groups who then need to examine their links with one another while simultaneously developing links with the savings and credit group. There are no such groups yet in Lakekamu; but their development is clearly a possible next step. This suggests that the kind of links that have been applied elsewhere between environmental foreign policy, economic development and micro-finance (for example, in Bangladesh and India) may be also beneficial for PNG.

In sum, CM activities have proved effective in reducing tensions and help-ing to build, protect or develop assets in Lakekamu. The process was, perhaps, driven by unvoiced needs to find ways forward amid a plurality of possible actions and to avoid possible violence. As the ICAD proceeds, further training and enhanced capacity for FPCD and other stakeholders will be important. These require appropriate policy support.

Conclusion

If CM activities applied within an SL framework have provided learning for local decision-making, what are the implications for international environmental policy development? The sequence of events described in the case study ran more or less in the following order, although, in practice, the training and analysis were often undertaken concurrently.

Within and among each village/language group:
- establish trust and confidence (cognitive social capital) within and then among groups to address local disputes;
- build on existing rules, roles and networks (structural social capital);
- develop, where necessary, new structural social capital where appropriate rules, roles and networks are absent;
- verify through iterative experience that people have the trust and confidence to use structural social capital and that the rules, roles and networks are appropriate for everyone.

Within and among local and provincial governments, NGOs and businesses:
- establish trust and confidence among local and provincial governments, national NGOs and relevant businesses (see Figure 14.2) through information-sharing, regular meetings, and identifying and acting upon needs and concerns;
- build capacity within and among these groups where necessary, including information-sharing, CM training, collaborative research, workshops and structured meetings;
- develop, where necessary, new rules, roles and networks;
- verify that each group has the trust and confidence to use among-group structural social capital;
- develop means, where necessary, for facilitated interaction between stakeholders at this level and those at local level through establishing, developing and verifying cognitive and structural social capital.

While CM principles may apply at all levels, the approaches taken need to vary. Brief workshops, mentoring, facilitated training within small groups and other approaches are more relevant for some stakeholders. However, where it has been possible to bring higher-level officials to the field, or vice versa, even for brief periods, CM activities have often advanced the resolution of a particular conflict and identified mechanisms for managing future ones. This process of interaction, advocated also by Tyler (1999), also permits policy-relevant information to reach policy-makers directly, and provides them with the chance to explain the policies to an audience often eager to learn. Indeed, the few examples that exist suggest that relevant CM work can be one 'policy pathway' for the feedback loops and dialogue advocated by Filer and Sekhran (1998) to link local, national and global debates (see Figure 14.2).

This chapter does not suggest that a conflict, once resolved, is over forever. Outcomes may not carry the permanence of solution that may be required in a 'shifting patchwork of relatively autonomous, small-scale, kinship-based societies' such as PNG (Dinnen and Ley, 2000, p4). But, as in economics and personal relationships, trust and confidence seem to be essential to successful conflict management. The establishment of this cognitive social capital was a necessary first step for people managing environmental changes facing Lakekamu. Local contexts certainly alter the specifics. However, to the conclusions of Tyler (1999) mentioned previously, we may add that CM tools and principles, appropriately applied within an SL framework, provide flexible entry points to developing policy pathways 'along which the dialogue develops through the making and testing of claims to productive (*policy*) innovation, and the continual reinforcement of feedback loops between local, national and global levels of debate' (Filer and Sekhran, 1998, pxix).

Over time, with sound facilitation, the training itself (like Tyler's participatory research) starts to build processes for collective stakeholder and conflict analysis. As a diversity of solutions is generated and consensus is built, next steps are identified that often include some of the structural issues which international policies seek to address. It is at this moment, as dialogue matures and confidence grows, where interaction among local, national and global levels may be effective. Policy frameworks should not only emphasize the building of structures and institutions. They might often be better targeted at support processes that focus on building social capital, particularly trust and confidence, among stakeholders facing conflicts in a broad context of environmental change.

Three environmental foreign policy implications emerge from this case study. First, for environmental foreign policy to have any meaning, it must be possible to *implement* it. To achieve this, policy must engage with community conflicts and priorities in ways that allow local peoples to respond to policy and that allow policy-makers to respond to local peoples. Second, whatever agency is responsible for facilitating the implementation of environmental foreign policy on the ground (for example, NGOs, government, private business), that agency requires support to develop its capacity to manage conflict. This includes being able to recognize and respond to issues of legitimacy, neutrality and technical ability. Third, environmental foreign policy cannot stand alone. Such policies are typically situated in a broader development context that benefits from holistic analysis and inter-agency collaboration. Sustainable livelihoods approaches that are suited for grassroots development can point to policy linkages that may be required to improve environmental foreign policy design. Policy support is required for the use of SL approaches and conflict management tools. This will provide practical ways forward for locally relevant policy implementation and a vehicle for information that is relevant to environmental foreign policy-makers.

Notes

Chapter 4

1 This chapter is based on several previous studies (Ohta, 1995, 2000, 2001).
2 In January 2001, MITI became the Ministry of Economy, Trade and Industry (METI) and the EA was upgraded to the Ministry of the Environment.
3 Interview with Dr Ichikawa Hiroya, then director of industrial policy of Keidanren (Federation of Economic Organisations), 2 June 1993.
4 Interview with Ambassador Akao, 23 February 1993.
5 Refer to www.env.go.jp/en/w-paper/1994/eae230000000015.html (1 October 2002).
6 Regarding the question on 'internationalization' of Japan, 42.4 per cent of the respondents to this public opinion poll felt obligation as a great power and 42 per cent favoured it for the maintenance of Japan's prosperity (Sorifu, 1997, p99).
7 Refer to www.kantei.go.jp/jp/ondan/suisinhonbu/9806/taikou.html (6 February 2002).
8 Takashi Imai (chairman, Keidanren), 'Request for Calm and Patient Negotiations on the Issues of Global Warming', www.keidanren.or.jp/english/speech/20010615.html (15 June 2001)
9 Regarding the question on 'internationalization' of Japan, 45.6 per cent of the respondents to this poll favoured for the maintenance of Japan's prosperity and 42.3 per cent felt obligation as a great power.

Chapter 5

1 Judith Shapiro is the author of *Mao's War Against Nature: Politics and the Environment in Revolutionary China* (Cambridge University Press, 2001), from which this chapter is adapted. Reprinted with the permission of Cambridge University Press.
2 Barry Naughton (1991, p157) calls the Third Front 'a military metaphor with economic resonance'. He also explains (Naughton, 1988, pp355–356) that the Third Front referred variously to the investment programme, the geographic area and the period (1965–1971) during which investment was a national focus.
3 According to Naughton (1988, p373), the Third Front was not in itself irrational; but the scale on which it was pursued certainly caused China long-term economic damage and setbacks.
4 'Directive about Attacking the Destructive Activities of Counter-revolutionaries' (*guanyu daji xianxing fangeming pohuai huodong de zhishi*) (cited in Shi and He, 1996, p161).
5 In addition to works cited, this chapter draws on two other hagiographic works, Jinse de Panzhihua Bianweihui (1990) and Zhonggong Panshihua Shiwei dangshi yanjiushi (1994).

6   Dukou's name was officially changed to Panzhihua in 1987, although both names had been used freely. It is claimed to be the only city in China named after a flower (Foreign Investment Office of Panzhihua Municipal Government, undated, p12).

7   According to one of the Panzhihua hagiographies, 'Some leading comrades wondered whether there shouldn't be less emphasis on construction, more emphasis on the question of the masses' food, clothing and consumer goods.' But after Mao spoke, they were persuaded that there should be no further delays (Jinse, 1990, p59). See also Naughton (1988, p332).

8   No explanation is given for the extremely high death rate in 1965, although we can easily imagine the numerous deadly accidents, infectious diseases and limited medical facilities. The decrease in subsequent years is attributed to an improvement in healthcare and social welfare measures.

9   Naughton (1991, p168) states that steel production was not regularized until 1978.

10 Naughton (1991, pp179–180) points out that the huge investments in the southwest caused a tremendous drain on the rest of the country. Railroads in the east were neglected for almost ten years, creating bottlenecks and long-term distortions in China's investment structure.

Chapter 6

1   The objective of the regime is taken as a benchmark for 'cooperativeness' of the actor (China).

2   Other sources are crude oil (19 per cent), natural gas (2 per cent) and hydroelectric (5 per cent). See Smil (1998, p937).

3   *Fa shi tongzhi jieji de gongju* ('law is an instrument of the ruling class'). See Chinese Communist Party (1985, p93).

Chapter 8

1   This dispute involves a unilateral trade embargo imposed by the US on the import of tuna from Mexico on the grounds that Mexico failed to meet the US standard for incidental killing of dolphin while catching tuna. This dispute sparked keen debate between environmentalists and free traders concerning the compatibility between the GATT and TREMs. For more discussion, see, for example, Mayer and Hoch (1993) and Hurlock (1992).

2   Statement from the Ministry of Foreign Affairs, 27 January 1997; the full statement (in Mandarin) is available at www.mofa.gov.tw/news/decl0127.htm.

3   Report from the Taiwanese media *Central Daily News*, overseas edition, 30 December 1998, in which the head of Taiwan's Environmental Protection Administration was quoted as insisting that the handling of the toxic waste by the Formosa Plastics Group should comply with the Basel Convention.

4   According to the 1999 Administrative Procedure Act, which only came into effect on 1 January 2001, administrative rules and regulations adopted by the executive need to have clear authorizations from the relevant legislation (Article 150, Taiwan's 1999 Administrative Procedure Act).

5   Report from the Taiwanese media *Liberty Evening News*, 8 July 1994, in which government officials from the COA expressed their concern that, if the Legislative Yuan did not speed up its process of discussing the amendments to the Wildlife Conservation Act, CITES might impose trade sanction on Taiwan at COP9 in November 1994.

6 There is no official English translation of the White Paper on Foreign Policy. The Mandarin version can be viewed at www.elearn7.com/abian/webook/.
7 See the following sources: United States Restrictions on Imports of Tuna, 33 *I. L. M.* 842, 1994; Dispute Settlement Panel Report on United States Taxes on Automobiles, 33 *I. L. M.* 1397, 1994; United States – Standards for Reformulated and Conventional Gasoline, 35 *I. L. M.* 274 and 603, 1996; EC – Measures Concerning Meat and Products (Hormones), WT/DS26/R/USA and WT/DS48/R/CAN (18 August 1997); US – Import Prohibition of Certain Shrimp and Shrimp Products, 37 *I. L. M.* 832, 1998; and Australia – Measures Affecting Importation of Salmon, WT/DS18/R, WT/DS18/AB/R.
8 For a brief discussion on these cases, see Kennedy (1998, pp430–471).
9 Footnote 174, US – Import Prohibition of Certain Shrimp and Shrimp Products, 37 *I. L. M.* 832, 1998.
10 Paragraph 130, US – Import Prohibition of Certain Shrimp and Shrimp Products, 37 *I. L. M.* 832, 1998.
11 Item 1 discusses 'the relationship between the provisions of the multilateral trading system and trade measures for environmental purposes, including those pursuant to multilateral environmental agreements' and Item 5 focuses on 'the relationship between the dispute settlement mechanisms in the multilateral trading system and those found in multilateral environmental agreements'. For more discussion on the work of the CTE, see, for example, Tarasofsky (1999).
12 *An Agenda on the WTO Committee on Trade and Environment*, in which main conclusions reached and current status of debate on the various items on the CTE working programme are reviewed. The full text is available at www.wto.org/english/tratop_e/envir_e/cte01_e.htm; visited 30 March 2001.
13 Letter from Alexander Timoshenki, officer-in-charge, Environmental Law and Institutions of the UNEP, to Dennis T C Tang at the Academia Sinica and Professor Daniel C K Chow at the Ohio State University College of Law. The letter is cited in Chow (1995).
14 Paragraph 6, 'Decisions of the Standing Committee on Trade in Rhinoceros Horn and Tiger Specimens', Brussels, 6–8 September 1993. Cited in Shih (1996, pp121–122).
15 For example, in a Mandarin article discussing environmental protection and trade sanction, a commentator stated that: 'The main response the government can take is to speed up the process of our GATT/WTO application so that negotiation or conciliation can be initiated if Taiwan is being trade sanctioned in the future' (Lu, 1995, p56; translated by the author).
16 For example, in 1992 the Commission of the European Communities proposed that the GATT should condition the use of trade measures upon the existence of a pertinent MEA. Cited in Blank (1996, pp101).
17 Australia versus France, 1974, ICJ REP 253, and New Zealand versus France, 1974, ICJ REP 457.

Chapter 10

1 The bureaucratic polity approach to studying Thai politics was developed by F W Riggs (1966).
2 Various interviews (anonymity requested).
3 Letter from the Office of the Council of State to the Cabinet Secretary, No 0601/765, 7 November 1996 (in Thai).

4   Letter from the Ministry of Science, Technology and Environment to the Cabinet Secretary, No 0803/4243, 28 March 1997 (in Thai).
5   Letter from the Ministry of Foreign Affairs to the Cabinet Secretary, No 0605/179, 28 January 1998 (in Thai) and memorandum of the Office of the Secretary-General to the Prime Minister, 31 July 1998 (in Thai).
6   Letter from the Office of the Cabinet Secretary to the Ministry of Foreign Affairs, No 0206/14599, 3 November 1998 (in Thai).
7   Various interviews (anonymity requested).

Chapter 11

1   The author thanks the Social Science and Humanities Research Council of Canada and Concordia University for funding, and the following people for research assistance: Michael Innes, Dwayne Pretli, Regis Loreau and Althea Riveas.

Chapter 13

1   Professor David Bell, York University, provided these three points to the author during a stay at the York Centre of Applied Sustainability, 1999.
2   Interview with Chih-Yuan Yang, director of Technology Advisers, Environmental Protection Agency, Taipei, Taiwan, 28 June 1999.
3   Interview with Beatrice Olivastri, chief executive officer, Ottawa, 21 July 1999.
4   Interview with Peter Hall, national director, Canadian Environmental Network (CEN), Ottawa, 21 July 1999. For more information about CEN, see CEN's website at www.cen.rce.org.
5   For the detailed activities and annual reports of TEAN, refer to its website at www.tean.formosa.org.

Chapter 14

1   The author thanks the people of Tekadu and Kakoro, and the staff of the Foundation for People and Community Development, for their support and participation in this research. Special thanks to Katherine Yuave and staff of Just World Partners, Michael Warner and Bruce Baker. This chapter is based on work for the UK Department for International Development's Conflict and Humanitarian Affairs Department, which provided funding.
2   The main sources for this analysis are FPCD project documents and staff; discussions with villagers in Tekadu; Salafsky and Paka (1999); and Conservation International (1998, pp8–24, 71–80). The section on resource rights owes much to conversations with André Iteanu, an anthropologist working near Lakekamu for over 20 years.

References

Adkin, L (1998) *The Politics of Sustainable Development: Citizens, Unions and the Corporations*, Black Rose Books, Buffalo

Akaha, T (1999) 'Environmental Policy in Japan: From Domestic Pollution to Global Environment' in Soden, D and Steel, B (eds) *Handbook of Global Environmental Policy and Administration*, Marcel Dekker, Basel, pp529–548

Alker, E and Haas, P (1993) 'The Rise of Global Eco-politics' in Haas, P, Keohane, R and Levy, M (eds) *Institutions for the Earth: Sources of Effective Environmental Protection*, MIT Press, Cambridge, Massachusetts, pp220–245

Allison, G (1971) *Essence of Decision: Explaining the Cuban Missile Crisis*, Little Brown, Boston

Asahi Shimbun (1992) Takeuchi, K and Yoshida, T 'Kankyokoken mienu "Nippon"' ['Japan's environmental contribution is invisible', 6 June 1992; A report crew for the Earth Summit, 'NGO inarabu seifu zaikaijin' ['NGO, government officials and industrialists are all present'], 8 June 1992

Asahi Shimbun (2000) 'Nihonkeizai-no ushinawareta 10-nen' ('A Lost Decade of the Japanese Economy') in *Asahi kuronikuru: shukan 20 seiki (The Asahi Chronicle: Weekly the 20th Century)*, vol 95, December 3, Asahi Shimbun, Tokyo

Bachman, D (1998) 'Structure and Process in the Making of Chinese Foreign Policy' in Kim, S (ed) *China and the World: Chinese Foreign Policy Faced the New Millennium*, Westview Press, Boulder, Colorado, pp34–54

Bacon, A et al (1996) *Estimating Construction Costs and Schedules: Experience with Power Generation Projects in Developing Countries*, World Bank, Washington, DC

Bakker, K (1999) 'The Politics of Hydropower: Developing the Mekong', *Political Geography*, vol 18, pp209–232

Barkdull, J and Harris, PG (2002) 'Environmental Change and Foreign Policy: A Survey of Theory', *Global Environmental Politics*, vol 2, no 2, pp63–91

Barnes, W (1999) 'Dam Talks Exclude Minority Groups', *South China Morning Post*, 15 September, www.probeinternational.org/pi/Mekong/index.cfm?DSP=content &ContentID=961

Barouin, B and Yu, C (1998) *Chinese Foreign Policy During the Cultural Revolution*, Kegan Paul International, London

Bartke, W (1991) *Who's Who in the People's Republic of China*, K G Saur, London

Battersby, P (1999) 'Border politics and the broader politics of Thailand's international relations in the 1990s', *Pacific Affairs*, vol 71, no 4, pp473–488

Baum, R (1994) *Burying Mao: Chinese Politics in the Age of Deng Xiaoping*, Princeton University Press, Princeton

Bell, D, Halucha, P and Hopkins, M (1999) 'Sustainable Development Concept Paper', Unpublished report for the Canadian government

Berger, J (1999) 'Unilateral trade measures to conserve the world's living resources', *Columbia Journal of Environmental Law*, vol 24, pp355–410

Blake, D (2001) 'China's Mekong River dam plans', Mekong Forum website, www.mekongforum.org/chinadam.html

Blank, D (1996) 'Target-based environmental trade measures', *Stanford Environmental Law Journal*, vol 15, pp61–129

Bodansky, D (1994) 'Prologue to the Climate Change Convention' in Mintzer, I and Leonard, J (eds) *Negotiating Climate Change: The Inside Story of the Rio Convention*, Cambridge University Press, Cambridge, pp45–74

Bowder, G, and Ortolano, L (2000) 'The Evolution of an International Water Resources Management Regime in the Mekong River Basin', *Natural Resources Journal*, vol 40, no 3, pp499–531

Boyd, E, Hanks, J, Chipper, L, Sell, M, Spense, C and Voinov, J (2001) 'Summary of the Seventh Conference of the Parties of the UN Framework Convention on Climate Change', *Earth Negotiations Bulletin*, vol 50, no 189, pp1–16

Brack, D (1996) *International Trade and the Montreal Protocol*, Earthscan, London

Breslin, S (1990) 'The Foreign Policy Bureaucracy' in Segal, G (ed) *Chinese Politics and Foreign Policy Reform*, Royal Institute of International Affairs, London, pp115–134

Breslin, S (1997) 'The China challenge? Environment, development and national security', (Norway) *Security Dialogue*, vol 28, no 4, pp497–508

Brocheux, P (1995) *The Mekong Delta: Ecology, Economy, and Revolution*, 1860–1960, University of Wisconsin-Madison, Madison

Brock, L (1991) 'Peace through parks: the environment on the peace research agenda', *Journal of Peace Research*, vol 28, no 4, pp407–423

Brooke, J (2002) 'A big mouth behind Japan's whaling', *International Herald Tribune*, 21 October, p9

Brunner, A. (1997) 'Conflicts between international trade and multilateral environmental agreements', *Annual Survey of International & Comparative Law*, vol IV, pp74–102

Buckles, D (ed) (1999) *Cultivating Peace: Conflict and Collaboration in Natural Resource Management*, International Development Research Centre, Ottawa

Buszynski, L (1994) 'Thailand's foreign policy: management of a regional vision', *Asian Survey*, vol 34, no 8, p722

Byers, B (1991) 'Ecoregions, state sovereignty and conflict?' *Bulletin of Peace Proposals*, vol 22, no 1, pp65–76

Calder, K (1997) 'The Institutions of Japanese Foreign Policy' in Grant, R (ed) *The Process of Japanese Foreign Policy: Focus on Asia*, Royal Institute of International Affairs, London, pp1–24

Canadian Environmental Network (CEN) (1998) *Canadian Environmental Network Newsletter*, Autumn

Cao, F, Zhao, F and Tian, C (1998) 'Zhongguo huangjing waijiao celiu' ['China's Strategy in Environmental Diplomacy'], in Kun, Z (ed) *Huangjing yu ke chixu fazhan–xu [Environment and Sustainable Development (Sequel)]*, Chixiang Chubanshe, Beijing

Carney, D (1999) *Livelihood Approaches Compared*, Department for International Development, London

Carpenter, C, Chasek, P, Cherian, A and Wise, S (1995) 'Summary of the First Conference of the Parties for the Framework Convention on Climate Change', *Earth Negotiations Bulletin*, vol 12, no 12, pp1–12

Central Communist Party (1985) *Faxue Jixu [Basics of Law]*, Central Communist Party, Beijing

Central News Agency (CNA) (2001) 'The unprecedented summer hit Beijing due to weather extreme' (in Chinese), Taipei, 18 May, No M47

Chambers, R and Conway, G (1992) *Sustainable Rural Livelihoods: Practical Concepts for the 21st Century*, Institute of Development Studies Discussion Paper 296, University of Sussex, Brighton, UK

Chang, P (1997) 'Vietnam and China: new opportunities and new challenges', *Contemporary Southeast Asia*, vol 19, no 2, pp136–151

Chao, Y (1993) 'Burning coal and pollution control' (in Chinese), *Energy in China*, April, p5

Chapman, E and Daming, H (1996) 'Downstream Implications of China's Dams on the Lancang Jiang (Upper Mekong) and their Potential Significance for Greater Regional Cooperation, Basin-wide' in Stensholt, B (ed) *Development Dilemmas in the Mekong Subregion*, Monash University, Clayton, Victoria, pp19–29

Charnovitz, S (1996) 'Trade measures and the design of international regimes', *Journal of Environment and Development*, vol 5, no 2, pp168–196

Chasek, P (ed) (2000) *The Global Environment in the Twenty-First Century*, United Nations University Press, Tokyo

Chayes, A and Kim, C (1998) 'China and the United Nations Framework Convention on Climate Change' in McElroy, M, Nielson, C and Lydon, P (eds) *Energizing China: Reconciling Environmental Protection and Economic Growth*, Harvard University Press, Cambridge, Massachusetts

China Daily (1992) 'Chinese premier meets foreign leaders in Rio', *China Daily*, 26 June 1992, p1

China Daily Index Project (1990–1994) Index to the *China Daily*, Nathan, Queensland

China Statistical Publishing House (1988, 1991, 1995, 1998, 2000, 2001) *China Statistical Yearbook*, China Statistical Publishing House, Beijing

China Times (2000) 'Unavoidable global warming, Everest summit shifting and salmon appearing in North Pole' (in Chinese), *China Times*, Taipei, 24 November, p10

Chinese Communist Party (1985) *Faxue Jichu* [*Basic Law*] Chinese Communist Party, Beijing

Chow, D (1995) 'Recognizing the environmental costs of the recognition problem', *Stanford Environmental Law Journal*, vol 14, no 2, pp256–299

Churie, A, Hanks, J, Schipper, L, Sell, M, Spense, C and Voinov, J (2000) 'Summary of the Sixth Meeting of the Committee of the Parties for the Framework Convention on Climate Change', *Earth Negotiations Bulletin*, vol 12, no 163, pp1–14

Comisso, E, Hardi, P and Bencze, L (1998) 'Hungary: political interest, bureaucratic will' in Weiss, E and Jacobson, H (eds) *Engaging Countries: Strengthening Compliance with International Accords*, MIT Press, Cambridge, pp327–352

Conservation International (1998) *A Biological Assessment of the Lakekamu Basin, Papua New Guinea*, Rapid Assessment Program Working Paper No 9, Conservation International, Washington, DC

Constitutional Court of Thailand (2000) Decision No 33/2543, 5 October (in Thai), www.concort.or.th/decis/y2000d/d03343_1.html

Cormick, G, Dale, N, Emond, P, Sigurdson, S and Stuart, B (1996) *Building Consensus for a Sustainable Future: Putting Principles into Practice*, National Round Table on the Environment and the Economy, Ottawa

Council for Economic Planning and Development (CEPD) (2001) *Proposal of Building a Green Silicon Island Economy in Taiwan*, www.cepd.gov.tw/eco-plan/greenisland/bludmap.htm

Crawford, C (1995) 'Conflicts between the convention on international trade in endangered species and the GATT in light of actions to halt the rhinoceros and tiger trade', *Georgetown International Environmental Law Review*, vol 7, p555

Crispin, S et al (2000) 'Choke point', *Far Eastern Economic Review*, vol 163, no 41, 12 October, pp22–24

Cumpeeraparp, J (1995) *Biological Resources and Thai Society* (in Thai), Local Community Development Institute, Bangkok

Cumpeeraparp, J (1998) 'Biopolicy in Thailand', *Thai Development Newsletter*, January–June, pp31–36

Cuong, N (1997) *Forest Mapping In Vietnam: Remote Sensing For Tropical Ecosystem Management*, United Nations, New York

Dai, Q (1994) *Yangtze! Yangtze! Debate Over the Three Gorges Project*, Earthscan, London

Daily Yomiuri (2001) 'Poll: record number favour cut in foreign aid', 22 January, p2

Dale, A (1995) 'Multistakeholder Process: Panacea or Window Dressing', Unpublished manuscript

Dasgupta, C (1994) 'The Climate Change Negotiations' in Mintzer, I and Leonard, J (eds) *Negotiating Climate Change: The Inside Story of the Rio Convention*, Cambridge University Press, Cambridge, pp129–148

Dauvergne, P (1997) *Shadows in the Forest: Japan and the Politics of Timber in Southeast Asia*, MIT Press, Cambridge, MA, and London

Day, D (1987) *The Whale War*, Douglas and MacIntyre, Toronto

Delsi, D (2000) 'Financing environmental moderation in China', *Dollars and Sense*, vol 4, no 9, pp44–55

Department for International Development (DFID) (1999) *Sustainable Livelihoods Guidance Sheets*, Introduction and Overview Section 1.1, www.livelihoods.org/info/guidance_sheets_pdfs/section1.pdf

Department for International Development (DFID) (1999, 2000) 'Sustainable Livelihoods Guidance Sheets', www.dfid.gov.uk/public/what/advisory/group6/rld/pdf/sectiont.pdf

Dieu, L, Luu,V and Trang, C (2000) 'Some Remarks on the Tendency of Marine Environment Quality Change in Vietnam' in Hoi, N (ed) *Marine Resources and Environment*, Science and Technology Publishing House, Hanoi

Dinnen, S and Ley, A (2000) *Reflections on Violence in Melanesia*, Asia Pacific Press, Canberra

Dore, R (1997) *Japan, Internationalism and the UN*, Routledge, London

Doyle R (2002) 'Greenhouse Follies', *Scientific American*, vol 286, no 4, p29

Dreyer, J (2000) *China's Political System: Modernization and Tradition* (3rd edition), Macmillan, Basingstoke

Drifte, R (1996) 'Japan's Power in the Post-Cold War Era: From Economic to What Power?' in Rumley, D, Chiba, T, Takagi, A, and Fukushima, Y (eds) *Global Geopolitical Change and the Asia Pacific: A Regional Perspective*, Avebury, Aldershot, pp85–92

Drifte, R (1998) *Japan's Foreign Policy for the 21st Century: From Economic Superpower to What Power?* Macmillan, London

Dryzek, J (1987) *Rational Ecology*, Blackwell, Oxford

Easterbrook, G and Palmer, B (1997) 'Greenhouse common sense: why global warming economics matters more than science', *US News and World Report*, 1 December, pp58–62

Eckholm, E (2001) 'China said to sharply reduce carbon dioxide emissions', *New York Times*, 15 June, www.nytimes.com/2001/06/15/world/15CHIN.html

Economy, E (1994) *Negotiating the terrain of global climate change policy in the Soviet Union and China: Linking international and domestic decision making pathways*, PhD thesis, University of Michigan, Michigan

Economy, E (1997a) 'Chinese Environmental Diplomacy' in Schreurs, M and Economy, E (eds) *The Internationalization of Environmental Protection*, Cambridge University Press, Cambridge

Economy, E (1997b) 'Chinese Policy-Making and Global Climate Change: Two-Front Diplomacy and the International Community', in Schreurs, M and Economy, E (eds) *The Internationalization of Environmental Protection*, Cambridge University Press, Cambridge and New York, pp19–41

Economy, E (1998) 'China's environmental diplomacy' in Kim, S (ed) *China and the World: Chinese Foreign Policy Faces the New Millennium*, Westview Press, Boulder, Colorado, pp264–286

Economy, E (1999) 'Painting China green', *Foreign Affairs*, vol 78, no 2, pp14–20

Economy, E and Oksenberg, M (1998) 'China: Implementation Under Economic Growth and Market Reform' in Weiss, E and Jacobson, H (eds) *Engaging Countries: Strengthening Compliance with International Environmental Accords*, MIT Press, Cambridge

Economy, E and Oksenberg, M (eds) (1999) *China Joins the World: Progress and Prospects*, Council on Foreign Relations Press, New York

Edmonds, R (1998) 'Studies on China's environment', *China Quarterly*, vol 156 (December), pp725–732

Elvin, M and Liu, T (1998) *Sediments Of Time: Environment And Society In Chinese History, Studies In Environment And History*, Cambridge University Press, Cambridge

Energy and Resources Laboratories (1997) *Sustainable Development in Taiwan: Report to RIO+5*, Industry Technology Research Institute, Taipei

Environmental Protection Administration (Taiwan) (EPA) (2000, 2001) *Environment White Paper 1999, 2000*, EPA, Taipei

Evans, P B, Jacobson, H K and Putnam, R D (1993) *Double-Edged Diplomacy: International Bargaining and Domestic Politics*, University of California Press, Berkeley, California

Faust, J and Kornberg, J (1995) *China in World Politics*, Lynne Rienner, London

Filer, C with Sekhran, N (1998) *Loggers, Donors and Resource Owners: Policy that Works for Forests and People*, International Institute for Environment and Development , London, www.iied.org/ptw/png.html

Fisheries Office, Cambodia (2000) *A Study of the Downstream Impacts of the Yali Falls Dam in the Se San River Basin in Ratanakiri Province, Northeast Cambodia*, Cambodian Fisheries Office, Phnom Penh

Flavin, C (1997) 'The Legacy of Rio' in Brown, L R et al (eds) *State of the World 1997 – A Worldwatch Institute Report on Progress Toward a Sustainable Society*, W W Norton and Company, New York, pp3–23

Fletcher, K (2001) 'The International Whaling Regime and American Foreign Policy' in Harris, P (ed) *The Environment, International Relations, and US Foreign Policy*, Georgetown University Press, Washington, DC, pp217–237

Foreign Investment Office of Panzhihua Municipal Government (undated) *A Guide to Investment in Panzhihua* (brochure)

Foreign Ministry of Japan (1997) *The Keizaikyoryoku Keikusetteiu no tame no Kiso Chousa [Studies for the Planning of Economic Cooperation]*, Mitsui Sougou Kennkyuujyo, Tokyo

Forests.org (2001) 'NGOs Battle for Papua New Guinea's Forests', *Worldwide Forest/Biodiversity Campaign News*, http://forests.org/recent/2001/envngosb.htm

Fox, J and Ledgerwood, J (1999) 'Dry-season flood-recession rice in the Mekong Delta: Two thousand years of sustainable agriculture?', *Asian Perspectives*, vol 38, no 1, pp37–50

Framework Convention on Climate Change (FCCC) (2002) 'Guide to the Climate Change Convention and Its Kyoto Protocol', http://unfccc.int/resource/convkp.html#bg

Friedman, J (ed) (1996) *The Rational Choice Controversy: Economic Models of Politics Reconsidered*, Yale University Press, New Haven, Connecticut

Genetic Resources Action International (GRAIN) (1997) *Signposts to Sui Generis Rights*, Background discussion papers for the international seminar on *sui generis* rights, Bangkok, 1–6 December, Thai Network on Community Rights and Biodiversity (BIOTHAI), Bangkok

Gerner, D (1995) 'The Evolution of the Study of Foreign Policy' in Neack, L, Hey, J and Haney, P (eds) *Foreign Policy Analysis: Continuity and Change in Its Second Generation*, Prentice Hall, Englewood Cliffs, New Jersey, pp17–31

Gibbons, J (1997) 'The United States and China take on global warming', *New Perspectives Quarterly*, vol 14, no 3, pp25–27

Gibbs, W (2002) 'Panel's vote on Iceland gives boost to whalers', *International Herald Tribune*, 22 October, p3

Gold, T (1986) *State and Society in the Taiwan Miracle*, M E Sharpe, New York

Goldman, M (2001) 'Constructing an environmental state: eco-governmentality and other trans-national practices of a "green" World Bank', *Social Problems*, vol 48, no 4, pp499–523

Gonsalves, P (2000) 'Water security and the Mekong', *Jane's Intelligence Review*, June, pp24–25

Gourevitch, P (1978) 'The second image reversed: the international sources of domestic politics', *International Organization*, vol 32, no 4, pp882–910

Government of Australia (2002) 'Papua New Guinea Country Brief', Australian Department of Foreign Affairs and Trade, www.dfat.gov.au/geo/png/png_brief.html

Green, D P and Shapiro, I (1994) *Pathologies of Rational Choice Theory: A Critique of Applications in Political Science,* Yale University Press, New Haven, Connecticut

Greenfield, J (1979) *China and the Law of the Sea, Air, and Environment*, Sijthoff and Noordhoff, Germantown, Maryland

Groom, A, and Taylor, P (eds) (1975) *Functionalism: Theory and Practice in International Relations*, University of London, London

Guowuyuan Guoji Jishi Yanjiusuo [State Council International Technology and Economics Research Institute] (1996) *Quanqiu Wenti yu Zhongguo* [*Global Problems and China*], Hebei Education Publishers, Beijing

Guy, R (ed) (1997) *Formal and Informal Social Safety Nets in Papua New Guinea*, National Research Institute, Papua New Guinea

Haas, P (1993) 'Epistemic Communities and the Dynamics of International Environmental Cooperation' in Rittberger, V (ed) *Regime Theory and International Relations*, Oxford University Press, Oxford, pp168–201

Hagan, J (1995) 'Domestic political explanations in the analysis of foreign policy' in Neack, L et al (eds) *Foreign Policy Analysis: Continuity and Change in its Second Generation*, Prentice Hall, Englewood Cliffs, pp205–230

Haggard, S (1990) *Pathways from the Periphery*, Cornell University Press, Ithaca

Haggard, S and Kaufman, R (1995) *The Political Economy of Democratic Transitions*, Princeton University Press, Princeton

Hanks, J, Schipper, L, Sell, M, Spense, C and Voinov, J (2001) 'Summary of the Resumed Sixth Session of the Conference of the Parties to the UN Framework Convention on Climate Change', *Earth Negotiations Bulletin*, vol 12, no 176, pp1–15

Hao, Y (1992) 'Environmental Protection and Chinese Foreign Policy' in Robinson, T (ed) *The Foreign Relations of China's Environmental Policy*, American Enterprise Institute, Washington, DC

Harland, D (1990) 'Jumping on the "Ban" Wagon: Efforts to Save the African Elephant', *Fletcher Forum on World Affairs*, vol 14, Summer, pp284–300

Harrington, J (2000a) 'State environmentalism in the People's Republic of China' in Nagel, S (ed) *Handbook of Technology Policy*, Marcel Dekker, New York City, pp156–170

Harrington, J (2000b) *Democratization and the Environment: Understanding the Determinants of State Environmental Policy Outputs in Communist and Post-Communist Societies*, PhD thesis, Loyola University of Chicago, Chicago

Harris, L (1990) 'Directions of Change' in Segal, G (ed) *Chinese Politics and Foreign Policy Reform*, Royal Institute of International Affairs, London, pp256–272

Harris, P G (1996) 'Considerations of Equity and International Environmental Institutions', *Environmental Politics*, vol 5, no 2, pp274–301

Harris, P G (1997) 'Affluence, Poverty and Ecology: Obligation, International Relations and Sustainable Development', *Ethics and the Environment*, vol 2, no 2, pp121–138

Harris, P G (ed) (2000a) *Climate Change and American Foreign Policy*, St Martin's Press, New York

Harris, P G (2000b) 'Climate Change and Foreign Policy: An Introduction' in Harris, P (ed) *Climate Change and American Foreign Policy*, St. Martin's Press, New York, pp2–25

Harris, P G (2001a) *International Equity and Global Environmental Politics: Power and Principles in US Foreign Policy*, Ashgate Press, Aldershot

Harris, P G (ed) (2001b) *The Environment, International Relations, and U.S. Foreign Policy*, Georgetown University Press, Washington

Harris, P G (ed) (2002) *International Environmental Cooperation: Politics and Diplomacy in Pacific Asia*, University Press of Colorado, Boulder, Colorado

Harris, P G (ed) (2003) *Global Warming and East Asia: The Domestic and International Politics of Climate Change*, Routledge, London

Hasenclever, A, Mayer, P and Rittberger, V (1997) *Theories of International Regimes*, Cambridge University Press, Cambridge

Hatch, W and Yamamura, K (1996) *Asia in Japan's Embrace: Building a Regional Production Alliance*, Cambridge University Press, Cambridge

Hempel, L (1996) *Environmental Governance: The Global Challenge*, Island Press, Washington, DC

Hermann, C (1969) 'International Crisis as a Situational Variable', in Rosenau, J (ed) *International Politics and Foreign Policy*, Free Press, New York, pp409–421

Herranz, A (2001) 'Argentine lawmakers approve Kyoto Climate Protocol', http://ens–news.com/ens/jun2001/2001–06–22–02.asp

Hess, M and Howlet, M (1997) *Canadian Natural Resource and Environmental Policy*, University of British Columbia Press, Vancouver

Hicks, B (1996) *Environmental Politics in Poland*, Columbia University Press, New York City

Hirsch, P (2001) 'Globalisation, regionalisation and local voices: the ADB and rescaled politics of environment in the Mekong region', *Singapore Journal of Tropical Geography*, vol 22, no 3, pp237–251

Hirsch, P and Cheong, G (1996) 'Natural Resource Management in the Mekong River Basin: Perspectives for Australian Development Cooperation', Sydney: website, AusAID/University of Sydney, www.usyd.edu.au/su/geography/hirsch/index.htm

Hishida, K (1998) 'Japan: China's largest donor', *China Environmental Review*, vol 1, no 3, Overseas Economic Cooperation Agency, Tokyo, pp10–11

Hoi, N (1995) 'Vietnam' in Hotta, K and Dutton, I (eds) *Coastal Management in the Asia–Pacific Region: Issues and Approaches*, Press of Japan International Marine Science and Technology Federation, Tokyo

Hoi, N, Yet, N and Thanh, D. (2000) 'Initiative Results Of Marine Protected Area Planning In Vietnam' in Hoi, N (ed) *Marine Resources And Environment*, Science and Technology Publishing House, Hanoi

Hong, P and San, H (1993) *Mangrove of Vietnam*, International Union for Conservation of Nature, Bangkok, Thailand

Hook, G (1996) 'Japan and Contested Regionalism' in Cook, I, Doel, M and Li, R (eds) *Fragmented Asia: Regional Integration and National Disintegration in Pacific Asia*, Avebury, Aldershot, pp12–28

Hook, G, Gilson, J, Hughes, C and Dobson, H (2001) *Japan's International Relations: Politics, Economics and Security*, Routledge, London

Houghton, J et al (eds) (1996) *Climate Change: The Science of Climate Change*, Contribution of WGI to the Second Assessment Report of the Intergovernmental Panel on Climate Change, Cambridge University Press, Cambridge

Huber, S and Douglas, C (1998) *Two Perspectives on Global Climate Change: A Briefing Book*, Center for the Study of American Business, Washington University, St Louis

Huntington, S (1991) *The Third Wave: Democratization in the late Twentieth Century*, University of Oklahoma Press, Norman

Hurlock, M (1992) 'The GATT, US Law and the environment: A proposal to amend the GATT in light of the tuna–dolphin decision', *Columbia Law Review*, vol 92, pp2098–2161

Ikenberry, G, Lake, D and Mastanduno, M (eds) (1988) *The State and American Foreign Economic Policy*, Cornell University Press, Ithaca, New York

Information Office of Sichuan Provincial People's Government (undated) *Panxi: A Land Richly Endowed by Nature*, Sichuan meishu chubanshe, Chengdu

Information Office of the State Council of the People's Republic of China (1996) 'Environmental Protection in China', Beijing, June, www.china.org.cn/e-white/environment

Inoguchi, T and Purnendra, J (eds) (2000) *Japanese Foreign Policy Today*, Palgrave, New York

Institute of Thai Traditional Medicine, Ministry of Public Health (2000) 'Operations against Bio-pirates' (in Thai), *Matichon Weekly*, 28 March, p19

Intergovernmental Panel on Climate Change (IPCC) (1997) *The Regional Impacts of Climate Change*, www.grida.no/climate/ ipcc/regional/260.htm

Intergovernmental Panel on Climate Change (IPCC) (2001) IPCC reports, www.ipcc.ch/pub.reports.htm

Intergovernmental Panel on Climate Change (IPCC) (2002) IPCC reports, www.ipcc.ch/pub.reports.htm

International Conventions on Environmental Protection (ICEP) (1995) *International Conventions on Environmental Protection*, National Politics Publishers, Hanoi

Interview with Dr Ampon Kittiampon, Assistant Permanent-Secretary, Ministry of Agriculture and Cooperatives; and Director, Institute of Natural Resources and Biological Diversity, 8 February 2000, Bangkok

Interview with Dr Pennapa Subcharoen, Assistant Director-General, Department of Medical Services; and Director, National Institute of Thai Traditional Medicine, Ministry of Public Health, 7 February 2000, Bangkok

Interview with Dr Sirikul Bunpapong, Chief, Biological Resources Section, Natural Resources and Environment Management Division, Office of Environmental Policy and Planning, Ministry of Science, Technology and Environment, 13 March 2000, Bangkok

Interview with Dr Sunee Mallikamal, Associate Professor, Centre of Law and Environmental Development, Faculty of Law, Chulalongkorn University, 12 November 1999, Bangkok

Interview with Dr Utis Kutintara, Associate Professor; Dean, Faculty of Forestry, Kasetsart University; and Chairman, Thailand's SBSTA (Subsidiary Body for Scientific and Technical Advice) Committee on the Convention on Biological Diversity, 28 March 2000, Bangkok

Interview with Anand Panyarachun, former Prime Minister; President, Saha-Union Public Company Limited; and Chairman, the Council of Trustees of Thailand Environment Institute, 29 February 2000, Bangkok

Interview with Suvat Poopatanapong, First Secretary, International Development Division, Department of International Organizations, Ministry of Foreign Affairs, 22 December 1999, Bangkok

Interview with Thitiphan Pookpakdi, Environmental Officer, Biological Resources Section, Natural Resources and Environment Management Division, Office of Environmental Policy and Planning, Ministry of Science, Technology and Environment, 16 February 2000, Bangkok

Interview with Wichar Thitiprasert, Director, Plant Varieties Protection Office, Department of Agriculture, Ministry of Agriculture and Cooperatives, 23 March 2000, Bangkok

Interview with Witoon Lianchamroon, Coordinating Officer, Thai Network on Community Rights and Biodiversity, 16 March 2000, Bangkok

Itoh, M (2000) *Globalization of Japan: Japanese Sakoku Mentality and US Efforts to Open Japan*, Macmillan, London

Jacobson, H and Oksenberg, M (1990) *China's Participation in the IMF, the World Bank and GATT*, University of Michigan Press, Ann Arbor

Jahiel, A (1998) 'The Organization of environmental protection in China', *China Quarterly* vol 156, pp757–787

Jancar-Webster, B (1998) 'Environmental movement and social change in the transition countries', *Environmental Politics*, vol 7, pp69–90

Japan Environmental Council (JEC) (2000) *The State of the Environment in Asia 1999/2000*, Springer-Verlag, Tokyo

Japan Times (1997) 'Spotlight Centers on Japan', 12 December 1997

Jian, S (1992) 'China's position on Environment and Development', *Beijing Review*, 5 June, pp8–12

Jinse de Panzhihua Bianweihui (ed) (1990) *Jinse de Panzhihua* [*Golden Panzhihua*], Sichuan kexue jishu chubanshe, Chengdu

Johnson, T, Liu, F and Newfarmer, R (1997) *Clear Water, Blue Skies: China's Environment In The New Century*, World Bank, Washington, DC

Johnston, A (1998a) 'China and International Environmental Institutions: A Decision Rule Analysis' in McElroy, M, Nielsen, C and Lydon, P (eds) *Energizing China: Reconciling Environmental Protection and Economic Growth*, Harvard University Press, Newton, pp555–600

Johnston, A (1998b) 'International Structures and Chinese Foreign Policy' in Kim, S (ed) *China and the World: Chinese Foreign Policy Faced the New Millennium*, Westview Press, Boulder, Colorado, pp55–87

Jones, P S (1998) 'Conflicts about Natural Resources' *Footsteps No 36: Coping with Conflict*, Tear Fund, Teddington, Middlesex

Katzenstein, P (1996) 'Introduction' in Katzenstein, P (ed) *The Culture of National Security: Norms and Identity in World Politics*, Columbia University Press, New York City, pp1–32

Keidanren (1991) *Keidanren Global Environmental Charter*, April 23, Keidanren, Tokyo

Keizai-kikakucho (1993) *Kokuminkeizai keisan nenpo* [*Economic Planning Agency Annual Report of National Economic Account*], Okurasho insatsukyoku, Tokyo

Kennedy, K (1998) 'The illegality of unilateral trade measures to resolve trade-environment disputes', *William and Mary Environmental Law and Policy Review*, vol 22, pp375–506

Keohane, R (1986) 'Realism, neo-realism and the study of world politics', in Keohane, R (ed) *Neo-Realism and its Critics*, Columbia University Press, New York City, pp1–33

Keohane, R, Haas, P and Levy, M (1994) 'The effectiveness of international environmental institutions', in Haas, P, Keohane, R and Levy, M (eds) *Institutions for the Earth: Sources of Effective International Environmental Protection*, MIT Press, Boston, pp3–27

Kim, S (1992) 'Environmental Security in Chinese Global Policy' in Robinson, T (ed) *The Foreign Relations of China's Environmental Policy*, American Enterprise Institute, Washington, DC

Kim, S (1994) 'China's international organizational behavior' in Robinson, T and Shambaugh, D (eds) *Chinese Foreign Policy: Theory and Practice*, Clarendon Press, Oxford, pp401–434

Kim, S (1998) *China and the World: Chinese Foreign Policy Faces the New Millennium*, Westview, Boulder, Colorado

Kingdom, J (1984) *Agenda, Alternatives, and Public Policies*, Harper Collins, New York

Kirkpatrick, C and Lee, N (eds) (1997) *Sustainable Development in a Developing World: Integrating Socio-Economic Appraisal and Environmental Assessment*, Edward Elgar, Cheltenham

Kirsch, S (1998) *A Biological Assessment of the Lakekamu Basin*, Conservation International Rapid Assessment Programme Working paper No 9, Conservation International, Washington, DC

Kitagawa, H (2000) *Yameru Kyyuryu: Chugoku* [*Environmental and Ecological Problems of China*], Bengeisha, Tokyo

Kitô S (1999) '*Kankyô o mamoru to wa dô iu kotoka*' in Kitô, S (ed) *Kankyô no yutakasa o motomete*, Shôwadô, Kyoto, pp5–28

Kluger, J (2001) 'A Climate of despair', *Time*, 9 April, pp34–35

Kobayashi, Y (2003) 'Navigating between "Luxury" and "Survival" Emissions: Tensions in China's Multilateral and Bilateral Climate Change Diplomacy' in Harris, P G (ed) *Global Warming and East Asia*, Routledge, London

Kreisberg, P (1994) 'China's Negotiating Behavior' in Robinson, T and Shambaugh, D (eds) *China's Foreign Policy: Theory and Practice*, Oxford University Press, Oxford

Krishna, A and Uphoff, N (1999) *Mapping And Measuring Social Capital: A Conceptual And Empirical Study Of Collective Action For Conserving And Developing Watersheds In Rajasthan, India*, World Bank, Washington, DC, www.worldbank.org/poverty/scapital/wkrppr/index.htm

Kristof, N D (2000) 'The Filthy Earth' in Kristof, N D and WuDunn, S (eds) *Thunder from the East: Portrait of a Rising Asia*, Alfred A Knopf, New York, pp291–313

Lambrecht, C (1999) 'Destruction and Violation: Burma's Border Development Policies', *Watershed*, vol 5, no 2, www.nextcity.com/ProbeInternational/Mekong/articles/990111.html

Lan, T (2000) 'Marine Protected Area as an Initiative for Sustainable Development in the Coastal Zone of Vietnam: Hon Mun Marine Protected Area Pilot Project' in Kerker, E, Foth, M Schipmann, C and Caspari, A (eds) *Sustainable Development of Coastal Zones and Instruments for Its Evaluation*, Carl Duisberg Gesellschaft, Bremerhaven

Lane, N and Bierbaum, R (2001) 'Recent advances in the science of climate change', *Natural Resources and Environment*, vol 15, Winter, pp147–151

Latiffe, G (1996) 'Upper Mekong: Ethnicity, Identity and Economy', in Stensholt, B (ed) *Development Dilemmas in the Mekong Subregion*, Monash Asia Institute, Monash University, pp64–69

Lazaroff, C (2001) 'China beats US in greenhouse gas cuts', *Environment News Service*, http://ens–news.com/ens/jun2001/2001–06–15–06.asp

Lemonick, M (2001) 'Life in the Greenhouse', *Time*, 9 April, pp28–33

Leng, T (May, 1998) 'Dynamics of Taiwan–Mainland China Economic Relations: the Role of Private Firms', *Asian Survey*, vol 38, pp494–509

Leng, T (2002) 'Sovereignty at Bay? Business Networking and Domestic Politics of Informal Integration between Taiwan and Mainland China' in Regnier, P and Liu, F (eds) *Regionalism in East Asia: Paradigm Shifting?* Curzon, London, pp230–250

Letter of Ministry of Foreign Affairs to the Cabinet Secretary, No 0605/179, 28 January 1998 (in Thai)

Letter of Ministry of Science, Technology and Environment to the Cabinet Secretary, No 0803/4243, 28 March 1997 (in Thai)

Letter of Office of the Cabinet Secretary to Ministry of Foreign Affairs, No 0206/14599, 3 November 1998 (in Thai)

Letter of Office of the Council of State to the Cabinet Secretary, No 0601/765, 7 November 1996 (in Thai)

Li, J (2000) 'An analysis of Taiwan's participation on CDM', *Working Paper*, National Policy Foundation

Li, P (1997) *Li peng jiu huanjing baogao xianzai* [*Selected Essays on the Environment*] (in Chinese), China Environment Press, Beijing

Lianchamroon, W (1998) *Bio-piracy: Case Study in Thailand* (in Thai), Thai Traditional Medicine Development Foundation, Bangkok

Liang, C (1999) 'Lanzhou: An environmental disaster', *Time International*, vol 154, no 13, pp113–114

Liang, H and Shapiro, J (1986) *After the Nightmare: A Survivor of the Cultural Revolution Reports on China Today*, Alfred A Knopf, New York

Lieberthal, K (1995) *Governing China: From Revolution through Reform*, Norton, New York

Lien Ho Pao [*United Daily News*] (2000a) 17 January 2000, p14

Lien Ho Pao [*United Daily News*] (2000b) 28 October 2000, p8

Lien Ho Pao [*United Daily News*] (2000c), 14 August 2000, p15

Lien Ho Pao [*United Daily News*] (2000d), 26 May 2000, p4

Lilienthal, D (1944) *TVA: Democracy on the March*, Harper and Brothers, New York

Linnerooth-Bayer, J (1999) 'Climate Change and Multiple Views of Fairness' in Toth, F (ed) *Fair Weather? Equity Concerns in Climate Change*, Earthscan, London, pp44–64

Lipshutz, R (1996) 'Environmentalism in one country: the case of Hungary' in Lipshutz, R (ed) *Global Civil Society and Global Environmental Governance*, SUNY Press, Albany, pp127–168

Logan, J et al (1999) 'Climate action in the United States and China', *Working Paper*, Battelle Memorial Institute and Woodrow Wilson International Center for Scholars, May, www.pnl.gov/china/pubs.htm

Lowi, M (1993) *Water and Power: The Politics of a Scarce Resource in the Jordan River Basin*, Cambridge University Press, Cambridge

Lu, G and Walsh, K (1992) 'The Foreign Relations of China's Environmental Policy' in Robinson, T (ed) *The Foreign Relations of China's Environmental Policy*, American Enterprise Institute, Washington, DC

Lu, S (1995) 'Environmental Protection and Trade Sanction' (in Chinese), *Today's Economy*, vol 333, pp49–52

Ma, X and Ortolano, L (2000) *Environmental Regulation in China: Institutions, Enforcement, and Compliance*, Rowman and Littlefield, Lanham, Maryland

Mainichi Shimbun (2002) 'Koizumi gaining support for North Korean stance', http://mdn.mainichi.co.jp/news20020923

Malanczuk, P (1997) *Akehurst's Modern Introduction of International Law* (7th edition), Routledge, London

Mao Zedong (1974) *Miscellany of Mao Tse-tung Thought, 1949–1968, Part I,* Joint Publications Research Service, Arlington

Marland, G et al (1999) *Global, Regional, and National CO$_2$ Emissions*, Oak Ridge National Laboratory, Oak Ridge, Tennessee

Martinot, E (2001) 'World Bank energy projects in China: influences on environmental protection', *Energy Policy*, vol 29, pp581–594

Matsushita, K (2000) 'Environment and Development in Asia', *Japan Echo*, vol 27, no 3, pp14–18

Maull, H (1991) 'Japan's Global Environmental Policies', *The Pacific Review*, vol 4, no 3, pp254–262

Mayer, D and Hoch, D (1993) 'International environmental protection and the GATT: the tuna–dolphin controversy', *American Business Law Journal*, vol 31, pp187–244

McCully, P (1996) *Silenced Rivers: The Ecology and Politics of Large Dams*, Zed Books, London

McDougall, D (1997) *The International Politics of the New Asia Pacific*, Lynne Rienner Publishers, Boulder, Colorado

McElroy, M, Nielsen, C and Lydon, P (eds) (1998) *Energizing China: Reconciling Environmental Protection and Economic Growth*, Harvard University Press, Newton

Mekong River Commission (MRC) (1995) *Agreement on the Cooperation for the Sustainable Development of the Mekong River Basin*, Mekong River Commission, Bangkok

Mekprayoonthong, M (2002) 'Thailand and the Convention on Biological Diversity' (in Thai), *Saranrom* (February), pp107–109

Memorandum of Office of the Secretary-General to the Prime Minister (1998) 31 July 1998 (in Thai)

Merviö, M (2002) '*Nihon no kokusai kankei ni okeru ningen no anzen hoshô to kankyô anzen*' in Uno, S (ed) *Hokutô ajia kenkyû to kaihatsu kenkyû*, Kokusai shoin, Tokyo, pp419–448

Miller, F (2000) 'Environmental Threats to the Mekong Delta', *Watershed* (17 February), www.nextcity.com/ProbeInternational/Mekong/articles/000217b.html

Miller, M (1995) *The Third World in Global Environmental Politics*, Open University Press, Buckingham, UK

Milner, H (1997) *Interests, Institutions, and Information: Domestic Politics and International Relations*, Princeton University Press, Princeton, New Jersey

Minh, N, Son, N, Thang, H (2001) 'Implementation of the case demonstration project on ICM in da nang', *Journal of Scientific Activity*, vol 3, pp19–20

Minh, T (1996) 'Sources and Oil Pollution Potential in the Vietnam Sea', *Journal of Meteorology and Hydrology*, vol 432, pp8–14

Ministry of Fisheries (1996) *Aquatic Resources in Vietnam*, Agriculture Publishing House, Hanoi

Ministry of Foreign Affairs (MOFA) (1994) *Japan's ODA: Annual Report 1993*, Government of Japan, Tokyo

Ministry of Foreign Affairs (MOFA) (1996) *Japan's ODA: Annual Report 1995*, Government of Japan, Tokyo

Ministry of Foreign Affairs (MOFA) (2000) *The Diplomatic Yearbook*, Urban Connections, Tokyo

Ministry of Foreign Affairs (MOFA) (2002) 'China's Participation in Multilateral International Agreements', www.fmprc.gov.cn/chn/premade/24475/dabiao.htm

Ministry of Planning and Investment (MPI) and United Nations Development Programme (UNDP) (1999) *A Study on Aid to the Environment Sector in Vietnam*, MPI Press, Hanoi

Ministry of Science, Technology and Environment (MOSTE) (1999) *Laws and Regulations on Environment*, The World Publishing House, Hanoi

Mitchell, R (1995) 'International Oil Pollution of the Oceans' in Haas, P, Keohane, R and Levy, M (eds) *Institutions for the Earth: Sources of Effective International Environmental Protection*, MIT Press, Cambridge, Massachusetts, pp184–247

Mizutani, Y (ed) (2000) *2010 nen chikyu ondanka boshi shinario* [*The Year 2010: A Scenario to Prevent Global Warming*], Jitsugyo Shuppan, Tokyo

Moser, C and McIlwaine, C (2000) *Perceptions of Urban Violence: Participatory Appraisal Techniques*, LCR Sustainable Development Working Paper No 7, The World Bank, Washington, DC

Murray, F, Reinhardt, F and Vietor, R (1998) 'Foreign Firms in the Chinese Power Sector: Economic and Environmental Impacts' in McElroy, M, Nielsen, C and Lyon, P (eds) *Energizing China: Reconciling Environmental Protection and Economic Growth*, Harvard University Press, Cambridge, Massachusetts, pp639–692

Narayan, D (1999) *Bonds and Bridges: Social Capital and Poverty* (World Bank Working Papers on Governance), August, World Bank, Washington, DC

National Environmental Protection Agency (NEPA) (1993) *China Country Program for the Phaseout of Ozone-Depleting Substance under the Montreal Protocol*, Report submitted to the Ninth Meeting of the Executive Committee of the Multilateral Fund of the Montreal Protocol, Montreal, March

National Round Table on the Environment and the Economy (NRTEE) (1999) *NRTEE Sustainable Cities Initiatives Final Report and Recommendations*, NRTEE, Ottawa

Naugton, B (1988) 'The Third Front: Defence industrialization in the Chinese interior', *China Quarterly*, vol 115, pp351–386

Naugton, B (1991) 'Industrial policy during the Cultural Revolution: military preparation, decentralization, and leaps forward' in Joseph, W, Wong, C and Zweig, D
(eds) *New Perspectives on the Cultural Revolution,* Harvard University Press,
Cambridge, pp153–187

Newhous, J (1992) 'The diplomatic round: Earth Summit', *The New Yorker,* 1 June, p68

Ng, I and Turner, M (1999) 'Toxic China: as breakneck growth transforms the country
into an environmental disaster zone, a few devoted activists are struggling to turn
things around', *Time International,* vol 153, no 20, pp16–17

Nguyen, V, Ta, T, Tateishi, M and Kobayashi, I (1999) 'Coastal Variation and
Saltwater Intrusion on the Coastal Lowlands of the Mekong River Delta, Southern
Vietnam' in Saito, Y, Ikehara, K and Katayama, H (eds) *Land–Sea Link in Asia,*
Press of Geological Survey of Japan, Tsukuba

Nissen, J L (1997) 'Achieving a Balance Between Trade and Environment: The need to
amend the WTO/GATT to include multilateral environmental agreements, *Law
and Policy in International Business,* vol 28, pp901–928

Oberthur, S (2000) 'Ozone Layer Protection at the Turn of the Century: The Eleventh
Meeting of the Parties', *Environmental Policy and Law,* vol 30, no 1–2, pp34–42

Office of the Council of State (2000) 'The Constitution of the Kingdom of Thailand
1997', www.krisdika.go.th/law/text/lawpub/e11022540/text.htm

Ohta, H (1995) *Japan's Politics and Diplomacy of Climate Change,* PhD Dissertation,
Columbia University, New York

Ohta, H (2000) 'Japanese Environmental Foreign Policy' in Inoguchi, T and
Purnendra, J (eds) *Japanese Foreign Policy Today,* Palgrave, New York pp96–121

Ohta, H (2001) 'Japan's domestic politics of global climate change: a research design',
The Aoyama Journal of International Politics, Economics and Business, no 54,
pp225–240

Oksenberg, M, Sullivan, L and Lambert, M (1990) *Beijing Spring, 1989:
Confrontation and Conflict, the Basic Documents,* M E Sharpe, Armonk

Osborne, M (2000a) *The Mekong: Turbulent Past, Uncertain Future,* Atlantic Monthly
Press, New York

Osborne, M (2000b) 'The Strategic Significance of the Mekong', *Contemporary
Southeast Asia,* vol 22, no 3, pp429–444

Ottawa Citizen (1999) 18 October

Paarlberg, R (1995) 'Managing Pesticide Use in Developing Countries' in Haas, P,
Keohane, R and Levy, M (eds) *Institutions for the Earth: Sources of Effective
International Environmental Protection,* MIT Press, Cambridge, Massachusetts,
pp309–350

Pacific Northwest National Laboratory (PNNL) (2001) 'China E-News Energy,
Environment, Economy', 8 May, www.pnl.gov/china

Palmer, M (1998) 'Environmental regulation in the People's Republic of China: The
face of domestic law', *China Quarterly,* vol 156, no 3, pp788–808

Panzhihua shiwei dangshi yanjiu shi (ed) (1997) *Cong Shenmi Zou Xiang Huihuang
[From Mysterious to Glorious: The Story of the Construction of Panzhihua],*
Hongqi chubanshe, Beijing

Parker, R (1999) 'The use and abuse of trade leverage to protect the global common:
what can we learn from the tuna–dolphin conflict', *The Georgetown International
Environmental Law Review,* vol XII, no 1, pp1–123

Parson, E (1995) 'Protecting the Ozone Layer' in Haas, P, Keohane, R and Levy, M
(eds) *Institutions for the Earth: Sources of Effective International Environmental
Protection,* MIT Press, Cambridge, Massachusetts, pp27–73

Peking Review (1972) 3, 16 and 23 June, Peking

Permpongsacharoen, W (1999) 'Comment: Nam Theun 2 Hydropower Project – At what price electricity?' *Bangkok Post*, 30 October, p17

Peterson, M (1995) 'International Fisheries Management' in Haas, P, Keohane, R and Levy, M (eds) *Institutions for the Earth: Sources of Effective International Environmental Protection*, MIT Press, Cambridge, Massachusetts, pp249–305

Pharr, S and Wan, M (1998) 'Yen for the Earth: Japan's Pro-active China Environment Policy' in McElroy, M, Nielson, C and Lydon, P (eds) *Energizing China: Reconciling Environmental Protection and Economic Growth*, Harvard University Press, Cambridge, Massachusetts, pp602–638

Porter, G, Brown, J and Chasek, P (2000) *Global Environmental Politics* (3rd edition), Westview Press, Boulder, Colorado

Putnam, R (1988) 'Diplomacy and domestic politics: the logic of two-level games', *International Organization*, vol 42, no 3 (Summer), pp427–460

Pyle, K (1998) 'Restructuring Foreign and Defence Policy: Japan' in McGrew, A and Brook, C (eds) *Asia–Pacific in the New World Order*, Routledge, London, pp121–136

Qin, Y (1992) 'GATT membership for Taiwan: an analysis in international law', *New York University Journal of International Law*, vol 24, pp1059–1105

Qu, G and Li, J (1994) *Population and Environment in China* (translated by Jiang, B and Gu, R), Lynne Rienner, Boulder, Colorado

Rajan, M (1997) *Global Environmental Politics: India And The North–South Politics Of Global Environmental Issues*, Oxford University Press, Delhi

Ramses, A (1997) 'The Territorial Disputes Between China and Vietnam and Regional Stability', *Contemporary Southeast Asia*, vol 19, no 1, pp86–113

Revkin, A (2001) 'Warming threat requires action now, scientists say', *New York Times*, New York, 12 June, p12

Ricoh Corporation (2001) *Environmental report*, www.ricoh.co.jp/ecology/e–/report /index.html

Riggs, F (1966) *Thailand: Modernization of A Bureaucratic Polity*, East–West Center Press, Honolulu

Robinson, T and Shambaugh, D (1994) *Chinese Foreign Policy: Theory And Practice*, Clarendon Press, Oxford

Rosenau, J (1987) 'Introduction: New Directions and Recurrent Questions in the Comparative Study of Foreign Policy' in Hermann, C, Kegley, C and Rosenau, J (eds) *New Directions in the Study of Foreign Policy*, Unwin Hyman, Winchester, Massachusetts

Ross, L (1998) 'China: Environmental Protection, Domestic Policy Trends, Patterns of Participation in Regimes and Compliance with International Norms' in Edmonds, R (ed) *Managing the Chinese Environment*, Oxford University Press, Oxford

Ross, L and Silk, M (1985) 'Post-Mao China and Environmental Protection: The Effects of Legal and Politico-Economic Reform', *Pacific Basin Law Journal*, vol 40, no 3, p67

Ross, L and Silk, M (1987) *Environmental Law and Policy in People's Republic of China*, Quorum, London

Ross, L and Silk, M (1988a) *Environmental Policy in China*, Indiana University Press, Bloomington, Indiana

Ross, L and Silk, M (1998b) 'China: Environmental Protection, Domestic Policy Trends, Patterns of Regime Participation and Compliance with International Norms' *China Quarterly*, vol 156 (December), pp799–835

Roy, D (1998) 'Restructuring Foreign and Defence Policy: The People's Republic of China' in McGrew, A and Brook, C (eds) *Asia–Pacific in the New World Order*, Routledge, London, pp137–157

Rutgeerts, A (1999) 'Trade and environment: reconciling the Montreal Protocol and the GATT', *Journal of World Trade*, vol 31, pp61–86

Salafsky, N and Paka, T (1999) 'Learning Conservation Lessons the Hard Way' in Biodiversity Conservation Network (ed) *Final Stories from the Field: Evaluating Linkages Between Business, the Environment and Local Communities*, Biodiversity Conservation Network, Washington, DC

Sandoz, M (1996) 'Agriculture Water Use in Vietnam' in World Bank, ADB, FAO/UNDP and NGO Water Resources Sectoral Group (eds) *Vietnam Water Resources Sector Review*, World Bank, Washington, DC

Sanwa Sougou Kenkyujyo (1997) *Teninoruyouni Kankyomondai ga wakaru hon* [*Understanding the Basics of Environmental Problems*], Kanki, Tokyo

Sato, A (1992) 'Seito kaitai-no zenya' ('The Eve of Dissolution of a Political Party'), *AERA*, vol 5, no 13, 24 March, p7

Scalapino, R (1992) 'The Foreign Policy of Modern Japan' in Macridis, R (ed) *Foreign Policy in World Politics*, Prentice Hall, Englewood Cliffs, New Jersey, pp186–221

Schnurr, J and Holtz, S (eds) (1998) *The Cornerstone of Development: Integrating Environmental, Social, and Economic Policies*, International Development Research Centre, Ottawa

Schraeder, P (1994) *United States Foreign Policy Toward Africa: Incrementalism, Crisis and Change*, Cambridge University Press, New York City

Schramm, G and Warford, J (eds) (1989) *Environmental Management and Economic Development*, Johns Hopkins University Press, Baltimore

Secretariat of the Convention on Biological Diversity (2002) 'Parties information', www.biodiv.org/world/parties.asp

Shi, W and He, L (1996) *Zhiqing Beiwanglu: Shangshan Xiaxiang Yundong Zhong De Shengchan Jianshe Bingtuan* [*Educated Youth Memoirs: The Production–Construction Army Corps in the Rustification Movement*], Zhongguo shehui kexue chubanshe, Beijing

Shibusawa, M, Ahmad, Z and Bridges, B (1992) *Pacific Asia in the 1990s*, Royal Institute of International Affairs, Routledge, London

Shih, W (1996) 'Multilateralism and the case of Taiwan in the trade environment nexus', *Journal of World Trade*, vol 30, no 3, pp109–139

Shih, W (1998) Multilateral Environmental Agreements and Taiwan *Asia Pacific Journal on Environment and Development* vol 5, no 1, pp39–52

Shih, W (2000) 'Taiwan and the 1992 UN Convention on Biological Diversity', Paper presented at the Annual Meeting of the Law and Society Association, 26–29 May, Miami

Shih, W (2002a) 'The implementation of the United Nations framework convention on climate change in a non-party state: Taiwan', *International Environmental Agreements: Politics, Law and Economics*, vol 2, pp69–98

Shih, W (2002b) 'The status of Taiwan in the international debate of free trade vs environmental protection' (in Chinese), *National Taiwan University Law Review*, vol 31, no 1, pp45–75

Shirk, S (1993) *The Political Logic Of Economic Reform In China*, University of California Press, Berkeley

Shirk, S (1994) *How China Opened Its Door: The Political Success of the PRC's Foreign Trade And Investment Reforms*, Brookings Institution, Washington, DC

Shoemaker, B (1998) 'Trouble on the Theun–Hinboun: A Field Report on the Socio-Economic and Environmental Effects of the Nam Theun-Hinboun Hydropower Project in Laos', International River Network, www.irn.org/programs/mekong/threport.html

Sichuansheng Panzhihuashi zhi biancuan weihuanhui (1994) *Panzhihuashi Zhi* (Panzhihua City Record), Sichuan kexue jishu chubanshe, Chengdu

Sinkule, B and Ortolano, L (1995) *Implementing Environmental Policy in China*, Praeger, Westport

Smil, V (1984) *The Bad Earth: Environmental Degradation In China*, ME Sharpe, London

Smil, V (1993) *China's Environmental Crisis: An Inquiry into the Limits of National Development*, Sharpe, Armonk, New York

Smil, V (1998) 'China's Energy and Resource Uses: Continuity and Change', *China Quarterly*, vol 156 (December), pp935–951

Snow, P (1994) 'China and Africa: Consensus and Camouflage' in Robinson, T and Shambaugh, D (eds) *Chinese Foreign Policy: Theory and Practice*, Oxford University Press, Oxford

Society for Environmental Economics and Policy Studies (1998) *Asia no Kankyou Mondai [Asian Environmental Problems]*, Toyo Keizai Shinnpousha, Tokyo

Solomon, R (1999) *Chinese Negotiating Behavior: Pursuing Interests Through Old Friends*, US Institute of Peace Press, Washington, DC

Sorifu (Prime Minister's Office) (1988–1993) *Seron chosa [Monthly Public Opinion Poll]*, Okurasho Insatsukyoku (Ministry of Finance Printing Bureau), Tokyo

Sorifu (Prime Minister's Office) (1997–1999) *Heisei 11-nen ban seron chosa nenkan [Public Opinion Polls Yearbook]*, Okurasho Insatsukyoku (Ministry of Finance Printing Bureau), Tokyo

Soroos, M (1992) 'Conflict in the Use and Management of International Commons' in Kakonen, J (ed) *Perspectives on Environmental Conflict and International Relations,* Pinter, London, pp31–43

State Environmental Protection Bureau (SEPA) and United Nations Environment Programme (UNEP) (1999) *State of the Chinese Environment 1998*, State Environmental Protection Bureau, www.sepa.gov.cn/soechina98

Steward, C (1999) Speech delivered by the Minister of the Environment Christine Steward at the Americana 1999 Conference, Montreal, 25 March, www.ec.ca/minister/speeches/amer99_s_e.html

Storey, I (2000) 'Living with the colossus: how Southeast Asian countries cope with China', *Parameters*, vol 29, no 4, pp111–125

Sun, Y (1993) 'A complete phase-out in 1996' (in Chinese), *Environmental Protection and the Economy*, vol 42, p24

Susskind, L E (1994) *Environmental Diplomacy: Negotiating More Effective Global Agreements*, Oxford University Press, Oxford

Susskind, L and Ozawa, C (1995) 'Negotiating More Effective Agreements' in Hurrell, A and Kingsbury, B (eds) *International Political Theory and the Global Environment*, Clarendon Press, Oxford

Tanabe, T (1999) *Chikyu ondanka to kankyo gaiko [Global Warming and Environmental Diplomacy]*, Jiji tsushin sha, Tokyo

Tanaka, S (2000) 'Japan and China and the Three Big Es', *Look Japan*, vol 46, October, pp32–33

Tang, C (2000) 'Democratic administration and sustainable development: comparing environmental impact assessments in Taiwan and Hong Kong', *Wenti Yu Yanjiu (Issues and Studies)*, vol 16, no 3, pp17–35

Tang, D (1993) 'The environmental laws and policies of Taiwan: a comparative law perspective', *Vanderbilt Journal of Transnational Law*, vol 26, pp521–580

Tang, W (1993) 'Post-Socialist Transition and Environmental Protection', *Journal of Public Policy*, vol 13, no 1, pp89–109

Tarasofsky, R (1999) 'The WTO Committee on Trade and Environment: Is it making a difference?', *Max Planck Yearbook of UN Law*, vol 3, pp471–488

Thanh, T (1995) 'Coastal Morphological Changes Concerning the Management Of Coastal Zone in Vietnam' in E Duursma (ed) *IOC/UNESCO Workshop Report No 105 Supplement*, pp451–462

Thanh, T, Huy, D, Nguyen, V, Ta, T, Tateishi, M and Saito,Y (2002) 'The Impact of Human Activities on the Vietnamese Rivers and Coasts' in Hong, G H, Kremer, H H, Pacyna, J, Chen, C T A, Behrendt, H, Salamon, W and Cressland, J I M (eds) *East Asia Basins: LOICZ Reports and Studies*, Land–Ocean Interactions in the Coastal Zone International Project Office, Texel, The Netherlands, pp179–184

Thi Dieu, N (1996) 'State versus indigenous peoples: the impact of hydraulic projects on indigenous peoples of Asia', *Journal of World History*, vol 7, no 1, pp101–130

Thi Dieu, N (1999) *The Mekong River and the Struggle for Indochina: Water, War, and Peace*, Praeger, Westport, Connecticut

Thuy, N and Khuoc, B (1994) 'El-Nino phenomenon, global climate warming, and sea level in Vietnam Sea and South China Sea', *Journal of Meteorology and Hydrology*, vol 5, pp16–23

Tien Long, N (2000) 'Review of Solar and Wind Energy Development in Viet Nam' in United Nations (ed) *Economic and Social Commission for Asia and the Pacific, Commercialization of Renewable Energy Technologies for Sustainable Development*, Energy Resources Development Series no 37, New York, pp171–175

Tolba, M K with Rummel-Bulska, I (1998) *Environmental Diplomacy: Negotiating Environmental Agreements for the World*, MIT Press, Cambridge, Massachusetts

Torode, G (1998) 'New dam takes toll on livelihoods', *South China Morning Post*, 4 April, www.probeinternational.org/pi/Mekong/index.cfm?DSP=content&ContentID=994

Tsai, H (2001) 'Global trend of environmental protection and Taiwan's energy policy' (in Chinese), *National Policy Forum*, vol 1, no 1, pp3–10

Tseng, E (1999) 'The Environment and the People's Republic of China' in Soden, D and Steel, B (eds) *Handbook of Global Environmental Policy and Administration*, Marcel Dekker, Basel, pp381–392

Tyler, S (1999) 'Policy Implications of Natural Resource Conflict Management' in Buckles, D (ed) *Cultivating Peace: Conflict And Collaboration In Natural Resource Management*, International Development Research Centre, Ottawa, Chapter 14

Unger, D (1993) 'Japan's Capital Imports: Moulding East Asia' in Unger, D and Blackburn, P (eds) *Japan's Emerging Global Role*, Lynne Rienner, Boulder, pp155–170

United Nations (UN) (1973) *Report on the Human Environment*, UN Doc A/Conf.48/14/Rev.1

United Nations Conference on Environment and Development (UNCED) (1992) *Earth Summit: Convention on Biological Diversity*, Rio de Janeiro, Brazil, 3–14 June, Department of Public Information, United Nations, New York

United Nations Development Programme (UNDP) (1999) *Compendium of Environmental Projects in Vietnam*, UNDP, Hanoi

United Nations Environment Programme (UNEP) (1999) *Global Environment Outlook,* Earthscan, London

Van Liere, W (1980) 'Traditional water management in the lower Mekong basin', *World Archeology*, vol 3, p267

Van Rooy, A (1997) 'The Frontiers of Influence: NGO Lobbying at the 1974 World Food Conference – The 1992 Earth Summit and Beyond', *World Development*, vol 25, no 1, pp93–114

Victor, D (1999) 'The Regulation of Greenhouse Gases: Does Fairness Matter?' in Toth, F (ed) *Fair Weather? Equity Concerns in Climate Change*, Earthscan, London, pp193–206

Walker, J (1974) 'Performance gaps, policy research, and political entrepreneurs', *Policy Studies Journal*, no 3 (Autumn), pp112–116

Walker, J (1981) 'The diffusion of knowledge, policy communities and agenda setting' in Tropman, J, Dluhy, M and Lind, R (eds) *New Strategies, Perspectives on Social Policy*, Pergamon Press, New York

Wallerstein, I (1980) *The Modern World System II: Mercantilism and the Consolidation of the European World Economy, 1600–1750*, Academic Press, New York City

Waltz, K (1979) *Theory of International Politics*, Addison Wesley, Reading, MA

Wan, Y (1990) 'Xiujian Cheng–Kun lu, jianshe Panzhihua: Lu Zhengcao Jiangjun fang-wen ji' ('Building the Chengdu–Kunming railroad, constructing Panzhihua: Interview with General Lu Zhengcao') in Jinse de Panzhihua Bianweihui (ed) *Jinse de Panzhihua [Golden Panzhihua]*, Sichuan kexue jishu chubanshe, Chengdu, pp141–142

Wang, J, Xia, G, and Jia, F (1999) *ADB Staff Consultant Report: PRC Environmental Profile Final Report* (draft copy), ADB/SEPA, Beijing

Wang, M (ed) (1998) *Shangshan Xiaxiang – Yichang Jueding 3000 Wan Zhongguo Ren Mingyun De Yundong Zhi Mi [Up to the Mountains and Down to the Countryside – The Conundrum of a Movement that Determined the Fate of 30 Million Chinese]*, Guangming ribao chubanshe, Beijing

Wang, W, Liang, X and Dudek, M (1994) 'Effect of Global Warming on the Regional Climate in China' in Zepp R (ed) *Climate–Biosphere Interactions: Biogenic Emissions and Environmental Effects of Climate Change*, John Wiley and Sons, New York, pp19–29

Wang, Z (1999) *China Environmental Diplomacy: Retrospect and Prospect of China Environmental Diplomacy*, Zhongguo huanjing kexue chubanshe (China Environmental Science Publishing Company), Beijing

Warner, M (2000) *Conflict Management in Community-Based Natural Resource Projects: Experiences from Fiji and Papua New Guinea*, ODI Working Paper 135, Overseas Development Institute, London

Watanabe A (1997) '*Gaikô seisaku kara kokusaiseisaku e*', in Watanabe, A (ed) *Gendai nihon no kokusai seisaku: Posto reisen no kokusai chitsujo o motomete*. Yûhikaku, Tokyo, pp1–16

Watson, R (2000) Presentation at the Sixth Conference of Parties to the UNFCCC, 13 November, www.ipcc.ch/press/sp–cop6.htm

Watson, R, Zinyowera, M and Moss, R (eds) (1998) *The Regional Impacts of Climate Change: An Assessment of Vulnerability*, Cambridge University Press, Cambridge, pp355–379

Webber, M and Smith, M (2002) *Foreign Policy in a Transformed World*, Prentice Hall, Harlow

Whimp, K (1997) 'Governance, Law, and Sovereignty: enforcing environmental objectives in Papua New Guinea', Chapter 16 in Filer, C (ed) *The Political Economy of Forest Management in Papua New Guinea*, National Research Institute and International Institute for Environment and Development, London

Whiting, A (1992) 'Foreign Policy of China' in Macridis, R (ed) *Foreign Policy in World Politics*, Prentice Hall, Englewood Cliffs, New Jersey, pp222–267

Wilson, J (1992) 'Green Lobbies: Pressure Groups and Environmental Policy' in Boardman, R (ed) *Canadian Environmental Policy: Ecosystems, Politics, and Process*, Oxford University Press, Toronto

World Bank (2000) *Violence in Colombia: Building Sustainable Peace And Social Capital*, World Bank, Washington, DC

World Commission on Environment and Development (WCED) (1987) *Our Common Future*, Oxford University Press, Oxford

World Resource Institute (WRI) (1997) 'President Calls Kyoto Protocol a Historic Step for Humankind', 11 December World Resource Institute, Washington, DC

Xie, J (1999) 'Humanity and nature: A review of development and environmental degradation of contemporary China', www.chinaenviro.net

Xinhua (1994) 'Agenda for 21st century announced', *China Daily*, 26 March, p1

Xinhua (1997) 'China's role key in global environment', *Xinhua English Newswire*, 22 August

Xinhua (1998) 'Li Peng on environmental protection', *F B I S China Report*, 7 November

Xinhua (1999) 'Official says China, India can work together', *Xinhua News Agency*, 22 November

Xinhua (2000) 'Chinese Environment News Weekly Highlights', *Xinhua News Service*, 18 December

Yamada, I (1997) *Tropical Rain Forests of Southeast Asia: A Forest Ecologist's View* (translated by P Hawkes), University of Hawaii Press, Honolulu

Yao, K (1997) 'Recent Sewerage Development in Taiwan', *Asian Water and Sewage*, May, pp12–14

Yasutomo, D (1995) *The New Multilateralism in Japan's Foreign Policy*, Macmillan, London

Yeh, J (1999) *Global Environmental Issues: Taiwan Perspective* (in Chinese), Chu–liou Publishing, Taipei

Yoshida, T (1992) 'Chikyu samitto waremo waremo' ('Vying with one another to go to the Earth Summit'), *Asahi Shimbun*, March 3

Young, C (1999) 'International Environmental Politics and Diplomacy: Taiwan's Situation and Future Outlook', Unpublished manuscript

Young, O (1989) *International Cooperation: Building Regimes for Natural Resources and the Environment*, Cornell University Press, Ithaca

Zhang, W and Li, Y (eds) (1998) *Kouhao yu Zhongguo [Slogans and China]*, Zhonggong dangshi chubanshe, Beijing

Zhang, W, Vertinsky, I, Ursacki, T and Nemetz, P (1999) 'Can China be a clean tiger? Growth strategies and environmental realities', *Pacific Affairs*, vol 72, no 1, pp23

Zhao, F, and Li, L (1998) 'Guanyu kongqi quanqiubiannuan de zaicikao ['Rethinking about the trend of global warming'] in *Huangjing yu ke chixu fazhan–xu: Zhongri youhao huangjing baohu zhongxin 1998 nian lunwenji [Environment and Sustainable Development (Sequel): 1998 Paper Collection of the Sino–Japanese Friendship Center for Environmental Protection]*, Chixiang Chubanshe, Beijing

Zhonggong Panshihua Shiwei dangshi yanjiushi (ed) (1994) *Panzhihua kaifa jianshe shi da shiji [Great Events in the History of Opening up Panzhihua]*, Chengdu keji daxue chubanshe, Chengdu

Index